Chicago's Reckoning

Chicago's Reckoning

*Racism, Politics, and the Deep History of
Policing in an American City*

John Hagan, Bill McCarthy, and Daniel Herda

OXFORD
UNIVERSITY PRESS

OXFORD
UNIVERSITY PRESS

Oxford University Press is a department of the University of Oxford. It furthers the University's objective of excellence in research, scholarship, and education by publishing worldwide. Oxford is a registered trade mark of Oxford University Press in the UK and certain other countries.

Published in the United States of America by Oxford University Press
198 Madison Avenue, New York, NY 10016, United States of America.

© Oxford University Press 2022

Library of Congress Cataloging-in-Publication Data
Names: Hagan, John, 1947– author. | McCarthy, Bill, 1958– author. |
Herda, Daniel, 1983– author.
Title: Chicago's reckoning : racism, politics, and the deep history of policing in an American city / John Hagan, Bill McCarthy, and Daniel Herda.
Description: New York, NY : Oxford University Press, [2022] |
Includes index.
Identifiers: LCCN 2021039948 (print) | LCCN 2021039949 (ebook) |
ISBN 9780197627860 (hardback) | ISBN 9780197627884 (epub) |
ISBN 9780197627891
Subjects: LCSH: Police brutality—Illinois—Chicago. |
Police corruption—Illinois—Chicago. | Discrimination in law enforcement—Illinois—Chicago. | Mayors—Illinois—Chicago.
Classification: LCC HV7936.P725 H34 2022 (print) |
LCC HV7936.P725 (ebook) | DDC 363.2/320977311—dc23
LC record available at https://lccn.loc.gov/2021039948
LC ebook record available at https://lccn.loc.gov/2021039949

DOI: 10.1093/oso/9780197627860.001.0001

1 3 5 7 9 8 6 4 2

Printed by Integrated Books International, United States of America

Contents

Acknowledgments

We are indebted to the many torture victims who shared their stories and to Jamie Kalven and the *Invisible Institute* for posting them online, along with other documents related to the Jon Burge case. We are also beholden to the many individuals who participated in interviews for the chapter on the Joseph White case. Our writing on the Jon Burge case as well as other topics was influenced greatly by the writings of John Conroy, G. Flint Taylor, Ralph Laurence, Andrew Baer, Eddie Glaude Jr., and Andrew Diamond. We are grateful to the Project on Human Development in Chicago Neighborhoods and the Chicago Community Adult Health Study teams who made their data publicly available and to the Inter-university Consortium for Political and Social Research for providing us with access to them. We are thankful to Robert Sampson for his encouragement and openness to our exploration of the ideas developed in this book, and to Doug Massey, Bruce Western, Andy Papachristos, Stephen Vaisey, Monica Bell, and anonymous reviewers for reading and reacting to an earlier draft of the book. We received tremendous support from the President of Oxford University Press, Niko Pfund, as well as its editors and production team, especially Meredith Keffer and Jeremy Toynbee. We received essential institutional support from the American Bar Foundation, Northwestern University, the University of California Davis, Rutgers University Newark, and Merrimack College, and from John Daniels at Davis who helped with geocoding. Ana Bettencourt's editing improved several chapters and our thinking throughout. Linda Hagan's listening skills and responsiveness at every stage were nothing less than essential. And Nico and Nathan Herda's patience and pretending to be interested, allowed Dan to make our maps.

Prologue: Daley's Law—Scandals in Black and White

This book is about the reckoning resulting from the racialized politics of policing and crime in Chicago as well as other American cities. Chicago, like many other cities, has a long history of police abuse of Black and Brown men, women, and communities. Yet it is unique in having ignored the systematic torture of more than one hundred Black men by Police Commander and Detective Jon Burge and a "midnight crew" of officers he supervised. The torture began in the 1970s and lasted for several decades. The full extent of the torture finally came to light through the determined efforts of lawyers, reporters, and activists (Baer 2020; Conroy 2000; Ralph 2020; Taylor 2019).

The Burge torture scandal was one among a number of scandals that occurred during Richard M. Daley's thirty years as Cook County state's attorney and then as mayor of Chicago. It was a scandal for which this mayor never accepted meaningful responsibility. Daley likely anticipated that in the racialized world of Chicago politics, he was unlikely to be held legally responsible for failing to stop Burge's supervision of racist torture. It is sometimes said that "Chicago works a little better crooked." This is a rationalization of a kind of "Big Lie" used to justify police brutality. The Burge torture scandal powerfully symbolizes the resulting racial reckoning that Chicago is today confronting.

In sharp contrast to his silence about Burge, RM Daley did apologize for his involvement in what became known as the city's Hired Truck Scandal. This apology avoided a reckoning of a different kind. This scandal lasted from the late 1990s into the early 2000s (Novak and Warmbir 2004a, 2004b) and was closely connected to the mayor's 11th ward Bridgeport neighborhood. Among those involved were RM Daley's brother John Daley, other friends of the mayor's "first family," and several city officials, politicians, and organized crime figures. The victims included White taxpayers spread across the city's middle- and upper-class neighborhoods that reliably delivered votes for RM Daley. Daley understood that this was a scandal for which he needed to make amends, and he resorted to a handy remedy: a public apology.

Apologies by powerful public figures can be self-selected restorative "punishments" which involve no real punishment at all. Consider the case of President Ronald Reagan. In the 1980s, he was implicated in the Nicaraguan Iran-Contra scandal. He responded with an oval office speech, apologizing for *indirectly* authorizing payments in a complicated "arms for hostages" deal. He said that if he had been more vigilant, he would not have authorized the payments. He also lamented that he couldn't actually recall where and when this authorization took place—a rhetorical device that we call the "I don't recall" defense. In his carefully worded apology, Reagan maintained a veneer of accountability, saying: "as disappointed as I may be in some who served me, I'm still the one who must answer to the American people for this behavior" (*New York Times* 1987, A 18). This indirect admission of responsibility was enough to blunt subsequent calls for Reagan's impeachment.

Offenders at lower levels of the social hierarchy sometimes also offer apologies, for example, in courtroom sentencing hearings that follow criminal convictions. However, these apologies rarely spare these less advantaged offenders from punishment. Instead, sentencing hearings are classically understood as "degradation ceremonies" (Garfinkel 1956) followed by harsh punishment (Rachlinski, Guthrie and Wistrich 2013).

Daley's involvement in the Hired Truck scheme involved convincing Chicagoans that selling the city's trucks and contracting with private companies would save money. However, a *Chicago Sun-Times* journalist, Tim Novak, lived in Daley's Bridgeport neighborhood and he noticed trucks were sitting idly on neighborhood streets. Novak, and fellow reporter Steve Warmbir (2004a, 2004b), exposed the scheme whereby trucking firms made campaign contributions in exchange for lucrative city contracts. Approximately $48 million went to companies located in Daley's 11th Ward. In return, the companies made over $800,000 in campaign contributions, including to the infamous Governor Rod Blagojevich and Illinois House Speaker Michael Madigan. Daley indirectly received more than $100,000 in campaign contributions.

When RM Daley realized that he could not dodge personal responsibility for the scandal and continue to win at the ballot box, he, like Reagan, offered a remorseful and carefully worded apology (Spielman 2004).

I am embarrassed. I'm angry, and I'm disappointed because I feel I have let the people down. I am responsible for everything that happens in city government ... When problems occur and change is needed, it is my responsibility to ensure that it is complete. In the case of the Hired Truck Program that did not happen, and, for that, I apologize.

This was a rare show of contrition by Daley, and it didn't last long. Within a year he was insisting that those close to him never personally benefitted, while insisting on his own innocence:

Anyone who believes that my interest in public life is in enriching my family, friends or political supporters doesn't know or understand me at all. My reputation and the well-being of this city are more important to me than any election (Spielman 2005).

However, he cared enough about elections to run twice for state's attorney and then six more times for mayor.

RM Daley was never prosecuted for his involvement in the Hired Truck Scandal. His apology was necessary, but also sufficient, to ward off his own criminal prosecution and insure further electoral success. Daley's survival illustrates a central theme of this book: that the law operates with a light touch for those in the upper reaches of the social hierarchy, while concealing as much or more than it reveals.

We show in this book that early in his career, RM Daley learned that his state's attorneys and legal advisors in the mayor's office could provide invaluable instruction about how to elude personal legal responsibility, while also enabling the prosecution and punishment of others. Thus, he learned that he could use the law advantageously to climb the social hierarchy, while simultaneously using it to punish and remove others. RM Daley learned how this was done from his father Richard J. Daley, among others.

RM Daley's apology for the trucking scandal was entirely different than his silence about Detective Burge's use of torture to coerce confessions from African American suspects. We demonstrate how the city's corporate counsel aided the mayor in concealing his knowledge of these events. We explain how counsel arranged financial settlements when Black victims filed civil suits against Burge, and how counsel accompanied Daley and provided cues that guided his sworn statements in a deposition about his actions involving Burge.

Yet this is hardly the full story of Daley's apology for the trucking scandal on the one hand, and his silence about police torture on the other. This disparity raises several questions: Was Daley's apology merely a response to allay the concerns of predominantly White citizens who realized that the trucking scandal had increased their taxes? And, did these same predominately White citizens remain silent about Detective Burge's torture because, as the journalist John Conroy (2003) insisted, they and their mayor *simply did not care* about the torture of Black men?

We argue that Daley's actions were actually more malign. Daley knew what happened under Jon Burge at the Chicago Police Department's Area 2 location. G. Flint Taylor (2019; Flint hereafter), a founding partner of the People's Law Office who brought civil suits on behalf of many of Burge's victims, regularly tried to impress on Chicagoans that Daley had many opportunities to mobilize a criminal prosecution of Burge for the torture crimes he supervised. Yet Daley's refusal to act meant that the statute of limitations ran out—one by one—on these racist torture crimes.

As a result, when U.S. Attorney Patrick Fitzgerald finally took over and charged Burge, it was for the derivative and more opaque crimes of perjury and obstruction of justice. We show how two compromised state prosecutors who took depositions in their investigation of Burge, and a judge who subsequently sidetracked a sidebar about the "code of silence" in his federal court trial, *both* obscured how this code was used by Burge to protect himself and other officers from meaningful prosecution. We explain how this code of silence continues to be a key source of racial disparities in Chicago policing and the racial reckoning that confronts this city as well as others.

As early as 1982, a letter from Chicago's Police Superintendent Richard Brzeczek had informed Daley that a detainee, Andrew Wilson, showed tell-tale signs of having been tortured at an Area 2 police station. Daley was state's attorney and should have responded by investigating the torture; however, he and his staff largely ignored the letter and instead prosecuted Wilson using what the Illinois State Supreme Court later ruled was a tortured confession. More than a decade later, following the further torture by White officers of many more Black detainees, the Chicago Police Department finally fired Burge for overseeing and supervising this torture.

Yet Daley still did not press for criminal charges. Over the next two decades, Daley again stood idly by, for example, when the previously noted special state prosecutors failed to charge Burge with any crimes. By that time, several decades had passed since the Burge torture story began. During this period, torture produced forced confessions that persuaded judges and juries to impose numerous life, as well as death, sentences, and Jon Burge began to collect a city pension. It is a remarkable story of how American criminal law can brutally push downward through the social hierarchy while it simultaneously protects and advances individuals and groups who are more advantageously positioned.

Daley came closest to accepting responsibility for Burge's torture crimes when, twenty-five years after the torture started, he campaigned for re-election in Chicago's African American neighborhoods. In a 2006 speech, Daley finally referred directly to the torture as "this shameful episode in our history." He then added: "I'll take responsibility for it. I'll apologize to anyone . . . It should never have happened . . . Everybody should be held accountable . . . The system could have broken down" (Spielman 2008). Daley's suggestion that he had an unfulfilled desire to hold Burge accountable strained credulity, and his observation that the system *could* have broken down was actually an odd confirmation of the importance of Daley's refusal to criminally pursue Burge. The system *was* broken, and in a horrific way. The same legal system that left RM Daley free from prosecution in the Hired Truck Scandal was busily imposing its most severe punishments downward against those with few resources to defend themselves from torture.

But Daley's decades of denial were not over. In 2008, with the 2007 election now behind him and with Burge finally going to trial in Fitzgerald's federal courtroom, reporters pressed Daley to speak out about Burge's long record of torture (Spielman 2008). Yet again, Daley did not accept responsibility. Instead, he offered a sarcastic "apology" followed by a claim that "I didn't do it":

> The best way is to say, Okay. I apologize to everybody [for] whatever happened to anybody in the city of Chicago . . . So, I apologize to everybody. Whatever happened to them in the city of Chicago in the past, I apologize. I didn't do it, but somebody else did it . . . I was not the mayor [at the time the torture started]. I was not the [directly responsible] police chief. I did not promote him [Burge].

Daley's claim that he did not know about the ongoing torture, and his obvious omission that he was the Cook County state's attorney when most of this torture occurred, were highly misleading. Soon after making his sarcastic statement, Daley announced he would not seek a seventh term as mayor of Chicago. Why did Daley make this oddly defensive denial, and what did it mean?

We argue that there was a fundamental contradiction at the core of Daley's police department throughout his more than 30 years as Cook County's state's attorney and Chicago's mayor, and lasting into the present. We explain how the father, Richard J. Daley, and especially his son Richard M. Daley, expanded a law and order regime that allowed the Burge torture team and others to subvert the Chicago Police Department's professed mission "to serve and protect" citizens. Ironically, Chicago was sometimes described during Daley's tenure as "the city that worked." In a perverse sense, this was true: if the goal was increased imprisonment of Black and Brown defendants, Richard M. Daley delivered.

Daley created a tightly coupled criminal justice regime that produced the volume of law and order arrests and convictions needed to stock a rapidly growing mass incarceration system that persists today at a still massive level (Simon 2007, 2014). A tightly coupled system is one in which decisions and actions of official actors and agencies are closely, efficiently, and purposefully connected. In following chapters, we show that RM Daley used the knowledge he gained when he was first elected to the state senate to reorganize the Cook County State's Attorney's Office into a tightly coupled system.

This reorganization, for example, involved creating an entire stand-alone department inside the state's attorney's office to draft laws linking police and prosecutors into a system of arrests and prosecutions producing rapid and predictable sentences—overwhelmingly on Black and Brown citizens. We show, for example, how the system was tightened by passing laws such as the Gang Loitering Ordinance. This law allowed the police to charge youth for posing ill-defined threats while congregated, often in small groups, on neighborhood street corners.

We present and apply an exclusion-containment theory of legal cynicism to further explain how Daley's tightly coupled system of law and order operated. According to this theory, Daley's system worked largely to benefit and protect White residential neighborhoods and the central business districts of Chicago; at the same time, it excluded Black and Brown Chicagoans from these areas, concentrating them in highly segregated neighborhoods. Burge's torture team was an unsparingly vicious part of this exclusion-containment machine, with a repressive reputation that persists to this day—striking fear into South and West Side Chicago neighborhood residents.

The torture, as many Black Chicagoans saw it, was part of a broader contradictory message: *Chicago's police department promised to serve and protect all of the city's residents, but its day-to-day policing more narrowly involved monitoring and punishing—through exclusion and containment—the disadvantaged residents of the city's most highly segregated neighborhoods.* Increasingly over the last century, these hyper-segregated neighborhoods separated residents from the cultural and economic resources available in the city's more advantageously located White neighborhoods.

As we demonstrate, *highly segregated minority neighborhoods are characteristically and understandably cynical about police promises to serve and protect their residents. Residents see the police as ineffective in—if not incapable of—preventing crime or protecting victims from criminal harm, not only from conventional street crimes but also from the abuse and brutality perpetrated by police officers like Jon Burge.* These abusive patterns and practices are more about monitoring neighborhood boundaries than they are about preserving neighborhood safety. These patterns and practices are further assisted by a code of silence that protects police when they engage in abuse, brutality, corruption, and criminality.

The structural contradictions that dominate the city of Chicago subject police to intense cross-pressures: between the demands of the city's more affluent residential communities and business districts and its segregated Black and Brown neighborhoods that are excluded and contained outside—to the south and the west—of this city's protected areas of privilege. The police are key institutional players positioned in the cross-hairs of the oppositional pressures that play out across this predictably tense urban divide. *Until this city—as well as cities in other parts of the country—come to terms with the racial and economic divisions that shape our everyday lives, our police will continue to be caught in cross-pressures that produce many of the tragic results considered in this book.*

Our epilogue shows that the Chicago Police Department's use of violence against Black and Brown residents and its cover-up by politicians did not stop with the end of the second Mayor Daley's tenure. They persisted through Rahm Emanuel's two terms as a successor mayor who followed in the footsteps of RM Daley—having served as the chief fundraiser for Daley's original election as mayor. The low point of Emanuel's tenure involved concealing evidence about how a police officer pumped sixteen shots into the dying body of a teenager, Laquan McDonald. It was yet another episode involving a continuing code of silence: in this case including a thirteen-month cover up made possible by Emanuel's refusal to release a police dash-cam video, and dubious police testimony about the last moments leading to McDonald's death.

The drawn-out cover-up of this killing was a continuing example of how the upward bias of law can conceal and protect powerful persons at the highest levels of the social hierarchy. Emanuel eventually acknowledged that he, like Daley before him, would be departing as mayor while leaving unresolved the problem of the code of silence in the Chicago Police Department. In the process, Emanuel offered a belated admission that this code and its silence remained stubbornly in place and awaiting his successor, Lori Lightfoot. It was a reminder that, in the prophetic words of James Baldwin (2010:154), "history is not the past." As we show in this book, history threatens to be a problematic predictor of Chicago's future, as well as the future of many other American cities.

A police code of silence and a resulting legal cynicism among South and West Side neighborhood residents are among the most pernicious and persistent systemic problems of contemporary Chicago law enforcement. At its heart, this system is increasingly seen from the South and West Sides as governed by a version of what Princeton historian Eddie Glaude, Jr. (2020) calls "The Lie." The giveaway is that, instead of acting "to serve and protect" the residents of highly segregated neighborhoods, this system has enforced their hyper-segregated exclusion and containment.

This overview is the foundation for the analysis we present about more than a century of racial exclusion and containment in Chicago, a pattern that also occurred in many other American cities. This analysis builds on the work of a growing collection of scholars who are documenting how America's cities have arrived at a time of reckoning when, if this nation is to succeed, its citizens must, in meaningful and lasting ways, confront the racial and ethnic problems that date from our country's origins. If we can meaningfully confront these beginnings, perhaps this country can, as James Baldwin and as his intellectual heir Eddie Glaude, Jr. (2020) implore us, *Begin Again*.

1

Two Mayors and "The Midnight Crew"

Columnist Mike Royko had his finger on the pulse of Chicago throughout his coverage of the raucous 1968 Democratic Convention. His follow-up book, *Boss* (1971), connected the Convention's "police riot" to Mayor Richard J. Daley's evolving White backlash politics. Royko put it succinctly: "The political winds were blowing from the right," and Mayor Daley "was as much a part of it as Wallace, Agnew, or Strom Thurmond" (1971:194). Royko should have added presidents Ronald Reagan and Richard Nixon to the list.

Two years before the Chicago Democratic Convention, Reagan was elected governor of California on a "law and order" platform. By adopting Reagan's law and order strategy, Nixon was elected president, and the politics of the "Age of Reagan" were upon us. Today, Royko would need to add Reagan and Nixon to his list, along with the Bushes, George H.W. and George W., as well as Donald J. Trump.

It was Reagan who introduced "Let's Make America Great Again" as his 1980 campaign slogan, which Trump barely bothered to modify for his 2016 red hat MAGA campaign. Mayor Richard J. Daley (RJ) shared Reagan's "law and order" politics, despite being a Democrat, and his son, Richard M. Daley (RM), adopted the same law and order position in his own election as Cook County state's attorney in 1980—the same year Ronald Reagan won the presidency. RJ and RM's law and order instincts were a match for Reagan's, and they anticipated Trump's future campaign and election. But RJ and RM understood that state and city governments, more than the presidency, controlled the levers of power that made the politics of punishment happen.

Trump would have admired RJ Daley's power to dominate Chicago politics, and Trump took obvious pride in emblazoning his own name in larger-than-life letters on his Chicago hotel tower. For his part, RJ valued his powerful grip on Chicago more highly than the idea of ever holding national office. The prospect of his two-decade domination becoming a half-century dynasty through the electoral success of his son was an Irish American father's dream. To RJ and RM Daley, Chicago was so much more than a "Second City."

The Quintessential American City

Robert Sampson (2012) drew from Norman Mailer's "new journalism" of the late 1960s when he titled his landmark book about Chicago the *Great American City*. Sampson reminded his readers, "to be great is hardly to be flawless" (77). Among the city's flaws he identified are its inequality, violence, segregation, and corruption. It is likely that these failings—amidst its other claims to greatness— led Sampson to suggest that Chicago "is arguably the quintessential American city" (76).

In his book of essays, *Chicago, City on the Make* (1951), Nelson Algren argued that this metropolis mixed grand ambition with world class moral indiscretion. Algren, one of Chicago's great writers and author of *Walk on the Wild Side* (1956*)*, as well as *The Man with the Golden Arm* (1949), could write in shimmering prose, but he was also a brutal realist about his city by the lake. It was Algren's descriptions of Chicago as the "city second to none" that inspired singer-songwriter Lou Reed to borrow from *Walk on the Wide Side* to describe the seductive pleasures of his own first city, New York. This book is about Chicago's "darker shades of grey" that Nelson Algren and others so eloquently describe.

At the center of our study are Chicago's hyper-segregated policies of racial exclusion and containment. Alongside and connected to this racial reality, we focus on Chicago's history of politics and crime—a history that includes prominent criminal cover-ups during the reigns of both RJ and RM Daley. The first included the shooting of the Black Panther activists Fred Hampton and Mark Clark, while the second featured the torture crimes of police detective Jon Burge, crimes that were covered up for nearly thirty years.

This history has fueled a persistent cynicism about law and its racially divisive enforcement. Our analysis probes the consequences of this cynicism over several recent decades. The consequences we document are part of what makes Chicago a quintessential American city. They underline James Baldwin's insistence that "history is not the past," while also helping us to answer Donald Trump's 2017 imploring question: "What the hell is going on in Chicago?" (Raymond 2017).

The exclusion-containment theory of legal cynicism we advance focuses on a succession of events and problems that unfolded for more than a century (Balto 2019), making Chicago a persistently racially conflicted and violent place, as well as an incongruously proud metropolis. Our findings suggest that Chicago's present—and America's future—cannot be understood without consideration of this archetypal city's past.

In this chapter, we consider the 1960s backdrop to the racially targeted police torture of more than one hundred Black suspects during RM Daley's tenure as state's attorney and mayor, from the 1980s through the 1990s, and the "midnight torture crew" led by police detective Jon Burge. Burge was hired in 1971, during the tenure of RJ Daley, and continued to lead his torture squad with the complicit knowledge of RJ's son, RM Daley. Police mistreatment has a long history in Chicago (Andonova 2017), but the torture of its African American residents may have peaked under Burge's direction in the mid-1980s; yet, its consequences and the legal cynicism it generated persisted not only throughout but also beyond the second Daley's three decades in public office.

Survivor testimonies and reports have identified scores of Chicago police officers who had direct knowledge of the torture that took place under Burge (Hunt n.d.).

As Laurence Ralph (2020:186) explained: "In Chicago, the belief that the police hate Black people and mistreat them, brutalize them, torture them and kill them is so commonplace as to be banal." Such practices represent recurring periods of poorly hidden political lawlessness that—masquerading behind badges and symbols of law and legality—we too often ignore with a naive belief in the rule of law.

The Quintessential City on Edge

A century after America fought its historic civil war—and in the midst of Lyndon Johnson's flawed efforts to create the "Great Society"—the racial and youth rebellions of the late 1960s captured America's attention. They highlighted our many lasting mistakes, including our original sin of slavery. Yet it is useful to recall that before this, for a bright but too brief moment, the mid-1960s also suggested more hopeful possibilities for Chicago.

Fresh from his leadership of southern mobilization efforts that successfully spurred President Johnson and Congress to pass the 1964 Civil Rights and the 1965 Voting Rights Acts, Martin Luther King, Jr. brought a new civil rights campaign to Mayor RJ Daley's Chicago. In 1966, King looked north to the city of "broad shoulders" and to its increasingly influential Democratic mayor, thinking that he had spotted a potential ally: a seemingly able and amenable Democrat who had helped get Presidents Kennedy and Johnson elected. Daley also enjoyed broad support among voters in Chicago's Black wards, and it was their votes which helped him win his first election as mayor in 1955 (Lemann 1991). King thought Daley could be persuaded to join in the challenge of reversing a half-century of Chicago's well-documented housing segregation (Austen 2018; Rothstein 2017).

King, of course, was not visually or politically impaired, and he saw Chicago for what it was: the intensely segregated endpoint of the pre- and post-World War II Great Migrations of many former slaves and their children from the American South (Lemann 1991; Wilkerson 2010). In his much-cited *Atlantic* magazine article, "The Case for Reparations," Ta-Nehisi Coates (2014) outlined the exclusionary housing practices in the west side Chicago neighborhoods that captured King's attention (also see Rothstein 2017). As Coates emphasized, and we will demonstrate, the imprint of racial segregation remains a dominant feature of Chicago life. And yet, the problems and prospects of this growing city seemed to make it and its Democratic mayor a plausible starting point for next steps in the civil rights movement. And King believed "that if the problems of Chicago, the nation's second largest city, can be solved, they can be solved everywhere" (Waxman 2018). He was sufficiently convinced to gather his family and move them to Chicago to launch a housing reform campaign called the Chicago Freedom Movement. It was the start of a new era for both King and Chicago, and it marked the period when many crucial policies and practices emphasized in this book began to take shape.

The Chicago Freedom Movement showed early signs of promise. King worked with Jesse Jackson and other local organizers to bring together leaders of several of

Chicago's prominent youth gangs—including the Blackstone Rangers—to form a unique security force to protect marchers. In the first major event, King drew 70,000 Black Chicagoans to a mid-summer rally at Soldier Field. The Chicago Historical Museum still prominently displays an iconic photo of this event. At the end of the rally, King and followers walked to City Hall and taped a list of demands to the door (Schlabach 2018). In addition to calling for an end to racist real estate practices, the list called for an end to police brutality and the creation of a civilian review board for the Chicago Police Department.

King's marches for open housing and to protest the city's social exclusion and containment policies followed on the heels of the Soldier Field rally. He worked with Jesse Jackson and others to keep Chicago's gangs aligned with the Blackstone Rangers during some of the first demonstrations for open housing; but the youth gang truce would ultimately prove impossible to sustain.

The marches succeeded in bringing out thousands of south and west side Black residents; yet these demonstrations also proved sobering in awakening King to exactly what he was up against. The marchers were assailed by "the thunder of jeering thousands, many of them waving Nazi flags" (Schlabach 2018). Andrew Diamond (2017:193) described a late summer rally on the west side in which "a number of Blackstone Rangers participating in the demonstration wore baseball gloves to catch bottles, bricks, and stones." They were confronted with shouts of "Kill those niggers!" and lynch mob echoes of "We want Martin Luther Coon." A well-aimed rock struck King in the head, leaving a bloody gash. Later, King would tell a reporter from the *New York Times*: "the people of Mississippi ought to come to Chicago to learn how to hate" (Fremon 1988:108).

King lauded the non-violent efforts of gang members who pledged to protect him during the march: "I remember walking with the Blackstone Rangers while bottles were flying from the sidelines, and I saw their noses being broken and blood flowing from their wounds; and I saw them continue and not retaliate, not one of them, with violence" (cited in Ralph 1993:137). However, this promise of disciplined defense proved to be a passing phase. Old gang rivalries, a rising mood of Black militancy, and the brutal tactics of the police could not be contained.

King's time in Chicago lasted little more than six months. By his own estimation, it ended in almost complete failure. This was despite a seemingly promising accord reached with RJ Daley in a high-profile "summit" that marked the culmination of King's local participation in the Chicago Freedom Movement. The summit included a commitment from the Chicago Housing Authority to build more low-rise public housing and from the Mortgage Bankers Association to stop using race as a factor in assessing mortgage applications (King 2020). Yet, in their aptly named book, *American Pharaoh*, Adam Cohen and Elizabeth Taylor (2000:428) concluded that actually, "[t]he Housing Summit was Daley's masterstroke, a way of ending the protests and driving the movement out of town in exchange for vague and unenforceable commitments." A year after leaving Chicago, King noted that public agencies had reneged on their promises, and he agreed with critics who called the document "a sham" made from "a batch of false promises" (King 2020). In retrospect, King's departure from Chicago marked a victory for the Daley dynasty's backlash politics.

Less than two years after his arrival in Chicago, and the promising rally at Soldier Field, King was assassinated in Memphis. In response to the racial rebellion that broke out in anger and protest over King's death, RJ Daley issued his infamous orders to police to "shoot to maim" looters and "shoot to kill" arsonists (Diamond 2017:208). Only four months later, the world watched as the infamous "police riot" unfolded at the 1968 Democratic Convention that nominated Hubert Humphrey to run unsuccessfully for president against Richard Nixon. The year after the Convention, a Yippie inspired "Days of Rage" mobilization in the downtown Loop resulted in broken store windows and further stunned Chicagoans.

In this atmosphere of instability and in the darkness of night, a Chicago police unit—with assistance from the Cook County State's Attorney's Office and the FBI—broke into the apartment of Fred Hampton, Chicago's rising young Black Panther leader. A barrage of nearly a hundred bullets killed Hampton and another fellow Panther, Mark Clark, and injured four other Panthers who were staying in the apartment. What Royko (1971) called Chicago's "White backlash" had taken a shadowy leap forward in the rising tide of Nixon and Reagan politics.

The Mayor's Man in the State's Attorney's Office

In the 1960s, Edward Hanrahan, not the Mayor's son RM Daley, seemed destined to be RJ's heir apparent. RJ had made his way to the mayor's office by mastering the finances of Chicago's patronage system, but in his first decade in office he also had learned the importance of law as an instrument of power. It was a lesson RJ passed on to his son, encouraging him to attend law school at Chicago's DePaul University. In the meantime, Edward Hanrahan was a lawman with the right credentials to take on the growing and changing legal issues confronting Chicago: in addition to being Irish Catholic and a conservative graduate of Notre Dame, Hanrahan had earned his law degree at Harvard.

In 1964, RJ Daley persuaded President Johnson to approve his recommendation of Hanrahan for U.S Attorney of the Northern District of Illinois. RJ proudly told the President that Hanrahan was not only a Harvard man, he was a precinct captain in the Chicago political machine, a machine that Johnson had learned to appreciate. Four years later, Daley convinced Hanrahan to give up his prestigious position as U.S. Attorney to run locally for Cook County state's attorney. In Daley's world, Cook County was more important than the U.S. Attorney's Office. He had a point: the Cook County State's Attorney's Office was, and still is, among the largest prosecutors' offices in the country and a powerful adjunct to the Chicago Police Department. Hanrahan understood this, while further appreciating that, with RJ Daley's support, the Cook County State's Attorney's Office could be a springboard to the office of mayor of Chicago, or perhaps governor of Illinois.

Hanrahan was elected to his new state office in a landslide. Race and gang-connected politics were much in RJ Daley's mind during this period. He could see an alarming alliance emerging between the leadership of the Black Panthers and the Black P Stone Nation street gang. Daley had seen the potential threat this posed from Martin Luther King, Jr.'s brief, but stunning, mobilization of gang support for his Chicago Freedom Movement. In the spring of 1969, Hanrahan and Daley joined forces to create a Special Prosecutions Unit in the state's attorney's office to work with the Chicago Police Department's Gang Intelligence Unit. Together they launched a highly publicized "war on gangs" (Hagedorn 2006), which prominently included the Black Panthers. The units were joined by their racist ideology and use of police terror, reinforcing Chicago's place at the forefront of America's backlash conservative politics (Diamond 2017).

RJ Daley and others singled out Black Panther Fred Hampton as a particular threat to his Democratic machine. Hampton's rise to leadership of Chicago's Black Panthers was remarkable. He was a charismatic and enthusiastic organizer in the Black community, coordinating a mosaic of previously racial and ethnically divided gangs, with the uplifting metaphor of a "Rainbow Coalition" (Balto 2019), the theme Jesse Jackson would take nationally in his 1988 presidential campaign. Hampton gained early South Side support with Panther-sponsored programs for free health care and other essential services. Thus, he earned attention not only from the national Panther organization that coveted his leadership skills, but also, and more ominously, from J. Edgar Hoover's racially and politically driven FBI.

As Cook County state's attorney, and previously as U.S. Attorney, Hanrahan was well positioned to address RJ Daley's political concerns by coordinating local and federal law enforcement. J. Edgar Hoover was simultaneously mobilizing an FBI program, COINTELPRO, to attack the leadership of the Black Panther Party and other radical groups. Hanrahan used his experience and contacts in the federal system to link Chicago to Hoover's plan.

These developments coincided with a summer shootout between members of the Black Panthers and Chicago police officers, leaving one Panther dead and several others facing criminal charges. The following fall, while Hampton was attending a meeting with national Black Panther leaders, a local Panther, Spurgeon Jake Winters, led a bloody shootout with Chicago police officers, injuring nine and killing two. Winters died from police gunshot wounds, and another Panther was charged with murder.

The shootings heightened Chicago's race- and fear-driven politics. On November 15, 1969, the *Chicago Tribune* played an incendiary role, publishing a racialized editorial titled, "No Quarter for Wild Beasts" (Editor 1969). Echoing Daley's call to arms following King's assassination, the *Tribune's* editorial encouraged Chicago police "to be ready to shoot" in encounters with the Panthers. The deaths of the two police officers at the hands of the Panthers intensified the pressure on State's Attorney Hanrahan, who took action less than a month later.

The Hampton Raid

In the dark hours of a late December night in 1969, an enforcement unit from Hanrahan's office joined with FBI agents and fourteen Chicago police officers to raid Fred Hampton's apartment. The official purpose was to confiscate illegal weapons, but it was also a show of force, a backlash response to the earlier Panther–Police shootout. Police fired nearly a hundred bullets from weapons, including a machine gun, killing the sleeping Hampton and his Panther colleague Mark Clark. Hampton's partner, Deborah Johnson, was eight months pregnant and asleep when the shooting began. She reported hearing voices during a lull in the attack and preceding a final round of gunfire:

> I heard a voice that wasn't familiar to me say, 'He's barely alive. He'll barely make it.' I assumed they were talking about Fred. The shooting started again, just for a brief period. It stopped. Then another unfamiliar voice said, 'He's good and dead now' (Taylor 2019:20).

The implication was that the singular goal of the raid was Hampton's assassination.

The next day, Hanrahan held a press conference to claim that his officers were the victims of a violent counterattack, narrowly escaping serious injury. There was immediate skepticism about Hanrahan's version, especially among a group of young Northwestern University law students, including Flint Taylor (2019). They suspected that Hanrahan's press conference was a pre-emptive step in a cover-up of the Hampton raid.

Hampton, Hanrahan, and the People's Law Office

Taylor would later become a founding partner of the Chicago-based People's Law Office which launched a five-decade battle against Chicago police brutality and torture. It soon became known to Taylor and his colleagues that only one of the nearly one hundred bullets fired in the Hampton raid came from a Panther weapon. When this was confirmed, the state's attorney's office dropped the initial charges they had filed against the surviving Panthers.

Yet, this was far from the end of the matter. Taylor and his colleagues subsequently filed a civil rights suit against Hanrahan on behalf of the Hampton and Clark families. The suit charged Hanrahan, and his first assistant, with a racially and politically motivated conspiracy to plan and undertake the raid (Taylor 2019:4). This was the first in a career-long succession of civil cases that Taylor and his office brought, many of which resulted in financial settlements that were at first small, but later grew in size and significance, eventually producing multimillion-dollar payments by the City of Chicago.

A Federal Grand Jury was also impaneled in the Hampton case, but despite the suspicious gunshot evidence, the panel concluded there was insufficient evidence to charge any of the police involved. Outrage followed in Chicago's Black community, and this led to the appointment of a local Cook County special prosecutor, who indicted State's Attorney Hanrahan and his assistant for obstruction of justice and conspiracy to present false evidence—although not for homicide.

The trial took place in the lead-up to the 1972 election in which Hanrahan was challenged for re-election as state's attorney by Republican Bernard Carey. The judge hearing the case, Philip Romiti, was known for his ties to the Democratic machine, and politically connected lawyers ultimately were paid more than a million dollars by the city to defend Hanrahan and his assistant. Hanrahan needed a favorable verdict before the election, and he miraculously got one: the judge found him innocent of all charges the day before voters went to the polls. This reliance on the city's financial coffers to defend police and politicians' wrongdoings anticipated similar cover-ups for decades to come.

Yet the vote still went heavily against Hanrahan, especially in Black precincts, and he badly lost his bid to stay in office. It was the effective end of Hanrahan's political career, and attention shifted instead to the federal civil suit filed earlier by Taylor on behalf of the Hampton and Clark families. The suit was slow-walked through its early stages, finally going to trial in 1976. Only a young Northwestern team of inexperienced attorneys would have been inclined to spend the time and forego the income necessary to sustain it. It became one of the longest trials in federal court history, lasting for more than a decade.

While the trial unfolded, additional evidence emerged from a post-Watergate senate committee led by Idaho Senator Frank Church. The committee was conducting a probe of J. Edgar Hoover's COINTELPRO program, and its report exposed the methods and means by which this FBI operation had set out to dismantle the national Black Panther leadership. Evidence revealed that the FBI had enlisted a Chicago informer to provoke violence by and against local Black Panthers. This had been the source of the plan that involved Chicago's police and State's Attorney Hanrahan's office in the raid that killed Fred Hampton.

The trial testimony in the Hampton–Clark case revealed the extent to which the raid had become a racial vendetta in response to the earlier shootout with members of the Black Panthers—even though Fred Hampton was not in the city on the day of the shootout. The racially driven nature and purposes of the raid were reflected in testimony by a wounded witness who reported the racial slurs and epithets he heard during the raid: "I remember hearing a voice say, 'If Panthers kill police, police will kill Panthers . . . They started calling me 'Nigger!' 'Black Bastard!' 'Mother-fucker!' " (Taylor 2019:18). This witness survived, but with wounds requiring partial removal of his colon. His testimony confirmed the deeper racialized politics that permeated the legal system.

Hanrahan and the Civil Suit

Hanrahan was ultimately called to testify in the case, but he refused to confirm or deny he had conferred with Mayor Daley about the raid. A suppressed FBI document spelled out elements of a deal in which charges against the surviving Panthers would be dropped in exchange for removing Hanrahan from the civil suit brought on behalf of the Hampton and Clark families. This proposal signaled the political, as well as legal, backdrop of Hanrahan's defense: to cover up politically connected motives of the Hampton assassination. It was a defense strategy that would become common-place in Chicago police brutality cases. RJ Daley's successful distancing of himself from the cases also foreshadowed his son's nearly thirty-year silence about the Burge torture cases.

The evidence against Hanrahan and his co-defendants was so strong that the U.S. Attorney and lawyers from Cook County and the City of Chicago agreed to enter negotiations for a cash settlement in the civil suit of nearly two million dollars. The Hampton–Clark case became the first of many litigated cases in which Taylor and other lawyers took Hanrahan and others to court. Chicago is not unique in this method of covering up criminal abuses of power; however, the Hampton–Clark case set an extraordinary precedent for a broader pattern that prevails in American police misconduct civil cases to this day. Many, if not most, of these cases ended in cash set-tlements to survivors and family members in compensation for police killings, abuse, and torture. These settlements paid by the city would become a growing and increas-ingly costly way of shielding high-level officials—such as Hanrahan and both RJ and RM Daley—from testifying in civil suites, and protect them from criminal charges and convictions. The most famous of these criminal cases, discussed in the final chap-ters of this book, was the case against Jon Burge for his role, both in directly torturing suspects and his supervision of torture by Chicago police officers.

The settlements not only provided significant compensation to the victims and families—who were also victims—but also payment of fees to Taylor and other lawyers, allowing them to sustain their activist practice that otherwise would have been impossible. However, because these were mostly civil cases, they also allowed Hanrahan and his co-defendants to escape criminal conviction. In this way, crim-inal responsibility and accountability for brutal racialized abuses of power and deadly backlash politics could be legally avoided.

The Emergence of RM Daley

RM Daley was in his late twenties when he sat beside his father in a special box at the 1968 Chicago Democratic Convention. He was elected to the Illinois State Senate in 1972, the year he turned thirty and Ed Hanrahan lost his re-election bid for state's at-torney. RM was not necessarily a quick study, taking three tries to pass his bar exam, and he was certainly a different person than Ed Hanrahan, the Harvard law graduate.

But he had the benefit of the many lessons learned in "real time" from his father in how the scandal-plagued game of Chicago politics was played.

As mayor, RJ Daley made it a trademark to not directly take bribes as other Chicago politicians often did. In this way, RJ avoided becoming directly involved in everyday Chicago corruption. Yet he was also well known for "looking the other way" when others around and below him were involved in illegal schemes. With this example, RM likely viewed Hanrahan as having been too smart by half when he directly enmeshed himself in the COINTELPRO plans leading to the killing of Fred Hampton. Not only would RM have learned that distancing oneself from direct involvement was an important way to avoid career-ending conflicts with the law, he was also entering Chicago politics with an awareness that gaining at least some level of credibility across Chicago's racial and ethnic divides was important to political success.

This is hardly to say that RM Daley foreswore White backlash politics and racialized abuses of power. The back and forth of racial polemics became key elements in RM's regime, first as state's attorney and then as mayor. When Hanrahan's successor, Republican Bernard Carrey, finished his second term as Cook County state's attorney, RM was more than ready to come to the aid of the Democratic Party by entering the race to replace him. Predictably, in his first successful run for political office in Chicago, RM campaigned for state's attorney with an explicit "Let's Get Tough on Crime" platform. Just two years later, he was already sufficiently confident to enter the race for the Democratic Party mayoral nomination against his father's former protégé, the incumbent Jane Byrne.

Jane Byrne had been elected in 1979, following RJ's unexpected death in 1976 and an ineffective interim mayor, Michael Bilandic. She was the Democratic machine candidate and first woman mayor of Chicago. However, she soon found herself spending much of her time looking over her shoulder to see if the young RM Daley, newly elected in 1980 as Cook County state's attorney, was gaining on her. An ensuing rivalry, and the unexpected and historic election of Harold Washington as Chicago's first African American mayor, would soon threaten to become the early undoing of both Byrne and Daley; but first, RM set about reorganizing the state's attorney's office.

Tightening Control and Intensifying Enforcement

In running for Cook County state's attorney, RM had promised to professionalize the office and, in doing so, he was quick to assert his law and order inclinations. Among his early steps was implementing the Automatic Transfer Act. This act assigned juveniles charged with violent crimes (murder, but also armed robbery and sexual assault) to criminal court (rather than juvenile court), thus making them vulnerable to imprisonment in adult institutions (we examine this process in Chapter Three with the case of 15-year-old Joseph White).

In his biography of RM Daley, Keith Koeneman (2013:81) observed: "After his first year in office, Daley had developed a reputation as a professional, competent state's attorney who ran a tightly controlled organization." The professionalization part was easy to understand and hard to question. However, RM's penchant for "tight control," combined with his resort to aggressive police tactics, were not the immediate sources of political success he might initially have expected.

Like Hanrahan, RM was confronted early in his tenure as state's attorney with responding to the shooting deaths of Chicago police officers. On a bleak winter day in February 1982, officers William P. Fahey and Richard O'Brien were returning from a funeral for a fellow officer when they stopped a vehicle for running a red light. The car was driven by Jackie Wilson, accompanied by his brother Andrew. Both were ordered out of the car. While being handcuffed, Andrew Wilson grabbed one of the officers' guns and shot both Fahey and O'Brien.

In the vernacular of law enforcement, it was a "heater crime" that called for a fast response from not only the police but also the state's attorney and the mayor. Mayor Byrne responded by instructing Chief Police Superintendent Richard Brzeczek and Officer (later Deputy Superintendent) Joseph McCarthy to lead probably the largest manhunt in the city's history. When Byrne appeared at Police Area 2 Headquarters on the South Side, after several hours at the hospital with the officers' families, she directed detectives "to solve the crimes by any means necessary" (Taylor 2019:37). She met three times with Area 2 officers in the following days and offered a $50,000 reward for evidence leading to arrests. When a lead emerged, she personally relayed the tip leading to the capture of the suspected killers, Andrew and Jackie Wilson.

The South Side Under Siege

From the time of the police killings to the apprehension of the Wilson brothers, Chicago's South Side neighborhoods were under siege. The police broke down doors, pointed guns at parents and children, and assaulted suspects (Ralph 2020). The police seemingly picked up suspects at random and took them to the Area 2 Police Headquarters for questioning. Up to this point, RM Daley had distanced himself from the manhunt, perhaps recalling the consequences of Hanrahan's too-conspicuous decision to directly involve himself in plans that led to the killing of Fred Hampton.

Byrne, on the other hand, was eager to implement the Age of Reagan law and order politics taking hold in the country. She chose Officer Joseph McCarthy, who was known for his rough treatment of minority youth, to lead the exhaustive South Side "house to house" search. McCarthy was a rising star, known for his use of disorderly conduct arrests with minority youth and for raiding gay bars. Aurie Pennick, head of an important activist group, Citizens Alert, called McCarthy's tactics "Gestapo" and noted that he had previously run a unit that called themselves the "ghetto raiders" (Cruz 1982).

After the siege, Pennick took the lead in sending a letter of complaint to Mayor Byrne on behalf of forty citizen groups. Byrne insisted McCarthy had her full support; she even later appointed him deputy superintendent of police and put him in charge of an anti-gang unit tied closely to her office. The president of the Afro-American Police League, Howard Safford, said, "McCarthy responds directly to the mayor. No one can touch him" (Cruz 1982).

McCarthy steadfastly insisted there was, "no more police brutality now than there ever was. And I don't know that there ever was any" (Cruz 1982). This was refuted when, following the Wilson manhunt, Citizens Alert received more than a hundred complaints of police abuse, with an equal or larger number received at Safford's Afro-American Police League.

From his position in Police Area 2, detective Jon Burge also played a leading role in the manhunt. Burge was already a favored figure in Daley's "war on crime," having increased arrests, confessions, and convictions on Chicago's South Side by spiking imprisonment of young Black males. Burge had joined the Chicago police force in 1971, having previously served as a military drill sergeant and then police officer in the 9th infantry in Vietnam. In all likelihood, this was where he learned about interrogation techniques, including torture.

Burge claimed to be a skilled interrogator who could produce confessions, and he joined eagerly in the dragnet investigation organized by Mayor Byrne, Superintendent Brzeczek, and Officer McCarthy. Burge ultimately gained infamy in Chicago for his use of an improvised device made unforgettable in John Conroy's (2005) essay about "Tools of Torture." Conroy reported that the device "bore a striking resemblance to what American troops [in the 9th infantry] called 'The Bell Telephone Hour'— shocking prisoners by means of a hand-cranked Army field phone."

In a story about the Chicago manhunt, Conroy (2000:24) reported that, "the Reverend Willie Barrow of Operation PUSH said that in the neighborhood . . . every young [B]lack male in sight was being stopped and questioned." Reverend Jesse Jackson similarly insisted that, "the [B]lack community was living under martial law, in 'a war zone.'" And it was clear, as Baer (2020:88) noted, that the Mayor's leadership team "knew what they were getting when they unleashed Burge that emotional afternoon." But it was not the police dragnet that broke the case. Following a citizen tip about where Andrew Wilson was hiding, Burge and McCarthy brought him in for questioning, while another tip led police to his brother Jackie.

The Torture of Andrew Wilson and the Unasked Question

When Andrew was taken to Area 2 Headquarters, he was suspected of shooting the police officers, with Jackie as his accomplice. According to Andrew, the police initially punched and kicked him in the face, injuring his eye (People v. Wilson 1987). The following account drew from several sources describing how the interrogation evolved:

> Burge said something on the order of 'My reputation is at stake and you are going to make a statement.' According to Wilson, Detective Yucaitis entered the room a short

time later carrying a brown paper bag, from which he extracted a black box. Yucaitis allegedly pulled two wires out of the box, attached them with clamps to Wilson's right ear and nostril, and then turned the crank on the side of the box . . . [Wilson reported] 'It hurts, but it stays in your head . . . It stays in your head and it grinds your teeth . . . All my bottom teeth were loose behind that' (Conroy 2000:69).

According to Andrew Wilson, Burge followed the electroshock by placing his revolver in Wilson's mouth and repeatedly pulling the trigger. The torture apparently stopped when Burge believed Wilson was ready to confess.

State's Attorney Daley's office now entered the case. His office took confessions through its "Felony Review Unit." Edward Hanrahan had started this unit in 1972. Contrary to its presumed intent, the program increased pressure on detectives to illegally coerce confessions. Confessions had increased because judges regarded them as strong evidence of guilt (see Baer 2020:68). Larry Hyman, who served as Chief of Felony Review, was waiting at Area 2 to take a confession from Wilson. Hyman waited in a separate room, presumably to avoid observing the torture. However, when Wilson entered the room he unexpectedly asked: "You expect me to make a statement after all of them tortured me?" Hyman responded by angrily telling detectives to "get the jagoff out of here" (Taylor 2019:39–40).

Wilson had breached the veil of secrecy surrounding his torture. Years later, as we explain in the final chapters of this book, this veil would be lifted further and it would become more widely assumed that State's Attorney RM Daley and lawyers from his office—beginning with Larry Hyman and reaching all the way to the top—were complicit in their knowledge that this confession had followed from Wilson's torture.

Confessions were taken later that day from both Andrew and Jackie Wilson. Later it would become apparent that Hyman had failed to ask Andrew Wilson a crucial question before taking his confession: that is, whether his statement was given voluntarily. Hyman would never explain this lapse, although the reason seemed obvious: he knew that Wilson had been tortured—because Wilson had told him, and there was bloody physical evidence of the torture.

Burge had by now told others that his reputation depended on delivering the confession, and this may be why he insisted on being in the room when Andrew's confession was delivered: "Hyman asked him to leave, but Burge remained, and after the statement was completed, triumphantly told Andrew, 'We're going to fry your Black ass now' " (Taylor 2019:41).

The Unanswered Letter and the Beginning of the Cover-Up

Two officers, Mario Ferro and William Mulvaney, transported Andrew Wilson to the police lockup, and they apparently also assaulted him (Ralph 2020:32–34). At the lockup, events began to veer further beyond control (Conroy 2000:71–72). The person in charge saw the condition Wilson was in and refused to admit him; he was taken instead to Mercy Hospital.

The police who took Wilson to the hospital told him that, if he knew what was good for him, he would refuse treatment; but, a Black orderly convinced Wilson he had a right to treatment. He was seen by a doctor who later testified that one of the officers had un-holstered his gun in front of Wilson. The doctor instructed him to re-holster the gun; however, when the doctor left the room, Wilson was again reportedly threatened with a gun. When the physician returned, Wilson stated he had been injured when he fell entering the police station (Ralph 2020).

The next morning the police took Wilson to Cook County Jail and photographed his injuries: "Ordinarily jail authorities take only a mug shot . . . . In Andrew's Wilson's case they took pictures of his whole body so as not to be blamed for his injuries" (Conroy 2000:72). A public defender, Dale Coventry, represented Andrew at his preliminary appearance, and he had Andrew show his injuries to the judge.

The police then took Andrew to Cermak Hospital, which was also part of Cook County Jail. The doctor who saw Wilson was alarmed by the injuries and also had them photographed. A description suggested the nature of the torture: "the shots of the ears . . . were the most curious: they showed a pattern of U-shaped scabs that seemed inexplicable unless one believed that alligator clips had indeed been attached to Wilson's ears" to deliver electric shocks (Conroy 2000:72).

Evidence of Wilson's torture now began moving up a procedural ladder of accountability. The Director of Medical Services, Jack Raba, was informed about the Wilson case, went to see him, and then took the extra step of examining him on two separate days (Ralph 2020; Taylor 2019). Concerned about Wilson's condition, Raba wrote a letter describing his injuries in detail and concluding, "all these injuries occurred prior to his arrival at the [Cook County] jail. There must [be] a thorough investigation of this matter" (Koeneman 2013:83–84). This letter became a central piece of evidence for three decades of litigation about the cover-up.

Raba directed the letter to Police Superintendent Richard Brzeczek, who became a center of attention in the fitfully evolving torture investigation. Brzeczek's response to Raba's call for an inquiry was to first file a notice initiating an internal investigation by the department's Office of Professional Standards [OPS]. He then sent a letter describing the situation and asking for advice from the next person in the law enforcement ladder: State's Attorney RM Daley. Brzeczek enclosed a cover letter to Daley informing him that he would not investigate Wilson's alleged torture unless Daley instructed him to do so.

Flint Taylor, who spent much of the next three decades litigating related cases, suggests that Brzeczek had "covered-his-flanks," and Byrne's as well, by passing the letter on to Daley. Taylor described Daley as being the perfect recipient, since he was increasingly regarded as "Mr. '[L]aw and [O]rder himself' " (Taylor 2019:45). Brzeczek further justified his decision to await Daley's response by noting the importance of the "heater case" and reasoning that, "I also do not want to jeopardize the prosecution's case in any way. I will forbear from taking any steps other than the one previously mentioned [i.e., the initiation of the internal police OPS investigation] in connection with these allegations" (quoted in Taylor 2019:46).

Daley was planning to campaign for the Democratic nomination to replace Byrne for mayor in the next election, and so he would have wanted the prosecution to move quickly to conviction and sentencing. Investigating the torture allegations and including a probe of Hyman's unexpectedly lengthy presence on the scene before taking the confession would have raised suspicions. Instead, Daley handed off the provocative letter to a trusted subordinate in his Special Prosecutions Unit, Frank DeBoni.

DeBoni apparently brought the prospect of an investigation to a close with the justification that Wilson would not cooperate with prosecutors. Indeed, Wilson was facing a capital murder charge, and his lawyer, Dale Coventry, probably did not want to put Wilson back in the hands of Daley's prosecutors, who likely would have wanted to extract further information for the prosecution. Meanwhile, Brzeczek did not move forward with the Chicago Police Department's OPS investigation, with the justification that he had not received a response to his letter from Daley. Neither Daley's nor Brzeczek's explanation indicated concern about the use of police torture to extract confessions (we return to the matter of the Brzeczek–Daley letter later in this chapter and again in Chapter Six).

The Confession in Political Context

Initially, Andrew's (and later Jackie's) confession appeared to be a triumph in the battle for White "law and order" votes in the approaching Democratic primary. On February 4, 1983, after a month-long trial, the Wilson brothers were convicted of murder; Jackie was sentenced to life in prison without parole and Andrew received the death sentence. The conviction that followed the dubious confession allowed both Byrne and Daley to take credit for apprehending and trying the Wilson brothers, with Andrew receiving a death sentence and Jackie sentenced to life imprisonment. It seemed a miraculously timely set of outcomes: the convictions were announced just three weeks before the February primary.

Both Byrne and Daley apparently assumed that the winner of the approaching Democratic mayoral primary would, at least in part, be determined by who gained the larger share of Chicago's White vote. Byrne rightly anticipated that she would be the target of primary challenges by Daley, as well as from the recently elected African American congressman, Harold Washington. Yet Byrne had difficulty seeing beyond Daley's threat to her hold on White Chicago voters in the all-important primary contest. Both Byrne and Daley underestimated how rapidly and successfully Harold Washington would mobilize a coalition of voters in support of his candidacy.

Byrne had made several critical errors as mayor, including replacing Black members of the Chicago Housing Authority, thereby undermining support from African American voters who occupied much of this housing. Sexist and racist slurs proliferated during the primary, with taunts of "Ditch the bitch and vote for Rich," "It's a racial thing, don't kid yourself," and capped with the accented syllables of the unabashedly racist slogan, "We don't want no Af-ri-can!" (Koeneman 2013:90). Flyers referred to Washington as "Mr. Baboon" and stoked fears about crime with claims that "[W]hite women will be raped" and that the city's police department would be renamed the "Chicongo Po-lease" (Marable 1986:18).

Byrne and Daley's underestimation of the depth and breadth of Harold Washington's electoral support was monumental, and Washington, to their surprise, was the easy winner of the primary. Undeterred, Daley challenged Washington in the general election as an un-nominated "independent" Democrat. But Washington won easily, becoming the first Black mayor of Chicago.

Not only did the coerced confession of the Wilson brothers not produce the antic-ipated primary victory for either Byrne or Daley, but because of the presumed part played by the forced confessions in the brothers' convictions, the guilty verdicts were later overturned in an Illinois Supreme Court decision. The coerced confessions were not reintroduced when the Wilson brothers were retried and reconvicted. *The irony was thus that the torture was counterproductive and unnecessary for purposes of gain-ing the desired convictions.*

This was obviously not the end of the story for RM Daley; but he would spend the following decades as state's attorney and mayor under a cloud of coerced confessions that became more widely known and difficult to excuse. In the following chapter, we show how Daley's electability in highly segregated Black neighborhoods was dam-aged by this and other aspects of his law and order regime. The cover-up of the Burge torture scandal haunted Daley for the entirety of his political career, leading up to and finally concluding with his eventual decision not to run for re-election as mayor in 2011.

"House of Screams"

In the late 1980s, Andrew Wilson, with the help of the People's Law Office, initiated a civil suit against the city and Jon Burge. Attorney William Kunkle represented Burge and the city. Kunkle had prosecuted Wilson's criminal case before leaving the state's attorney's office and entering private practice with Daley's first assistant in the office, Richard Devine. The judge in the case ruled that Wilson's lawyers could not intro-duce testimony from others who said they had been abused by Burge and his detec-tives, and the jurors in this civil case ultimately deadlocked, with the judge declaring a mistrial.

In a subsequent retrial, the jury found that Andrew Wilson's constitutional rights had been violated while he was in police custody and furthermore, that the City of Chicago had a "defacto policy, practice, or custom" of arrestee abuse (Ralph 2020:52). This finding made it more difficult for RM Daley to feign ignorance of the abuse. Yet juries are known for their unpredictability, and this case was no exception: the jury concluded that Wilson's mistreatment occurred outside the policy, and the police were acting "emotionally" in response to the killings of their fellow officers. As a result, Burge was not held legally responsible in this trial, and Wilson was not awarded any damages.

By 1990, there had been little progress in the torture cases of Black suspects. Yet there were scattered signals that this extraordinary scandal could not be completely covered up and permanently buried. The most important sign was the publication of John Conroy's (1990a) shocking essay, "House of Screams" in *The Chicago Reader.* Conroy was well known as a talented writer and respected for his exhaustive research. "House of Screams" provided an overview of the trials of Andrew and Jackie Wilson and was a key part of Conroy's (2000) book, *Unspeakable Acts, Ordinary People: The Dynamics of Torture.* In a closing chapter, Conroy protested that "the public is not aroused" by what he had reported in his earlier articles. But he also noted an exception involving an initiative undertaken by David Fogel, who had been appointed by Mayor Harold Washington as the chief administrator of the police department's OPS. Fogel had moved to reopen the OPS investigation that Police Superintendent Brzeczek had formally initiated without results eight years earlier.

Fogel had reached the conclusion that OPS essentially served within the Chicago Police Department, "to immunize police from internal discipline" (Conroy 2000:227). Nonetheless, he appointed two top investigators, Francine Sanders and Michael Goldston, to assess what was going on in Area 2. Fogel retired a few weeks later, but Sanders and Goldston continued their work and issued reports the following fall about the detectives named in Conroy's "House of Screams" article.

The *Invisible Institute* posted the reports on the web (Hunt n.d. OPS.Goldston. Sanders.Police Foundation Reports). Sanders directly confronted reports about Burge's torture of Wilson. She concluded: The only reasonable explanation for Wilson's injuries "was that they were sustained during Wilson's detention . . . at the hands of the police and under the sanction of the officer in charge . . . Lieutenant Jon Burge" (Conroy 1997). She noted that the abuse included electric shocks and recommended that the OPS charges against Burge be sustained, as well as against two other detectives among Burge's "midnight crew" of torturers.

Goldston's separate report implicated more officers by name and offered two broader substantive conclusions: "the preponderance of the evidence is that abuse did occur and that it was systematic," and furthermore, that "particular command members were aware of the systematic abuse and perpetrated it either by actively participating in same or failing to take any action to bring it to an end" (3). Goldston's report included six appendices that named names and included a spreadsheet data base, as well as statistical analyses.

Burge and the Midnight Crew

Police Superintendent LeRoy Martin received the Sanders and Goldston reports in the fall of 1990, but he waited an entire year before taking action. Martin was personally compromised by having been a commander in Area 2; however, in November 1991, he finally decided to act. He suspended Burge and two other "midnight crew" officers without pay and filed formal charges with the Police Board.

News stories based on the Sanders and Goldston reports focused new media attention on allegations of police brutality against Black Chicagoans. The columnist Mike Royko (1992), who earlier had exposed the White backlash politics of the Daley Democratic machine, surprised readers by denouncing the reports and praising the officers. However, the well-documented evidence spoke for itself: it linked Burge to half of the identified incidents. Notably, the Police Board process did not involve criminal charges and was not a criminal trial, and so Burge was subject to a judgment based on a "preponderance of evidence" rather than "beyond a reasonable doubt." The Board found Burge had failed to stop police brutality against Andrew Wilson, and it recommended that he be fired. This should finally have made it impossible for RM Daley to ignore the evidence of police brutality involving Burge, but it did not result in any criminal charges or convictions, and Daley continued to elude responsibility or accountability.

Conroy (2000) acknowledged the recommendation that Burge be fired, but he noted that the Police Board was still calling the brutality "physical abuse" rather than "torture." Conroy (2000:230) concluded: "it was a long wait, but eleven months later, on February 10, 1993, the Board issued a cautiously worded decision, as if they were afraid to shed too much light in so dark a corner." Although the Board fired Burge from the Chicago Police Department, it reinstated his associates, treating them much like bystanders who, if not innocent, had nonetheless already been sufficiently punished. It was as if the Board had finally discovered that torture was occurring (Ralph 2020:186) but still was not quite able to bring itself to see it (Baer 2020:191).

Burge was now out of work in Chicago, but he was not a convicted criminal, and he began to draw a city pension. Later, in the fall of 1993, the US Seventh Circuit Court of Appeals issued a ruling on Andrew Wilson's appeal of the decision in his civil case against Burge and the city (Ralph 2020). The chief judge, Richard Posner, was dismayed by the judge's decisions in the earlier case, including prohibiting testimony from other abuse victims and allowing Burge's lawyer, William Kunkle, to introduce questionable evidence. The Court of Appeals sent the case back to the federal district court, and Judge Robert Gettleman reheard it. He accepted the decision of the Chicago Police Board, and in the summer of 1995, he ordered the city to pay more than a million dollars in damages. Still, because it was a civil case, there were no criminal charges.

A New Demand to Investigate Jon Burge and RM Daley's Criminal Liability

Despite the civil settlement, a determined group of Chicago lawyers and activists, including Flint Taylor, persisted in demanding criminal charges in the Burge torture case. In spring 2000, the group petitioned the chief judge of the criminal court to appoint an independent special prosecutor. By now, a number of plea deals and settlements involving other torture cases had already been granted or were in the works through the state's attorney's office, and this threatened to diminish the consequences of the mounting torture revelations. John Conroy (2001) once again rose to the occasion by writing another important article, titled "A Hell of a Deal." The essay boldly took on the festering issue of the responsibility of the state's attorney's office under RM Daley for never meaningfully responding to Brzeczek's letter about Andrew Wilson's coerced confession. Conroy protested: "If the [s]tate's [a]ttorney's office has never investigated the policemen, how can you say there was no torture? If the only government bodies that have investigated it—the Police Board and the Office of Professional Standards—concluded that the police were guilty, how can you say they were not?"

Conroy reminded readers that two of Daley's former assistants at the Cook County State's Attorney's Office, William Kunkle and Richard Devine, worked for the firm that had received nearly a million dollars for defending Burge in the Wilson case. This was in addition to the substantial sum Devine had earlier received for defending Edward Hanrahan. The chief judge of the criminal court responded by implicitly acknowledging that the issue not only involved Burge and his officers, but also State's Attorney and now Mayor RM Daley, as well as his leadership team. The judge concluded that the matter required "the appointment of a special prosecutor to investigate the facts alleged by the petitioners and to determine if any prosecutions are warranted" (Conroy 2001).

Flint Taylor (2019:285) observed that this might finally be a crucial moment, but he also warned it would depend on who led the investigation. On this score, the results were disturbing. In 2002, the court appointed the retired Illinois appellate court Justice Edward Egan as special state prosecutor and Robert Boyle as assistant special state prosecutor. Egan had issued an appellate court decision denying one of Andrew Wilson's appeals, and Boyle had been involved as criminal division chief in the pursuit of the Panther survivors of the Fred Hampton raid. It would later also become known that many of Egan's family members were involved in the Chicago Police Department, including a nephew who worked in Division 2 under Burge (Ralph 2020). Taylor (2019:285) concluded: "These old-school prosecutors were, without a doubt, longtime Democratic machine operatives."

The Machine Marches On

The special state prosecutor took four more years to issue a report, and, in the end, he failed to recommend a single criminal charge. It would be another four years before Burge was finally convicted. In 2010, he was sentenced to prison for federal crimes for perjury and obstruction of justice, but not for torture. Both brothers filed multiple appeals of their convictions but Andrew died in prison in 2007. Jackie was released in 2018. In 2020, his murder charge was dismissed, and he was exonerated (Possley 2020).

Years earlier, in 1988, RM Daley had realized his goal of becoming mayor of Chicago, and he would serve in this office until 2012. Combined with his time as state's attorney, RM dominated Chicago politics for nearly a third of a century, despite, as state's attorney, overseeing the case of Andrew Wilson and many more African American torture victims of Jon Burge and his cohorts. All this, despite the growing number of cases and the enormous sums in court settlements for Chicago police abuse of Black suspects (Ralph 2020).

This chapter has only scratched the surface of this thirty-year saga of "the mayor and the midnight crew." In the following chapter, we begin to examine the cynicism toward the Chicago Police Department that this era provoked among the residents of the city's South and West Sides.

2
Politics and Punishment Chicago-Style

The tortured confession of Andrew Wilson under Police Detective Jon Burge is the case that most dramatically symbolizes the punitive politics of Richard M. Daley as state's attorney and then mayor of Chicago. Yet the Wilson case is only one among many of the laws and cases that trace the logics and trajectories of Chicago's modern political history of crime and punishment.

Law enforcement was central to both RJ and RM Daley. The patronage politics that RJ brought to the first Daley machine added growing numbers of police officers, prosecutors, and judges to its ranks, and RM Daley in turn escalated this growth trajectory. The latter Daley's punitive policies were therefore an important inflection point, building the city's criminal justice machine to unprecedented heights while extending its previously evolving perspectives and practices.

A Century of Conflict and Coercion

Christopher Muller (2012) has made the case that the explosive growth in Black arrests and mass imprisonment that occurred in the late 20th century—when RM Daley first became state's attorney and then mayor—had deep roots in successive waves of migration. These migrations included African Americans escaping the aftermath of slavery and Jim Crow in the South, as well as the immigration of European Americans, who also had come looking for work and better lives in America's growing cities. Chicago was positioned at the national crossroads of a century-long era of societal change.

Chicago's stockyards and steel mills were prominent among the powerful economic engines that attracted both European immigrants and African American migrants. However, the growing police and criminal justice systems were also attractive and particularly welcoming to White European immigrants, especially the Irish, who saw careers in law enforcement as offering opportunities for their socio-political and occupational advancement in American life. Steven Erie (1988) captured the arc of this aspirational era with his aptly titled book, *Rainbows' End: Irish Americans and the Dilemmas of Urban Machine Politics, 1840-1985*.

Irish police officers took occupational pride in providing protection for their fellow countrymen who, while seeking opportunity, also experienced mistreatment at the hands of American nativists. By contrast, Bryan Stevenson, of the Equal Justice Initiative, explained, African Americans coming to Chicago and other northern cities were motivated less by opportunity and more by fear: they were refugees and exiles from the torture and terror of the South (Capehart 2017). As the Great Migration grew into the tens of millions, the rising Irish increasingly saw the arriving African Americans as a threat, both to their recently gained economic success and to the safety of their neighborhoods (Wilkerson 2010). Law enforcement became a valued instrument for Irish neighborhood protection. A traditional Irish folk song boasted, "He's on the police force now," and Irish residents felt safer as a result.

Muller (2012) demonstrated that rates of non-White incarceration in the post–Civil War north grew significantly as foreign-born Whites became a majority of police officers. His quantitative evidence was consistent with findings of other scholars about the role of the police in the clash of arriving groups. For example, Neil Ignatiev (1995) observed that the Irish saw policing as a way of protecting their families from feared attacks by both White nativists and recently arriving African Americans, and as a way "to gain the rights of the white men" (140).

In his book, *Race Riot: Chicago in the Red Summer of 1919*, William Tuttle (1970) emphasized that legal cynicism was already instilled among African Americans fleeing the South during the early 20th century. The violence of slavery, the slave patrols, and the Klan made it clear that the state sanctioned White groups and White police officers' violence against African Americans. This violence ranged from isolated instances of assaults and lynchings of individuals to attacks on entire communities such as those in 1898 in Wilmington, North Carolina; in 1917 in East St. Louis, Illinois; and in 1921 in Tulsa, Oklahoma. As they made their way north during the Great Migration—for example, through the gateway of East St. Louis—African Americans were unprotected targets of brutality and abuse.

The Chicago police often did little to protect Black migrants from victimization by Whites. Indeed, Tuttle (1970:232) observed: "If East St. Louis shattered the trust of black men and women in the state's capacity to protect them, the behavior of Chicago's police only intensified their insecurity and readiness to furnish their own protection." Assaults by individual offenders and small groups were most common, but in July 1919, a conflict erupted that involved hundreds of White assailants and Black victims. The conflict began when Black bathers entered a Whites-only beach. In one area, a White man threw rocks at Black teenagers, striking one in the head and killing him. The dead boy's friends reported the death to police, but the police refused to arrest the rock thrower. News of the death spread, and within hours groups of Black and White Chicagoans took to the streets. The following five-day riot killed or injured 500 mainly Black victims. White Irish gangs, euphemistically known as "athletic clubs," were responsible for much of the violence.

One of the Irish gangs, the Hamburg Athletic Club in Bridgeport, was a training ground for RJ Daley's entry into Chicago politics (Cohen and Taylor 2000). Daley joined the club as an adolescent and rose to become its president. The club exposed RJ to political patrons who encouraged members to "defend" White South Side neighborhoods. In other words, these "patrons" sponsored White on Black violence, as reflected in a 700-page report, with graphic photos, "The Negro in Chicago: A Study of Race Relations and a Race Riot" (Tuttle 1970).

RJ's biographers, Cohen and Taylor (2000:36), speculated about the significance of his club experience with the 1919 riots:

> Daley's role, or lack of role, is likely lost to history, in part because the police and prosecutors never pursued the white gang members who instigated the violence. At the least, it can be said that Daley was an integral member of a youth gang that played an active role in one of the bloodiest anti-black riots in the nation's history—and that within a few years' time, this same gang would think enough of Daley to select him as its leader.

At a minimum, RJ and RM Daley had an up-close intergenerational familiarity with American acceptance of White on Black violence.

Legal Cynicism and Chicago Machine Politics

Once in office, RJ and RM Daley were proud to assist Irish Americans in securing municipal jobs, including positions in law enforcement. These officers were highly valued in communities like Bridgeport, where RJ and RM Daley both raised their families. These communities strongly identified as Irish American, and they were overt in their hostility to feared encroachment from nearby African American neighborhoods. A Bridgeport father, whose son attracted national attention by assaulting and seriously injuring a Black youth for simply walking through the neighborhood, explained that his son had acquired a "Bridgeport attitude" (Bogira 2005:278).

RJ and RM contributed to African American cynicism about law enforcement by allowing, if not encouraging, police misconduct. As we noted in our first chapter, this misconduct lasted decades. Along the way, Chicago paid millions of dollars in civil case settlements, which, over time, were recognized as a tactic of diversion and delay in dealing with police brutality and corruption. The long-term lingering effect of these cases was a legacy of cynicism about police law enforcement practices.

The Burge case uniquely linked RJ and RM Daley's political careers, with Burge's employment in the police department beginning during the father's time as mayor, and complaints and litigation continuing through RM's three-decade-long tenure as state's attorney and mayor. Both RJ and RM Daley were graduates of DePaul University Law School, and both first served in the state legislature. During his eight years in the Illinois Senate (1972–1980), RM was best known for blocking legislation opposed by his father's political machine. However, he also differed from his father in notable ways. For example, he did not follow the path to power through control of the patronage-rich clerkship of Cook County. Instead, RM chose law, and ran successfully in 1980 for Cook County State's Attorney.

The dynastic transition from father to son was temporarily interrupted mid-stream by several short-term serving mayors following the death of RM's father. This included election of the city's first woman mayor, Jane Byrne; the unpopular Michael Bilandic; and the first African American mayor, Harold Washington. Notwithstanding these milestone elections, gender bias and especially racial conflict persisted. Loïc Wacquant (2008, 2009) and Michelle Alexander (2010) note that in Chicago, as elsewhere, the rapid growth of exclusionary "hyper-segregated" housing policies, followed by the expansion of the "carceral state" and the rise of "mass incarceration," served to heighten racial conflict and legal cynicism.

Exclusion, Containment, and Public Housing

The construction of large public housing projects was a historically essential part of the separation, containment, and exclusion of African Americans from Chicago's downtown business district in the city's Loop and the Magnificent Mile shopping area near the lakefront (Austen 2018; Lemann 1995). Although RJ is known for deter-mining public housing policy in Chicago, his son, RM, recalls it somewhat differently. RM maintained his father accurately foresaw and therefore tried to warn lawmak-ers about the danger of high-rise designs and how they would isolate and concen-trate disadvantaged families in the massive new tower projects. "It's a big fallacy," RM insisted, "that he wanted all this. It's totally bullshit. He knew more about this than anybody else. He knew this would make them [the projects] like a prison" (cited in Austen 2018:42). RM's allusion to imprisonment was either a mental slip or an un-expected acknowledgment of the connection between the rising towers and the fol-lowing explosive growth of incarceration. It echoed the lament of a tenant who told a *New York Times* reporter her tower building was a "public aid penitentiary" (Belluck 1998). This characterization captured the implications of the towers for both spatial exclusion and coercive containment.

In the summer of 1959, RJ traveled to Washington to lobby for construction money to build public housing. He testified before a senate committee that Chicago needed "not only high risers but walk-up and row houses" (Austen 2018:42). The answer he received was that the dollar limits per unit would instead necessitate vertically stacked buildings. It was a plan that a 1966 federal senate commission on "executive reorgani-zation" heard described as "human filing cabinets" for the poor, another chilling sug-gestion of the containment involved in this form of public housing. RM recalled his father saying, "This is not going to go well" (Austen 2018:42).

Others were making the same point even more emphatically. In their book, *American Pharaoh*, Cohen and Taylor (2000:186) reported that RJ received many warnings. The warnings were prophetic: one prominent developer advised that the results would be, "to create further concentrations of high density . . . segregated housing on the Central South Side" (187). The containment effect of this segregation was confirmed by research showing that most residents rarely traveled outside their neighborhoods.

Even if RJ accurately foresaw the worst outcome—that the projects would prove to be criminogenic time bombs—it was also clear he was not going to turn down the federal funds to build them. Patronage jobs were the bread and butter of Chicago machine politics (Diamond 2017); besides, RJ argued, without the projects the growing Black population would either be crowded into rapidly deteriorating housing or wind up on the streets.

The first Mayor Daley doubled Chicago public housing in the 1950s and 1960s to nearly 40,000 units, second only to New York City and its Puerto Rican neighborhoods (Massey and Denton 1993; Sampson 2012). However, as RJ neared the end of his time as mayor, lower courts finally began to challenge the exclusive (and exclusionary) placement of the high-rise projects in Black neighborhoods. In *The Color of Law* (2017), Richard Rothstein explained how federal agencies joined forces with Mayor Daley to hold off lower court decisions requiring placement of public housing in White neighborhoods.

In 1976, a year before RJ's death, Robert Bork, President Reagan's solicitor general, defended the city's *de facto* discriminatory practices before the U.S. Supreme Court, arguing that building public housing in White neighborhoods would have "an enormous practical impact on innocent communities that will have to bear the burden of the housing" (Rothstein 2017:35). The Supreme Court ultimately rejected Bork's argument, but this did not improve the situation. RJ simply halted new public housing construction, which, as Rothstein noted, continued the *de facto* discrimination.

With the halt of new construction, Chicago's public housing boom was effectively finished. Douglas Massey and Nancy Denton (1993:76) used the 1980 decennial census to demonstrate just how "hyper-segregated" this construction boom had made Chicago. It placed the city among this nation's most segregated on five impactful dimensions: unevenness, isolation, clustering, centralization, and concentration. Poor construction of the towering projects further contributed to the problems that resulted from this hyper-segregation. The projects were plagued by poor design, inadequate funding for repairs, and mismanagement. Lawsuits claimed the housing strategy was explicitly racist in purpose and intent (Misra 2016).

President Bill Clinton's administration introduced a new housing policy: a market-based Hope VI program combining some mixed-income housing with vouchers that would allow some residents to move to private rental housing. However, the vouchers were typically too modest to allow movement to lower-crime neighborhoods and preferred schools. Yet the voucher values were nonetheless high enough to be attractive to landlords in only slightly more desirable neighborhoods (Rotella 2019). In 1998, the *New York Times* (Belluck 1998) published a special report that highlighted problems created by the Hope VI program. The report confirmed a recurring story: "the goal is to disperse the project's concentrated poverty . . . . But . . . tenants from housing projects [are] being moved mainly to poor black neighborhoods . . . as . . . unsafe as the high-rises they left."

Robert Sampson (2008) tested this reproduction of poverty thesis with data from a government experimental program in five cities, including Chicago. Called "Moving to Opportunity" (MTO), the program enlisted about 4,600 residents, and approximately one-third received vouchers to move from high- to lower-poverty neighborhoods. He noted that many families randomly assigned a voucher could not find suitable housing and did not move. As Ben Austen (2018:223; also Rotella 2019) observed: "this [program] had the effect of making the Housing Authority a source of growing problems in the private rental market."

Some encouraging evidence emerged in later studies indicating that some families with younger children might benefit from moving. Children of families who moved before their 13th birthday benefited in terms of college attendance and earnings, family life, and place of residence (Chetty, Hendren, and Katz 2015). Other research found evidence that violent crime arrests were lower for males in families that had access to a voucher. However, this benefit faded over time and did not occur for property crime or females (Kling, Ludwig, and Katz 2005; Sciandra et al. 2013); instead, some types of delinquency increased, particularly among males who moved into economically mixed neighborhoods (Graif 2015).

In 1999, RM Daley declared the public housing projects a failed experiment. He announced plans to tear down all the remaining decaying projects (Street 2007), concluding they were hazardous or beyond repair. These demolitions required relocating approximately 50,000 residents in a process that was chronically behind schedule and lasted upwards of five years; moreover, it mostly moved people to places they did not want to go.

Overall, there is little evidence that plans to rejuvenate and replace the projects resolved the city's problems of hyper-segregation. As Massey and Denton (1993:74–78) noted, RM Daley probably could have watched the disappointing results unfold, in real time, from the windows of his downtown fifth-floor mayor's office. The early 1990s was also a period in which unemployment was rising. In Chicago and elsewhere, racial implications of this problem were obscured by removing Black men from the unemployment rolls and placing them in jails and prisons, while simultaneously hiring increasing numbers of White men into law enforcement jobs (Western 2006). When White male employment markedly improved in the late 1990s, the joblessness of formerly incarcerated Black men continued to rise. As Western (2006:94–97) has demonstrated with national data, increases in Black job loss were linked to rising incarceration.

During this period of transition, RM shifted voters' attention from the failure of the projects to his "law and order" campaign. "Gangs, guns and drugs" was the repetitive mantra of his politics of punishment. RM saw the rising focus on punishment already happening elsewhere—with the new punitive turn gaining speed in the lead-up to "the Age of Reagan"—first in California and then New York. RM was determined to be the mayor who would bring punitive law enforcement to Chicago. He probably saw himself as a visionary, because he was expanding and intensifying the same rhetoric that he had introduced several years earlier during his campaign to become Cook County state's attorney.

RM's Punitive Politics in the State's Attorney's Office

When RM was first elected state's attorney in 1980, he won by just two-tenths of one percent (Street 2007). During his first years in office, he rolled out his "tough on crime" policy that increased arrests and convictions. Consistent with this approach, he was not inclined to reform the punitive culture of Chicago's police department, notably its established "code of silence" about brutal police misconduct.

Unlike his father, who relied on the implicit discretion granted to police officers to interpret and enforce the law, RM reduced this discretion to create a more tightly organized criminal justice machine. As state's attorney, one of his first goals was to increase the volume of cases his office handled. The Chicago journalist David Jackson (2011) offered a clear-eyed description of State's Attorney Daley as one of the toughest prosecutors in the country: "He . . . revamped the bureaucracy of his office—creating new units and tightening the chains of command—and left his stamp on large chunks of the Illinois criminal code: … from the way crimes are charged to the way judges mete out sentences."

This "tightening of the chains of command" reflected a kind of "tight coupling" found in Chicago and other modern, racially focused penal regimes (see also Beckett and Western 2001; Hagan 1989, 2010). In RM's first term as state's attorney, the Chicago Police Department was already making about 150,000 disorderly conduct arrests a year, with more than three times as many Blacks and Latinos arrested as Whites. A city task force report later observed that the focus on minorities totaled "almost half of all arrests . . . and therefore became one of the primary ways police interacted with minority communities" (Police Task Force 2016:34). In effect, as state's attorney, RM was reproducing the kind of racial animus that his father was still fostering at the end of his time as mayor.

An example of their parallel policies of coercion and containment was apparent in 1976, when the Afro-American Patrolmen's League won a court ruling ordering the Chicago Police Department to increase racial diversity in police officer hiring. As leverage, the court impounded federal revenue-sharing funds earmarked for the city. But RJ responded by borrowing $55 million from local banks to keep the department the way it was (Baer 2020:120). In turn, RM's regime used these funds to increase its focus on drugs: the year before he was elected, the office prosecuted about 900 defendants for drug-related felonies; but by the end of RM's first term, his office boasted nearly 4,500 drug-related felonies. RM touted the policy as both efficient and effective.

Daley and Cook County's criminal court judges were on the same page in their determination to advance Chicago's drug war. The remotely located courthouse at

26th and California was already bursting at the seams and leading the nation in felony cases. However, during Daley's second term, the court initiated a night court drug program that in its first year nearly doubled its felony caseload, from about 5,000 to nearly 10,000 cases. A 1992 U.S. Justice Department study praised this result, calling the program an "efficient and cost-effective approach available right now for replication in other jurisdictions" (cited in Bogira 2005:118). Chicago had gained a leadership position in America's escalating war on drugs.

Jackson (2011) reported that Daley was meanwhile reorganizing the Cook County State's Attorney's Office into a "veritable legislation mill," drawing on his experience and contacts in the Illinois legislature. He quadrupled the size of the office appeals division, putting it to work drafting "legislative concepts." This resulted in fifty or more newly drafted bills per year, which included changing the Automatic Transfer Act [ATA] to allow prosecution of juveniles as adults for nonviolent crimes, notably including drug violations, within 1,000 feet of a school. The revised ATA meant that any fifteen- or sixteen-year-old accused of possessing more than fifteen grams of cocaine could be transferred automatically—without judicial review—to adult court. Fifteen grams of cocaine mandated a minimum of six years in an adult institution.

A former chief of felony review under RM challenged the logic of these prosecutions in an interview (Jackson 2011; see also Van Cleve 2016).

> You're not getting the hard-core dealers .... You're getting the kid who has never been in trouble before. The narcotics officer buys a little bit from the kid, and keeps buying until finally he talks the kid into distributing a 'Class X' amount.

Even RM's aides were skeptical about this punitive turn. Jackson (2011) concluded: "The complaints about Daley, in one sense, all boil down to this: He is using the office for a steppingstone to the fifth floor [mayor's office] of City Hall." The resounding complaint from the South Side neighborhoods was that Daley was prosecuting young Black males to get himself elected mayor.

RM's Climb to the Fifth Floor

RM's desire to occupy his father's former office was already apparent by 1982, only a year after he was elected state's attorney. But, as we noted in Chapter One, he had misread the city's changing politics. Chicago's African American voters now numbered more than a half million, many of whom were anxious for change. These voters were already supporting a new "change" candidate, the charismatic Harold Washington, whose message was that "Chicago is a city where citizens are treated unequally and unfairly . . . women, Latinos, Blacks, youth and progressive [W]hites have been left out of the Chicago government" (cited in Koeneman 2013:89).

Progressive youth and minorities were increasingly skeptical about Chicago politics and formed a strong coalition of support for Washington. As noted in the previous chapter, after losing a primary bid, Daley persisted in running as an "independent Democrat" against Washington in the general election, which Washington won handily. RM kept his mayoral prospects alive with his re-election as Cook County state's attorney in 1984, and he resumed his quest to be mayor after Washington unexpectedly died of a heart attack in 1987.

Daley made limited efforts to address cynicism among minorities and progressives; he often mixed his war on drugs rhetoric with puzzling proclamations of being a progressive (Koeneman 2013:112–113). It was a blunt and instinctual speaking style with a delivery that somehow matched the city's insensitivity and racial intolerance, especially as linked to crime. Yet RM seemed to understand that going forward politically, he needed to find other ways to mute opposition in minority communities, so with an eye to public relations, he hired a respected Black radio reporter, Avis LaVelle, as his spokesperson.

Daley had considerable help in cultivating a new look for the general campaign. He enlisted Rahm Emanuel to expand his fundraising base, and Emanuel raised an unprecedented seven million dollars. Contributions still came from patronage workers and labor unions, but also from a growing class of private sector donors. As the political scientist Richard Simpson and colleagues (2004) noted, the latter source of funds included the rising business class of the global economy, including financial firms, securities traders, corporate law firms, bankers, and international manufacturers.

Other key additions to RM's team included his brother, Bill Daley, who later played a parallel role as strategist in Bill Clinton's ascent, and David Axelrod, who masterminded a remake of RM into an electable candidate. Bill Daley and David Axelrod developed a strategy that joined RM's Reagan-like appeal to less educated voters with a cooptation of the business class, plus a poll-tested calculation that, absent the charismatic Harold Washington, the African American vote could be outflanked.

Daley won the 1989 Democratic primary nomination and the general election as well. He took the White working-class wards, the White lakefront vote, and he swept the Latinx wards. Along the way, Daley discovered he was more appealing to Latinx than Black voters, and this became an enduring element in his electoral success.

Increased distrust remained concentrated among African American voters. Two Black candidates opposed Daley in the general election, the interim mayor Eugene Sawyer, and a more popular former ally of Mayor Washington, Tim Evans (whereas Ed Vrdolyak was the unlikely and unlikable Republican opponent). The election result was a racialized reversal of the electoral politics that had previously made Washington mayor: "The [B]lack vote was split between Sawyer and Evans, making 1989 the mirror image of Washington's 1983 victory" (Koeneman 2013:117). The lessons of this election served the new Daley machine well during the next five mayoral campaigns. The prosecution of drug crime continued to be a central theme, despite a lack of demonstrated success in providing citizens protection or prevention. Not surprisingly, Daley's drug policy would continue to be controversial in Chicago's Black neighborhoods.

RM's Governance through Race, Politics, and Crime

Chicago continued to be a leading city in the policing and prosecution of drug crime during RM's early terms as mayor. Between 1991 and 1998, the number of drug-related arrests rose from about 21,000 to more than 58,000. This was more than a 170 percent increase during a period of overall reductions in crime locally and nationally (Skogan 2007:16). Politicians of all stripes were now supporting more punitive crime policies in response to the public's unrelenting fear of crime, which the same politicians had helped to create.

Reminiscent of his father's 1959 trip to Washington in pursuit of funding to build public housing, RM traveled twice to Washington to deliver speeches in favor of President Clinton's massive 1994 crime bill. The first speech was comparatively restrained, emphasizing that the crime bill could bring a thousand more police officers to Chicago (Daley 1994a). The second speech was more ambitious, with Daley (1994b) mixing his support for more police with additional funding for prisons and gun control:

> It's not enough to put more police on the street—although that is vitally important. It is not enough to get guns off the street—although that's equally important. It's not enough to build more prisons and impose longer sentences—although we must do these things as well.

Daley wanted it all. He was joined by other big city mayors in supporting the legislation, and the Clinton-era crime bill wound up delivering substantial funding for both local policing and prison construction (Forman 2017; Western 2006). For RM in the 1990s, as for RJ in the 1950s, this was good patronage politics. Public housing projects and prisons were, in political terms, interchangeable. He could hire workers to tear down the housing projects, and construct new prisons while hiring police officers to fill them. Times may have changed, but patronage was still good politics in the city with broad shoulders.

Koeneman (2013) described how crowded the Cook County courthouse became in the 1990s, with drug and other cases. The courtrooms were routinely packed with defendants, witnesses, lawyers, judges, and clerks. "On a typical day," he observed, "the courts dealt with fourteen hundred cases and bond hearings," and "half of these cases involved drugs" (150). The machine-like handling of Cook County's tightly organized drug docket was both dramatic and disturbing: "the criminal courthouse in Chicago was like a huge, bureaucratic factory that constantly manufactured prisoners" (Koeneman 2013:151). The Chicago Police Department created named special teams—like Hammer Down, Iron Wedge, Clean Sweep, and Risky Business—to conduct dragnet sweeps through South Side neighborhoods and housing projects. The result was a growing supply of minor as well as more serious cases for the night court drug docket (Bogira 2005:118). RM's politics of punishment had successfully enlarged the city's incarceration machine.

Skogan (2007) highlighted how racially concentrated drug crimes had become. Nearly all the new arrests—approaching 80 percent—were of African Americans. Skogan observed that, under RM's direction, Chicago's courts were making Illinois one of the most racially disproportionate sites of mass incarceration in America.

The Gang Loitering Ordinances

In the 1990s, the new Daley machine added to its enforcement weaponry with a highly publicized gang loitering ordinance. With RM's aggressive support, the Chicago City Council passed the ordinance in 1992. The Council made clear that the intent was to increase policing in minority neighborhoods, using "dispersal orders" and arrests. From 1992 to 1995, police issued almost 90,000 dispersal orders and arrested more than 40,000 largely minority suspects (Police Accountability Task Force 2016:35).

In 1999, the U.S. Supreme Court ruled the ordinance unconstitutional on grounds that it violated due process rights, was excessively vague, and gave police too much discretion. The city council, at RM's urging, responded by drafting a new and more closely worded ordinance that was also enforced almost entirely in minority neighborhoods. It was as if the Supreme Court decision had given detailed instructions on how to make the revised ordinance legally defensible (see Schoenfeld 2018).

In 2014, nearly 85 percent of dispersal orders issued under the new gang ordinance targeted African American youth. This governing approach added to the growing skepticism about law enforcement in African American neighborhoods. Dorothy Roberts (1999; see also Harcourt 1998) called the gang loitering ordinance a form of "order maintenance policing" that was justified as offering protection to neighborhood residents. Advocates of the ordinance argued that crimes such as drug dealing were difficult for the police to intercept and therefore required vaguely framed statutory authority for enforcement.

The effect of the ordinance on crime was uncertain if not doubtful. An early study found that it reduced robberies (Skogan 1990), but subsequent research indicated little evidence of a link between aggressive order maintenance policing and a reduction in serious crime (Harcourt 2001; Harcourt and Ludwig 2006; also see Braga, Welsh, and Schnell 2015). Roberts (1999) provided a revealing evaluation of Chicago's experience with the gang loitering ordinance. The core of her critique questioned the assumption that police can accurately distinguish "visibly lawless people" from those who are lawful. Roberts argued this distinction incorporates "racist social norms that perpetuate stereotypes of Black criminality" (1999:803). She contended that gang loitering enforcement through dispersal orders and arrests actually helped to create— through its behavioral vagueness and focused concentration on minorities—the racialized categories of lawlessness that it claimed to deter.

Roberts further explained how order maintenance law enforcement—from disorderly conduct charges, through gang loitering arrests, to stop and frisk practices—was prioritized in RM's new law enforcement machinery and applied through drug law enforcement. She emphasized that it was well received in neighborhoods populated by White voters. While some academics as well as activists and residents from varied backgrounds also supported the ordinance, Roberts emphasized that opposition from the Black community was intense. Only six of eighteen Black council members voted for passage of the original gang loitering law.

Alderman John Steele grounded his opposition explicitly in its racial implications, asserting that the law was "drafted to protect the downtown area and the [W]hite community at the expense of innocent [B]lacks" (cited in Roberts 1999:824). A group of organizations filed an amicus brief claiming that the ordinance was the product of a neighborhood federation based in a predominately White part of the city; it was drafted by several White council members and endorsed by Mayor Daley (Roberts 1999:825).

The gang loitering ordinance is one of a succession of laws that RM's machine—first through the Cook County State's Attorney's Office and then through the mayor's office—employed to expand police powers over minority youth. These practices were among the enduring legacies of RM Daley's political career. This ordinance was another chapter in our national history of the racial gap between rich and poor, and the politics of crime and punishment. We will see that this resulted in rising levels of legal cynicism, particularly in Chicago's highly segregated neighborhoods..

The Beginnings of Our Exclusion-Containment Theory of Legal Cynicism

Our theoretical approach draws—but also differs in emphasis—from Sampson's (2012) influential theory of collective efficacy, legal cynicism, and crime. Sampson's theory prioritizes the positive effects of collective efficacy, a concept that builds on what criminologists have called "the willingness to intervene" to prevent crime, as well as the social trust involved in making these interventions impactful. We acknowledge the significance of collective efficacy, but we differ in assigning priority to the more ominous concept of legal cynicism, which Sampson included in his research but to which he gave less emphasis.

Studies of connections between legal cynicism and crime are grounded in two theoretical traditions. The first, David Matza's (1964) symbolic interactionist theory of *Delinquency and Drift*, focused on perceptions of legal injustice that can lead to involvement in crime. An important early paper by Sampson and Bartusch (1998) on causes of legal cynicism drew upon Matza's interactionist theory.

The second tradition has two interconnected threads, respectively focusing on neighborhood poverty and racial segregation. Sampson's work emphasized *the joint influence* of both poverty and segregation by building on William Wilson's (1987)) theory of economic and racially concentrated poverty (see also Sampson and Wilson 1995; Sampson, Wilson, and Katz 2018). As Wilson noted in his book, *The Truly Disadvantaged,* both race and poverty are strongly and positively associated with high crime rates. Sampson analyzed the joint impact of race and poverty by measuring their influence together (e.g., Sampson, Raudenbush, and Earls 1997). He did this with a joined conceptualization of concentrated disadvantage operationalized through a mixture of measures that included both neighborhood poverty and racial composition.

The second tread, which is central to our approach, differs in emphasis and draws from Massey and Denton's (1993) demographically driven theory linking high neighborhood racial segregation to high rates of crime, as reflected in their provocatively titled book: *American Apartheid.* We prioritize Massey and Denton's demographic attention to racial segregation by *separating* our measurement of neighborhood racial exclusion and containment from an index of concentrated disadvantage. Our measures of these concepts do not overlap. This allows us to better focus on the segregation effects of neighborhood exclusion and containment. Massey and Denton (1993:77) emphasized that the unique importance of racial segregation in the United States made many Black Americans "among the most isolated people on earth." This systemically imposed isolation is at the heart of our exclusion-containment theory.

Two Important Studies of Legal Cynicism and Crime

According to Google Scholar, two of the most (if not *the* most) influential empirical studies of legal cynicism are by Sampson and Bartusch (1998) and Kirk and Papachristos (2011). Perhaps surprisingly, neither of these studies made structural factors the sole or most important focus for their analyses of legal cynicism. Sampson and Bartusch (1998) placed their emphasis on Matza's interactionist version of anomie theory, and defined legal cynicism as the product of a "normless anomic neutralization process" in which rules of law prove ineffective in constraining criminal behavior. They argued that when law-related norms lose their force in neighborhoods, youth can become anomic—or normless—and can be drawn into crime.

More than a decade later, Kirk and Papachristos (2011) developed an alternative cultural framing theory emphasizing that people who perceive law enforcement practices as illegitimate, unresponsive, and ineffectual for crime prevention and protection are more prone to legal cynicism and may resort to crime in self-defense. Kirk and Papachristos maintained that social norms and cultural frames are subtly different in their relationship to legal cynicism and crime. They (2011:1207n) pointed out that Sampson and Bartusch's original scale of legal cynicism incorporated measures of anomie and moral cynicism. This served Sampson and Bartusch's goal of identifying and explaining *social psychological causes* of legal cynicism. Kirk and

Papachristos focused instead on the *consequences* of citizens' cynical responses to law enforcement. Their cultural framing approach involved a major modification of the measurement of legal cynicism. They explained: "We measure legal cynicism using indicators of resident *perceptions of the legal system and the police*, in contrast to earlier work that measured legal cynicism using indicators of social norms" (2011:1192, emphasis added).

More specifically, David Kirk and his colleagues (e.g., Kirk and Matsuda 2011; Kirk and Papachristos 2011;) measured legal cynicism with survey questions that asked about agreement with three statements: (1) the police are not doing a good job in preventing crime in this neighborhood, (2) the police are not able to maintain order on the streets and sidewalks in the neighborhood, and (3) laws are made to be broken. The latter is the only item that overlaps with Sampson and Bartusch's scale; nonetheless Kirk and Papachristos (2011) reported a high correlation (.75) between the two scales.

Kirk and Papachristos' conceptualization leveraged the explanatory power of their measurement of legal cynicism to answer a pressing question about crime in Chicago: Why did homicide rates remain high in some neighborhoods, despite their marked improvement in economic conditions? They took advantage of the versatility of the concept of legal cynicism for this purpose (see Hagan, McCarthy, and Herda 2020). They discovered that neighborhood legal cynicism rises when gaps emerge between citizen needs and expectations, and the police provision of crime prevention and protection. This cynicism, in turn, exerts an influence on neighborhood rates of violence. They underscored that this process can be "*independent of the structural circumstances that originally produced such cynicism*" (2011:1192, emphasis added). According to Kirk and Papachristos, this independence was the source of the otherwise unexpected persistence of continued high rates of homicide through the 1990s in some South Side Chicago neighborhoods such as Bronzeville.

In the early 1990s, Bronzeville's gentrification had increased home values, resident incomes, and home ownership. Yet legal cynicism remained high, and the homicide rate doubled. Bronzeville is suggestive of how relationships that can operate through intervening variables do not always or necessarily unfold as expected, and why reconceptualization and continued measurement of citizen skepticism about police law enforcement may be necessary in explaining such exceptions.

The modifications that Kirk and Papachristos introduced into the conceptualization and measurement of legal cynicism are an essential contribution, and their finding of its link to crime is fascinating and important; yet, we propose that the Bronzeville finding may be an important exception rather than the rule. We contend that legal cynicism more often operates as a mediator between structural conditions—such as poverty and racial segregation—and outcomes. These intervening effects are crucially important beyond the unique neighborhood circumstances observed in Bronzeville.

Legal Cynicism and Resistance to Daley's Law

Scholars have used legal cynicism to examine an array of problems, ranging from homicide (Kirk and Papachristos 2011) and police bias (Carr, Napolitano, and Keating 2007; Kirk and Matsuda 2011) to drug and property crime (Hagan, McCarthy, Herda, and Chandrasekher 2018), domestic violence (Emery, Jolley, and Wu 2011; Bell 2017), family problems (Bell 2016), and teen births (Sampson 2012). Our goal is to direct attention to the responsibility of elites for creating and neglecting conditions that contribute to feelings of neighborhood insecurity, perceptions of police ineffectiveness, and attitudes expressing legal cynicism. Our study extends attention to the highest levels in the hierarchy of law enforcement, including not only police but also elected political officials such as mayors. Our intent is to make explicit the coercive role of elite politicians and their powerful agents in structuring illegitimate, unresponsive, and ineffectual policing. These are the building blocks of what we call an exclusion-containment theory of legal cynicism and crime.

This theory of legal cynicism traces the causes of persistently high American crime rates to social exclusion and coercive containment of racial and ethnic minority communities. As indicated in the prologue to this book, the police operate at the apex of a contradiction between their promise to serve and protect citizens and their intense involvement in controlling and containing minority spaces in hyper-segregated neighborhoods. RM Daley's tenure as Chicago's mayor is a case in point: it offers a compelling illustration of how the tightened coupling of criminal justice practices, combined with policies of exclusion and containment, can result in police practices that lead to legal cynicism and crime.

Our theoretical emphasis on exclusion and containment is consistent with an important and evolving understanding of the relationship between law enforcement and crime, articulated by Chicago activists. This is reflected, for example, in the writing of Salim Muwakkil (2006) about the racially biased role of policing in Chicago. He argued,

> Racial bias is symptomatic because policing institutions were designed to contain rather than serve and protect the black community .... The job of racial containment has been White America's mandate to the police, and for the most part they have faithfully performed their duty.

Muwakkil emphasized that Chicago police perform this containment role as a means of enforcing barriers of access to the cultural and economic capital of this quintessential city.

Figure 2.1 introduces a conceptual overview of the exclusion-containment theory of legal cynicism and crime that we use. The outcomes emphasized in this model include calls by residents for police assistance, complaints about police misconduct, and attitudes toward Chicago's "law and order" mayor Richard M. Daley. However,

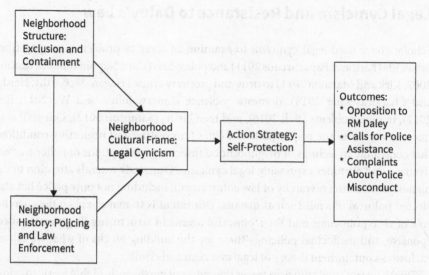

Figure 2.1 Exclusion-Containment Theory of Legal Cynicism

this summary figure does not include all the variables or theoretical pathways we consider in this and following chapters. The immediate purpose of this model is simply to identify and locate the influence of key concepts to which we attach special importance. Legal cynicism is the lynchpin in this exclusion-containment theory of crime and its control.

Exclusion, Containment, and Legal Cynicism in the 2003 Election

We begin this book's examination of legal cynicism and its consequences with an investigation of neighborhood support for RM Daley in the 2003 mayoral election. We hypothesized that variation in support for Daley in this election followed from the exclusion and containment of African American residents in hyper-segregated neighborhoods, as well as police relations with residents of these neighborhoods.

RM Daley won his first successful campaign for mayor in 1989 with 55 percent of the vote. In 2003, he won with 78 percent, and in 2007, in his final race for mayor, he had support from 71 percent of voters. In 2011, Daley announced he would not seek another term, in large part because of rising opposition to his political regime. However, signs of the end were already apparent in 2003, and these signs are what we aimed to capture in our focus on this election.

The 2003 election was unusual in several respects. Daley did not announce that he would seek re-election until late 2002. His wife Maggie Daley, a popular figure in Chicago, had been diagnosed with breast cancer earlier in the year, and this likely occupied his thoughts. Daley had won in the previous election with 71 percent of the vote, even though he had been challenged by Congressman Bobby Rush. Rush was well known as a co-founder of the Illinois Black Panther party and for his activism and public service. Furthermore, Rush had defeated challenger Barack Obama to retain his congressional seat. Rush won 17 of 50 Chicago wards when he challenged Daley. However, the betting was that, since Rush had lost by more than 20 percent in the popular vote, others would have trouble doing better.

Notwithstanding these odds, three Black candidates took up the challenge in 2003, including a businesswoman and two ministers. All three struggled to achieve name recognition and to raise campaign funds. Voter turnout was less than one-third, lower than in any previous election. Yet this was a significant time of change in South and West Side Chicago neighborhoods. As we noted early in this chapter, the preceding decade included the serial teardowns of the city's high-rise public housing projects, with only limited replacement through voucher and other programs. This intensified the exclusion and containment of the residents left behind in hyper-segregated census tracts.

Our theory predicts that the exclusion and containment of neighborhoods would intensify legal cynicism and in turn strengthen minority opposition to RM's machine. Thus, key links in our conceptual model presented in Figure 2.1 anticipate that census tracts high in African American representation would show weaker support for RM's re-election. The middle part of our conceptual model in Figure 2.1 indicates that census tract legal cynicism should help explain weakened support for Mayor Daley. This part of our model assumes that the consequences of Black social exclusion and containment should be positively associated with census tracts where segregation was increasing and where levels of legal cynicism were highest.

The Data Used in This Chapter

Our examination of these hypothesized relationships, as well as those in subsequent chapters, used data drawn from several sources. In this chapter, we analyzed data from the U.S. Census for 1990 and 2000, surveys of Chicago residents, and voting records (see Appendix A for details about these data sources).

Beginning with the 1990 census data (see Tables, Chapter 2 Table 1 for descriptive data), we used percent African American, as well as percent Hispanic, to measure social exclusion and containment at the census tract level. There are almost two dozen well-known measures of racial exclusion (Massey and Denton 1993). The percent Black and percent Hispanic in Chicago neighborhoods are highly skewed and so we divided them into quartiles; using quartiles provides a clear way to reveal the extent to which these communities are excluded and contained. There are also many ways to divide cities (e.g., into blocks, tracts, and collections of tracts). We used tracts because alternative measures (i.e., blocks) are too small to represent neighborhoods, while other measures (e.g., collections of tracts) may introduce problems when the tracts are not homogenous on variables of interest (Hipp 2007).

Figure 2.2 shows a map of the quartiles of percent African American across Chicago census tracts in 1990. In tracts in the first quartile, less than one percent (.65%) of residents were Black. For illustrative purposes, we disaggregated this first quartile further. This disaggregation showed that 72 percent (122/169) of tracts in this first quartile had no residents who identified as Black. Neighborhoods with the

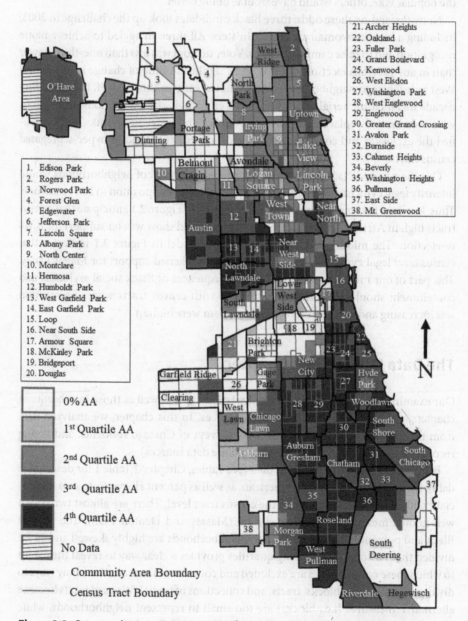

Figure 2.2 Community Area Tracts across African American Quartiles of Exclusion-Containment

most first quartile tracts were concentrated in the northwest, southeast, and central west parts of the city and included wealthy communities such as Forest Glenn and North Center, as well as more middle-class neighborhoods such as West Lawn and Archer Heights.

Tracts in the second quartile ranged from less than one (.66%) to 12 percent African American. Prominent neighborhoods in this quartile included Logan Square, Lincoln Park, Lakeview, and West Town. In the third quartile, tracts were between 12 and 97 percent Black. This group of neighborhoods includes South Chicago, South Shore, Humboldt Park, and Rogers Park. The fourth quartile was more than 97 percent African American and included many of the poorest neighborhoods in Chicago, such as Englewood, West Garfield, Washington, and Grand Crossing (about 21 percent of the tracts in this quartile were entirely Black).

The distribution for Hispanics was less skewed. In the first quartile, less than one percent (.75) of residents were Hispanic. In the second, residents who were Hispanic ranged from .76 percent to 6 percent. Tracts in the third quartile were more than 6 percent Hispanic, but less than 29 percent. The fourth quartile tracts were more than 29 percent Hispanic.

We also considered a second measure of social exclusion—economic exclusion—as measured by what Sampson, Raudenbush, and Earls (1997) call concentrated disadvantage. We included five of their dimensions: number of children under 18; percent of residents below the poverty line; percent receiving public assistance; percent in a female-headed household; and percent unemployed.

We measured legal cynicism using Kirk and Papachristos' scale that included items considered by Sampson and colleagues (1997) in their 1994–1995 Project on Human Development in Chicago Neighborhoods (PHDCN). We measured other variables, described below, with survey data collected in a follow-up project, the 2001–2003 Chicago Community Adult Health Study (CCAHS; House et al. 2012). The PHDCN included 8,782 respondents from 847 census tracts; the CCAHS was smaller with 3,782 respondents and 627 tracts.

Recall that Kirk and Papachristos' (2011) legal cynicism scale included three items. These came from the PHDCN. They measured agreement about police failure to achieve three goals: a just rule of law ("laws are made to be broken"), prevention ("the police are not doing a good job in preventing crime in this neighborhood"), and protection ("the police are not able to maintain order on the streets and sidewalks").

We also included two other variables as controls, both introduced by Sampson and colleagues (see Appendix). The first, collective efficacy, was the major concept in Sampson's (2012) theoretical approach. The second, tolerance for deviance, was central to Sampson and Bartusch's (1998) initial examination of legal cynicism. These measures were from the CCAHS.

We measured electoral support for RM Daley with data for the 2003 mayoral election. In this election, Daley received the highest citywide support of his career, thus reflecting his electoral popularity at its peak. Our measure was percentage of votes for Daley in each sampled census tract.

Our analyses also incorporated a number of control variables that measure neighborhood structural features and other conditions. We drew from Shaw and McKay's (1942/1972) theory of neighborhood social disorganization and included 1990 census measures of immigrant concentration (percent foreign born) and residential stability (percent of owner-occupied housing), as well population density. We controlled for crime with a measure of the number of homicides from 1980 to 1994 (from Block and Block 2005).

Our measures of neighborhood structural conditions used 1990 census data because these reflect structural conditions of Chicago at the time when the legal cynicism measures were collected. However, our second focus, support for Mayor RM Daley, used data from the 2003 election. We therefore supplemented our 1990 census measures with a series of variables that used 2000 census data to calibrate change over time. Some census tract boundaries were divided, joined, or altered in other ways. We addressed this with a "crosswalk" procedure that harmonized the 2010 tract boundaries with those used in 1990 (Logan, Xu, and Stults 2014). The 1990 and 2000 census variables were closely correlated, so we measured change as the difference between them (2000–1990). For racial exclusion we used dummy variables that distinguished tracts in which racial concentration increased (i.e., a positive change) or decreased (i.e., a negative change) compared to those that did not change.

Analysis of the 2003 Daley Election

As expected, our descriptive data indicated that, with each successive quartile of increased African American exclusion-containment, the average for legal cynicism displayed the anticipated step-like movement (see Tables, Chapter 2 Table 1). The average for legal cynicism was -.34 for tracts in the first quartile and -.19 for those in the second; it turned positive at .16 in quartile three and reached .29 in the fourth quartile. Again, this is the quartile in which the hyper-segregated level of exclusion-containment was 97 percent and above.

We next estimated a multivariate ordinary least squares (OLS) regression equation for legal cynicism (see Tables, Chapter 2 Table 2). As anticipated, our measure of racial exclusion-containment—the relative concentration of Blacks across tracts—was a striking predictor of legal cynicism: in the third and fourth quartiles, the predicted effect for African American concentration was statistically significant ($p<.001$), whereas it was non-significant for the second quartile (relative to the first quartile).

Figure 2.3 presents predicted margins based on the slopes from the OLS analysis. These show the predicted values for legal cynicism for each level of African American and Hispanic racial/ethnic composition, taking into account all control variables in the model (i.e., set to their means). The lines extending vertically from each bar indicate 95 percent confidence intervals. The results revealed a steady increase in predicted legal cynicism from the first quartile (i.e., -.224) to the fourth

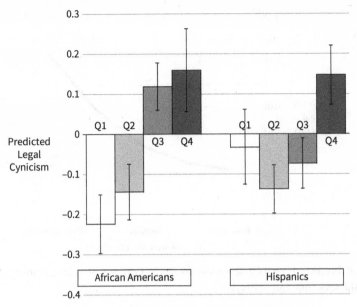

Figure 2.3 Predicted Means of Legal Cynicism across African American and Hispanic Quartiles of Exclusion-Containment (with 95% Confidence Intervals)

quartile (i.e., .160). A similar, more muted step-like pattern occurred for our measures of Hispanic concentration, but only the effect for the highest level of Hispanic concentration was significant (.148).

Our second measure of social exclusion—concentrated disadvantage—was also significantly associated with legal cynicism. Predicted margins presented in Figure 2.4 showed a value of -.19 for legal cynicism for privileged tracts that were at the fifth percentile in concentrated disadvantage, whereas the score for legal cynicism at the 95th percentile for economic disadvantage was .07. The other significant predictors of legal cynicism included number of homicides in the period before legal cynicism was assessed, percent foreign born, and population size.

We next turned our attention to the 2003 mayoral election (see Tables, Chapter 2 Table 3). The results from our OLS analysis showed the strong influence of Black exclusion-containment, with effects increasing in size from the second to the third and fourth quartiles for the percent African American (compared to tracts in the first quartile). As we expected, legal cynicism also had a sizable negative association with support for Mayor Daley, net of other predictors.

We show the magnitude of these effects with predicted margins and 95 percent confidence intervals (see Figure 2.5). These show the predicted values of electoral support for Mayor Daley, taking into account all control variables in the model (i.e., set to their means). Here we held legal cynicism at a high level and present margins

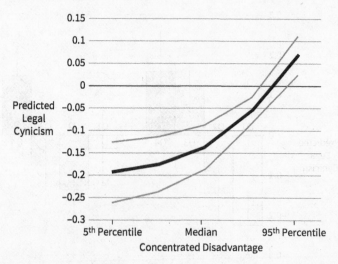

Figure 2.4 Predicted Legal Cynicism Values across Concentrated Disadvantage (with 95% Confidence Intervals in gray)

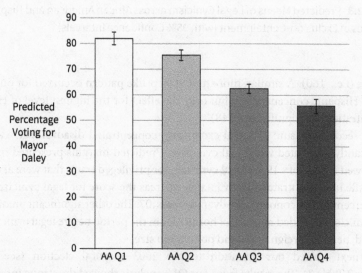

Figure 2.5 Predicted Percentage Voting for 2003 RM Daley across African American Quartiles of Exclusion-Containment (with 95% Confidence Intervals)

for each of the four quartiles of African American concentration (we used the 95th percentile in the distribution of legal cynicism for each quartile).

Recall that in the 2003 election, Mayor Daley won 78 percent of the vote, and won by the largest margin in any of his six campaigns. Our results show a predicted level of support for Daley at about 82 percent in the first quartile. The predicted level of support for Daley dropped to about 75 percent in tracts high in legal cynicism that were in the second quartile. Predicted support for Daley dropped precipitously to about 63 in the third quartile and declined even further to 56 percent in the high-cynicism tracts of the fourth quartile; the difference from the first to the fourth quartile was about 26 points.

Thus, even in Daley's most triumphant election, he received a smaller number of votes in hyper-segregated tracts where legal cynicism was particularly intense. In these highly segregated tracts of social exclusion, opposition to Daley was substantial. Looking back after the 2007 election, Reverend Jessie Jackson summarized the views of Black voters: "If people knew then what we know now, Daley would never have been elected in the first place" (Taylor 2019:351).

Our measures of change in census tract segregation provided further reason to believe that opposition to Daley was apparently growing. Recall that our model included a measure of change in the racial exclusion of Black residents between 1990 and 2000. Support for Mayor Daley is significantly and negatively associated with tracts that moved up a quartile (e.g., from second to third) in African American concentration, and it is significantly and positively associated with tracts that moved down a quartile. Predicted support for Daley was about 10 percent lower in tracts that increased in the proportion of African Americans. Thus, as anticipated, opposition to Daley in 2003 significantly increased in the tracts where segregation was growing and, as we have seen, where legal cynicism was highest.

In contrast to the effects for African American exclusion, the coefficients for Hispanic concentration were positive and significant, and increased in magnitude across the quartiles. These effects reflected the high level of Latinx support for Mayor Daley, which we discuss below. The results also showed that neither measure of change in Hispanic concentration (increase or decrease) was significantly associated with electoral support for Mayor Daley.

Exclusion-Containment Theory, Legal Cynicism, and Punitive Politics

During his tenure as mayor, RM Daley mobilized the massive machinery of the Chicago Police Department, the Cook County courts, and the state prison system in a coercive response to crime. This helped deflect attention from the teardowns of the towering housing projects that RM's father's administration had spent heavily in time, energy, and public funds to build, and from the subsequent failure of RM's administration to provide adequate replacement housing. RM shifted the focus from housing to crime and to a tightening of the criminal justice system that better aligned with the rising "politics of punishment" in America's Age of Reagan and RM's own emphasis on "gangs, guns, and drugs."

The policies and practices we have described are not inevitable. Robert Vargas (2016) reported that, in some Chicago Latinx neighborhoods, residents have perceived the city as supportive of community efforts to resolve crime problems without relying on arrests. For example, in the Little Village area, West Side residents had a strong relationship with their alderman. This council member was able to direct city-funded resources to crime prevention, and as a result, crime was less problematic. Moreover, access to resources for community-based prevention and protection efforts in some politically favored Latinx neighborhoods reduced reliance on more coercive police containment. However, Vargas noted that not all Latinx neighborhoods were so fortunate.

There is little or no convincing evidence that successive disorderly conduct arrests, automatic transfers of juveniles to adult court, or enforcement of the gang loitering ordinance demonstrably improved crime prevention or provided protection from crime in Chicago. Instead, these repressive legislative interventions likely contributed to legal cynicism in residentially segregated, excluded, and contained Black communities, as well as in some Latinx neighborhoods (Vargas 2016; also see Rios 2011).

This era of tightly organized and coercive law enforcement failed to attend to the strong desire in African American neighborhoods for investment in crime prevention and protection rather than punishment. Cynicism about the promise of policing to serve and protect was a reasonable response to the tightly coupled, coercive, and punitive policies in highly segregated neighborhoods. These coercive criminal justice policies are systematically organized and publicly rationalized from the top down by state authorities, while opposition to these programs is little recognized (and when recognized, typically ignored) because it is organized from the bottom up, by socially excluded groups who are disproportionately the targets of state-based police coercion.

The evolving conceptualization and measurement of the concept of legal cynicism, with its attention to police responsibility for prevention and protection, reveals the misconceptions involved in punitive, coercive law enforcement. Using official and unofficial data spanning two decades, we have begun to analyze how the concentration of legal cynicism about law enforcement in Chicago's socially excluded and coercively contained Black neighborhoods has played a significant but insufficiently understood role in opposition to RM Daley's tightly organized crime control machine. We demonstrate later in this book that this punitive approach provoked the rising and increasingly strident demands—especially from African American communities—for new mechanisms of police accountability in Chicago.

The long span of the father–son Daley dynasty in Chicago uniquely reveals how a self-reinforcing and tightly coupled system of crime control can serially amass counterproductive punitive policies. The ways in which the punitive politics of punishment were concentrated in Chicago's Black neighborhoods through the Daley years—and continued in the Emanuel years—underlies the importance of attending to the politics of race and crime in this city and beyond.

We have seen that state-based social exclusion, coercive containment, and legal cynicism have important race-connected roles to play in understanding American politics of punishment and crime. Yet we need to understand more fully the historically and culturally driven processes that explain relations with the police in America's Black communities. As we will see in the account of the prosecution of Joseph White in the chapter that follows, the police may often play an underestimated lynchpin role in crimes where their relevance is seriously misunderstood.

3
Two Mothers/Two Sons

With Carla Shedd and Paul Hirschfield

Shooting at Tilden High

On November 20, 1992, Joseph White shot and killed DeLondyn Lawson and wounded two others at Tilden High School on the South Side of Chicago. There was no question that Joseph White was the shooter; he fired at the top of a stairwell before a crowded hallway of witnesses. The questions concerned the charges Joseph would face and whether he would be tried in juvenile or adult court.

To explain the fate of Joseph White, we use information collected with a variety of methods (see Hagan, Hirschfield, and Shedd 2002 for details) in combination with the concept of a tightly coupled criminal justice system and the theory of legal cynicism. First, we recount the coverage of the shooting as a news story. Next, we combine court transcripts with interviews of the defense lawyer in the case. Then we connect information about the neighborhood and justice system to interviews conducted with the persons centrally involved in the case. We use this information to elaborate the racial, economic, and historical context of the shooting. These factors provide a broader social and historical explanation of the group-based legal cynicism that led to the shooting and to the sentencing of Joseph White to an adult prison for much of his young adult life (People vs. Joseph White 1994).

The News Story of a School Shooting

The first newspaper accounts of the shooting appeared the day it took place: Friday, November 21, 1992. The headline in the *Chicago Tribune* front-page wire services (no author) story read, "Boy Killed in Shooting at Tilden High School." The article described the shooting as possibly resulting from an argument over gambling. According to a commander of the Chicago Police Department's school patrol, the shooter "fired a handgun about four times randomly toward the skirmish." The article said that three teenagers had been shot, and one, 15-year-old DeLondyn Lawson, was fatally shot in the back. The shooter was not identified. The press noted that school metal detectors were not operating that day because they were being used randomly rather than daily.

The next day, the story was again on page one and the headline read, "Even Safety of Schools Shattered, Student Slain, 2 Others Wounded in Hallway at Tilden" (Lenhart and Kiernan 1992). In this article, the Chicago Police Department school patrol commander said that the skirmish in the hall had already started when a boy walked out of a classroom, "entered the hallway and randomly fired four shots." The article identified a 15-year-old freshman, Joseph White, as the shooter. The casting of the event, as an indiscriminate and unprovoked attack by a teenager, implied a senseless shooting familiar from accounts of rural and suburban school violence combined with urban gang violence.

There was little or no attention in the article to the systemic vulnerabilities of youth coming of age with gangs and guns on Chicago's South Side. The article included an interview with Linda Lawson, the mother of the deceased victim, DeLondyn Lawson. She asked, "What was I supposed to do with a 15-year-old? I drove him there in the morning, and I was there at 2:02 p.m. to pick him up. What else can you do? You have to send them to school." Friends and family of her son described him as a "great dancer and funny," a boy who liked football and video games, and who was trying to stay away from gangs. The mother of a sophomore at Tilden elaborated on the newspaper headline about school safety and underscored the presence of gangs. She observed, "It's bad enough they're [the gangs] taking violence into the neighborhoods, but when they're taking it into the schools, it's bad." She emphasized that schools are supposed to be different for the youth attending them: "They're just here to learn. They're not here to be dying."

Mayor RM Daley also quickly stepped into the politics of the shooting. His first comments appeared in the November 21 news report, criticizing the school's random use of metal detectors (Lenhart and Kiernan 1992). "They have to realize you have to run them every day," the mayor insisted. He asked rhetorically, "What's more important?" and then answered, "Children are more important than anybody else in society. And that shooting, the death of a young child, directly affects everyone." Comments from the mother, the mayor, and other parents combined with the framing of the news article to cast the incident as a failure of vigilance: sacred spaces—schools—had come under attack, just as the streets had fallen victim to violence before them.

The third day, Sunday, brought another page-one headline focused on the apparent randomness of DeLondyn's shooting: "Student was in the Wrong Place at Wrong Time" (Papajohn 1992). Joseph White again was identified as the charged assailant; he was now in jail, having been denied bond the previous day. The story raised the possibility that the shooting might have involved a dispute over a dice game.

The artcile then focused on the victim, DeLondyn, and his family. DeLondyn's mother described him as a child who cried easily and who recently had been attending funerals for boys he knew at a rate of one or two a month. "His friends are constantly dying around him," his mother reported. "They're getting shot on the corners. Every month somebody he knew in his age group was dying." The story reported that, while walking between classes, "a bullet tore through DeLondyn's back and through his heart," killing him almost instantly. DeLondyn had been staying with his aunt and then his father until his mother had retaken custody of him in the preceding weeks. She was trying to help DeLondyn keep out of trouble and get his grades up, picking him up after classes each day and then tutoring him for two hours of schoolwork. DeLondyn's former school principal called the violence an American tragedy.

This article seemed most intent on disclaiming any involvement of the victims in gang activity. Instead, DeLondyn came to symbolize a youthful innocent bystander randomly caught up in a scene of violence. According to the article, DeLondyn, "was like any boy his age, with innocent passions such as video games, basketball and pizza." The article reported that DeLondyn was not involved with gangs. It quoted a friend who said she "did not peg him as a gang member or much of a tough guy." Indeed, Michael Pearson, DeLondyn' father, described his son, as well as Joseph White, as "kids" and the tragedy as "Babies killing babies."

The final phase of the initial coverage of the shooting came the following Tuesday, November 24 (Hawes and Wilson 1992). Joseph White's family had retained Chicago attorney Robert Habib to represent their son, and he appeared in Cook County Circuit Court on Monday seeking to bar the news media from further reporting the boy's name because he was a juvenile. Yet, White had already been charged as an adult. Raising the media issue simply resulted in his name appearing once again in the same sentence as the report of the judge's refusal to suppress his identity. The article reporting the judge's refusal of the appeal for his release on bond repeated his name once again.

In an interview, White's lawyer Habib noted that in the bond hearing, the state's attorney declared, "White just walked in . . . and started shooting. [As a result], you had that image, right off the bat, that Joseph White had made an unprovoked attack in the school, literally just walked in and started firing." The media and legal reconstructions of the shooting now began to reinforce one another, with the image of Joseph White as a stone-cold killer of the kind often depicted in gang shootings. Habib later encountered the judge who had denied the suppression of Joseph White's name. According to Habib, the judge confided to him: "You know, quite frankly, had there been no publicity on the case, I probably would have granted your motion. But at this point, we'd look like total fools given the fact that everybody in Chicago knows his name." Habib felt he had probably already lost the case at this point: "He [Joseph White] was convicted in the media, before we had a chance."

Habib encouraged White's mother, Karen, to try to recast the public image of her son, and she appeared before television cameras to answer reporters' questions. "Any parent with kids understands there are no model kids," she began (Hawes and Wilson 1992). Picking up on the American tragedy theme introduced by Lawson's former school principal, she then said: "It's a tragedy for both and all parties concerned—for the families and the kids. He is a victim of a tragic situation that cannot be altered." Karen White then echoed Mayor Daley's pleas for the regular use of metal detectors. An editorial in the Chicago Tribune also took up Daley's theme, arguing, "had metal detectors been used routinely at Tilden, DeLondyn Lawson's killer might have been deprived of his weapon—or at least forced to use it elsewhere" (Green 1992).

Less frequent but continuing news stories appeared over the following days and weeks (e.g., Thompson 1992; Thornton 1992). Habib said he did not push for the case to go to trial quickly, hoping the intervening period would allow the effect of the pre-trial publicity to subside. However, the appearance of an article in mid-June in *People* magazine (1993:48–49) about DeLondyn Lawson and his mother Linda focused on the loss of her son and brought new attention to the shooting and to a national audi-ence. The article alluded to the possibility of gang involvement. This was the first real hint in the news media that Lawson, as well as White and the other victims, had more complicated gang affiliations.

Gangs and Schools in Chicago

In the early 1990s, shootings and homicides were escalating on the South and West Sides of Chicago. More than 900 homicides were occurring a year; yet, when Joseph White shot DeLondyn Lawson, it was the first fatal shooting in a Chicago school an-yone could remember.

Joseph and DeLondyn were both 15-year-old boys and on the periphery of the Mickey Cobra and Black P. Stone Ranger gangs. Sometimes the Cobras and Rangers joined forces to fight a common enemy—which could be an instance of Mark Granovetter's (1973) important insights about the strength of weak ties—but on this day, Joseph and DeLondyn were adversaries.

Tilden High was racially mixed, but Joseph's mother Karen worried about the Cobras and Rangers, which were both Black gangs. The racial issue was there too, but mainly below the surface. "We had learned to co-exist . . . the gang activities were the problem." The Mickey Cobras dominated Joseph's neighborhood, but Karen wor-ried about "a whole other faction"—the Black P. Stone Rangers—who were closer to Tilden. Hallway fights between gang members were common (Wilson 1994a). Before the shooting, a teacher reported fights breaking out more frequently: "You know, you've got your kids in the classroom and all of a sudden something goes on in the hall and then the whole class just runs out .... It was wearing on teachers. It hap-pened almost every day—some days more than once." The principal of Tilden also conceded that gangs were a big part of school life: "They roamed the halls; there were gang fights almost every day, teachers constantly locking their classroom doors." It became school policy to lock students into the classrooms during class time, "to close out the chaos in the halls."

The shooting involving Joseph grew out of money lost in a dice game that took place in the school locker room. Joseph was winning, and his counterpart, Dewaun Glover, was playing with gang money, losing twenty to thirty dollars with each throw of the dice. When the losses passed the hundred-dollar mark, the Black P. Stones demanded their money back. Fists began flying. A school security guard managed to stop the fight, but in the confusion, the money disappeared. Once things calmed down, the security guard took Joseph and Dewaun to the principal's office.

It was not a full-out gang fight. Karen White insisted her son Joseph was not a real member of the Mickey Cobra gang. In an interview from prison ten years after he was convicted, Joseph explained his affiliation: "I was a distant member, I was fifteen—so it wasn't no, it wasn't much, you know what I mean? I was really a member through association. O.K., you live here, so this is what you are. But I never wore any, I wasn't walking around with a gang insignia, no tattoos." Joseph speculated that if he had been a "for real" Mickey Cobra, he would have had backup and the shooting probably would not have happened.

DeLondyn, the shooting victim, was a friend of Dewaun. DeLondyn's mother, Linda Lawson, later insisted that her son was not a Black P. Stone either. Karen White and Linda Lawson saw the plight of their sons in much the same way. Linda made this clear when she talked about her son's growing up in their gang-dominated neighborhood: "The guys who are in the gang grew up with him [DeLondyn]. It's not like he don't know them. He's got to go through them. These are kids that he's seen all his life."

The school suspended Joseph and Dewaun for three days for fighting. The school hoped their time away would calm things between the Cobras and the Stones. It did not. While he was on suspension, Black P. Stone members found Joseph in the neighborhood and told him that he had to return the missing money, otherwise he was going to get "whipped or banged." Joseph thought he knew why: "They were trying to show how strong they were, trying to make an example out of me .... The Black P. Stones were the largest gang in the school and they wanted to show that they were in control." Joseph knew the Black P. Stones kept a cache of golf clubs and other weapons in their lockers. He knew he would be attacked if he looked weak and vulnerable. Karen White recalled: "they had bats, they had car antennas .... They were not coming to him for an old-fashioned fist fight." Joseph was terrified. His suspension would be ending the following week, so he began looking for a weapon to protect himself on his walk to school.

Tightening the Screws in the Justice System

Joseph White was a typical 15-year-old, making his way in the company of peers similarly awakening to rapidly changing hormones and surging adolescent impulses. Neuroscientists confirm what all parents of adolescent sons learn: 15-year-olds are not guided by careful calculation of the consequences of their acts; impulse control and long-term thinking come later (see Steinberg 2017), and Joseph was still far from that. His case begged the question of the difference between impulse and intention: Can 15-year-olds form adult criminal intent? If 15-year-olds are too young to buy cigarettes or vote, are they old enough to be found guilty and sentenced to lifetime prison terms in adult institutions for first-degree murder?

Ironically, almost a hundred years earlier, Joseph might have been better protected from his fate in adult court. The nation's first juvenile court was established apart from the adult criminal courts in Chicago in the early 20th century (Fox 1970; Platt 1969;

Sutton 1988). But, there were exceptions to this separation: Prosecutors retained some power to transfer children and adolescents from juvenile to the adult courts. This authority was granted in 1935 under what became known as the Lattimore ruling (Dodge 2000).

Fifteen-year-old Susie Lattimore was the same age as Joseph White, and she was also African American. She had stabbed another teenage girl during a fight in a bar where both had been drinking. The victim died several days later and, notwithstanding the unpremeditated nature of the attack, the state's attorney charged Lattimore with first-degree murder (rather than manslaughter); she was convicted in adult court. At that time, prosecutors rarely charged White women with first-degree murder, and it is likely that Susie Lattimore's race was a determining factor in her treatment. The Lattimore transfer set a precedent that would be followed for several decades.

In 1973, Illinois adopted the practice of "transfer by judicial discretion," giving judges authority over prosecutors' petitions to send juveniles to adult court. However, one of RM Daley's first initiatives as state's attorney was his restoration of prosecutorial control through implementation of the 1981 Automatic Transfer Act [ATA]. The ATA provided "Illinois with one of the harshest and most complex set of transfer provisions in the nation" (Clarke 1996:4). It allowed age 15 and older youths charged with homicide to be placed automatically under the control of adult court prosecutors.

Soon the list of automatic transfers included gun violations within 1000 feet of a school. Joseph White would still have been transferred to adult court even if he had used the gun to protect himself in a non-fatal incident near Tilden High. From this perspective, the prison door was already slamming shut on Joseph before he made the mistake of taking a gun anywhere near a school. Perhaps thinking that the gun was small, seeing that the metal detectors were not in use that day, and fearing being victimized all contributed to Joseph's decision to keep the weapon with him. It was unlikely that the threat of prison time occupied much, if any, of these anxious thoughts.

Prosecutors loved the ATA, but judges were less enamored. Automatic transfers are the difference between being legally defined as a criminal instead of as a delinquent. Youth in juvenile court are usually released without an official record when they turn 21; youth convicted in adult court can receive sentences of several decades, as well as life without parole, marking them with a permanent criminal record. The state's attorney's office soon expanded the ATA to additionally include possession of small amounts of drugs.

A judge lamented that adding drugs was an affront to the judicial system: "He's [Daley] undermined the credibility of the prosecutors in the court room and of his office" (Jackson 2011). According to the Cook County State's Attorney's Office, the number of children tried as adults doubled from 223 to 455 cases in the year before White's arrest. The majority (417) of these youth were transferred automatically to adult court under ATA (Fountain 1992). When RM Daley began to talk about running for mayor in 1988, he defended the ATA: "The Automatic Transfer was needed because discretion was terrible down there [juvenile court] . . . It didn't make sense."

The soon-to-be mayoral candidate summarized this part of his law and order campaign in customarily succinct fashion: "We see the mess out there today, because that was the attitude for too many years in this country" (Jackson 2011).

Black youth like Joseph were the most affected by ATA, especially when it came to prison sentences (Regulus, Stevens, and Faggiani 1988). An Amnesty International Report (2005) indicates that, in the 1980s, Black youth were ten times more likely than Whites to receive life prison sentences without parole. A study based in Cook County found that at the time of Joseph's case, 95 percent of the youth automatically transferred to adult court were Black (Clarke 1996). As we explain below, the difference between being defined as criminal versus delinquent greatly influenced the factors that could be introduced in Joseph's defense.

Fatal Mistakes

It is easy to get a lethal weapon in Chicago's South and West Side neighborhoods. Within days of Joseph's suspension, a youth in the neighborhood who had heard about the fight approached Joseph with a small, semi-automatic pistol. After loading and test firing the gun, Joseph bought it. To Joseph, it was an act of self-protection. The need for self-protection was obvious: there was a high likelihood that he would get jumped during his suspension from school, and he knew that Black P. Stone gang members were watching for him. Joseph recalled, "I knew that they were going to beat me, but I didn't know whether they would have a gun." He reported that, on the day his suspension ended, other youth chased him just a few blocks from home; nonetheless, Joseph made it to school without pulling the gun.

Joseph was not the only one worried that day. Linda Lawson would later report in the *People* (1993) magazine interview that DeLondyn had not wanted to go to school the morning he was shot. She asked herself, "Was he having problems he didn't want to tell me about?" After the shooting, she couldn't get this out of her thoughts.

DeLondyn Lawson was standing with Dewaun Glover on the school stairway, where the Black P. Stones typically hung out, when events began to spin out of control. Dewaun crossed in front of Joseph and Joseph remembered him saying something like, "Hey, man, what's up with my money." Joseph, probably emboldened by the gun in his pocket, responded provocatively, "I ain't giving your money back, pussy." A Black P. Stone member made their intentions clear: "Man, we didn't come here to talk. Let's do what we gone do so I can put this guy's . . . head up in his locker."

Joseph remembered the next part as if it unfolded in slow motion: "I began to get hit, and I fell. And when I fell I didn't fall flat: I kind of braced myself with my hands . . . I had no way of getting out. I tried, but I . . . couldn't." After recovering from his fall, Joseph rose and pulled the gun out. Within seconds, DeLondyn lay dying on the landing with two other injured youths, and Joseph was running down the stairs, out the school doors, and racing down the street. He had no preconceived plan. He took refuge under the porch of a house across the street from the school. Each of these movements would be dissected and interpreted in the trial that followed. These few moments became the focus of a self-defense claim, but without the help of attention to Joseph's larger social context. The prosecutor challenged the relevance of this line of testimony, and the judge concurred.

Worst Fears

Linda Lawson learned from a neighbor that DeLondyn was a victim of the shooting, and she rushed in panic to the school and then to the hospital. She remembered that, "When I came through the door, I knew . . . no one had to tell me." The scene was desperate: "Seeing my baby laying up there, that's a feeling I can't describe . . . I think the thing that hurt me most was that I wasn't there with him [when he died]."

Karen White was off work on the day of the shooting. She said that the police were at her doorstep within the hour because Joseph was identified as the shooter so quickly by other youths. "I was washing my hair when somebody was beating on the door. When I went downstairs and opened the door, there was just like police everywhere." They told her about the shooting and that Joseph was at large and armed with a gun. "The only thought that I was thinking was that my son was going to be killed. They said he had a gun and that if he came back, I needed to let them know because he was in danger of being killed if they saw him with that gun."

By the time Karen White arrived at the school, the police had found Joseph under the porch across the street. "They were laying him up against a car and they were handcuffing him .... My first thought was just being thankful to God that he was alive." They took him to the 51st Street police station, and Karen followed. When she arrived, "everything was just pandemonium." Joseph was already locked in a cell. "When I saw him he was scared, he just looked wild-eyed because he didn't know . . . the full ramifications of his actions." Karen recalled that she didn't initially have a chance to talk with her son as he was being processed. She contacted the attorney, Robert Habib, through a friend, and then stayed with Joseph. "We stayed there until maybe eleven or twelve o'clock at night, and finally the District Attorney came down and they told me that that they were indicting him for murder." This was Joseph's ATA ticket to adult court.

Linda Lawson's and Karen White's experiences underlined fears common among neighborhood parents for the safety of their sons. A cynical sense of futility was pervasive in the neighborhood about relying on the police for protection, much less prevention of violence. Joseph certainly did not regard the school, and especially the police, as sources of protection. He felt basically on his own, and that the possession of a weapon was his only protection. His act of self-help (Black 1983), associated with the focus on self-protection as the penultimate element in Figure 3.1, foretold the liability of the unfolding events.

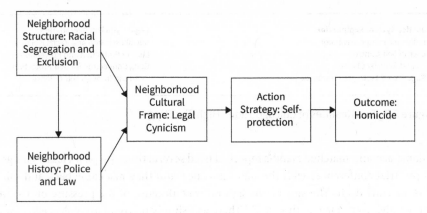

Figure 3.1 Causal Model of Legal Cynicism and Homicide

The People versus Joseph White

The ATA placed Joseph White in the crosshairs of the tightly coupled system that RM Daley had put in place as Cook County state's attorney. It put Joseph on track to a charge and trial in adult court that preordained a lengthy sentence. His transfer eliminated the protection that a more loosely configured juvenile court would likely have provided. Instead, Joseph was already condemned in the media as a crazed killer and a member of a violent gang, a portrayal that established a presumptive case for conviction and imprisonment. This characterization anticipated the first and second elements of the adult justice system explanation, identified in Figure 3.2, of Joseph White's individual responsibility for his assumed lack of self-control.

Joseph's attorney, Habib, could not fight the automatic transfer and had no alternative but to try to plea bargain the charge down from first-degree murder, in hopes of shortening his client's sentence. Under the circumstances, Habib argued that a plea of guilty to manslaughter or a weapons charge made more sense. He noted the unrealistic cognitive assumptions about the formation of criminal intent required to charge a 15-year-old defendant with first-degree murder. Yet, this plea-bargaining strategy was blocked by a tightened system that made charge and sentence reductions a rarity in the state's attorney's office. A veteran defense lawyer, Sam Adams, laid out the rigid system that Daley had built:

> If you tell the trial assistant that you're willing to plead to a lesser offense, he can no longer just say yes or no. He has to ask his wing boss, and his wing boss has to ask his floor commander, and the floor commander has to go to the assistant in charge of the criminal division, who has to go to the first assistant state's attorney, and then the two of them presumably look at the case and decide how it will look on Rich Daley's record, because three or four days or a week later the answer comes back on whether they'll accept it or not (Jackson 2011).

Justice System Explanation	Legal Cynicism Explanation
Individual Irresponsiwbility	Social Exclusion and Racial Isolation
Lack of Self-Control	Lack of Protection and Prevention
Joined Gang by Choice	Gang Connection for Self-Protection
Rage-Based 1st Degree Homicide	Self-Help through Self-Defense

Figure 3.2 Two Realities of Chicago Tilden High Shooting

Adams' account matched Habib's report: "I tried several times [to plea a lesser charge] in pre-trial conferences with the state's attorney, and they just came back and said, 'No, we can't do it. The supervisor says no way. Because of the pressure on us, we cannot give you a plea on this case.'" There was simply no room for a plea, even for a juvenile facing a trial and sentencing in adult court.

Plea negotiation would have offered an opportunity to emphasize the gang context of the shooting, the threat, and the absence of protection for Joseph White. These factors could potentially have "mitigated" several decades of prison time White was facing for first-degree murder. Instead, White was stonewalled by a system designed to narrowly impose Daley's "law and order" politics of punishment. A judge offered an unusually provocative summary of the politics involved: "When Daley became state's attorney, I talked to him in these chambers. He had no idea what he was doing. Since then, he's made politically expedient decisions that are frequently repugnant to the best interests of the judicial system" (Jackson 2011).

A guilty plea to a first-degree murder charge would almost certainly have resulted in decades in prison, and so Joseph's lawyer, Habib, recommended that he take his chances with a jury that might be sympathetic. Looked at from White's and Habib's side of the case, pleading not guilty and going to trial was the best hope of avoiding a life sentence in prison. Yet the combination of the semi-automatic weapon and the Automatic Transfer Act seemed to have sealed White's fate before the trial even began.

Two Realities on Trial

The prosecutor and defense lawyer in the Joseph White trial seemed to be operating with different conceptions of legal and social reality. The prosecutor, as part of the "courtroom workgroup" (Eisenstein and Jacob 1977), seemed much more aligned with the judge. Defense lawyers, on the other hand, are generally outsiders, challenging the system through the eyes of their clients, whose priorities and concerns differ from system insiders. Prosecutors and judges focus narrowly on the individual criminal responsibility of the offender, while defense lawyers bring a broader and legally more cynical view of the justice system and the place of the defendant in it. This dichotomy was especially evident in South Side Chicago.

The prosecutor and ultimately the judge saw Joseph White as lacking self-control, recklessly choosing to join a street gang, and becoming a violent gang member;

moreover, they concluded that he irresponsibly chose to draw and fire a gun and willingly committed a first-degree homicide. These are the key elements of the justice system framework of responsibility outlined in Figure 3.2.

Incongruously, the prosecutor cast Joseph White as both a member of the Mickey Cobra gang and yet as acting alone, and thus solely responsible for the murder of DeLondyn Lawson. He seemed to purposefully confuse these gang and personal identities in addressing the jury:

> There is only *one person* in the whole group that has a dead body to his credit, and that's that guy right over there, *Mickey Cobra*, who settles a dispute with a gun, and you cannot let him do that, and that's going to be your decision, and what you will decide is your message to the rest of society about what is, or is not, going to be tolerated (emphasis added).

This left unaddressed the alternative guilty plea to lesser charges that Habib had proposed. It ignored the dubious assumption that a 15-year-old would form criminal intent as envisioned in adult criminal law. It also disregarded, as Habib emphasized, the context of the shooting: "He did what any reasonable person would have done at this point . . . Joseph White, at this point, was a scared little kid" (Wilson 1994b).

It was ultimately the judge, Richard Neville, who summarized the logic of individual responsibility in an adult criminal court, a logic that made Joseph White legally guilty of first-degree murder. He did this while simultaneously and gratuitously disparaging the juvenile court system. Judge Neville recalled that White had engaged in earlier minor thefts for which he had suffered few consequences in juvenile court because, "15-year-olds know that when they steal, nothing happens to them. They go back home." This statement ignored the rehabilitation that occurs in some court-ordered treatment programs and juvenile detention centers, and that juveniles involved in shooting deaths are usually not released but are confined in juvenile detention until they reach adulthood and are then sent to adult prison to serve the remainder of their sentence. The John Howard Society reported that the number of youth sentenced to juvenile detention centers doubled in the first two years following RM Daley's election as state's attorney(Dodge 2000).

Despite his earlier insistence on individual responsibility, at the sentencing hearing Judge Neville emphasized that Joseph was associated with the Mickey Cobras gang. He speculated that it was "that gang in his school that allowed him certain leeway and rights regarding his conduct with other boys who belong to other gangs." He did not explain how he came to know Joseph White's thinking in the lead-up to the shooting, nor how the late consideration of the role of the gang conflicted with the individual responsibility argument. Finally, the judge noted that Joseph recently had fathered a child whom he clearly could not expect to support. This was offered as further evidence of Joseph's impulsiveness, lack of self-control, and irresponsible life choices—characteristics that otherwise might have been consistent with his treatment as a juvenile. Judge Neville used a "three strikes" logic to conclude, "I think society is tired of people who are 15 who make these kinds of judgments."

Most important, in terms of legal cynicism theory, the judge wondered aloud why Joseph had not tried to find other ways of solving the gambling dispute. He asked why Joseph had not gone to the police for assistance and protection, and complained: "He did not seek help from authorities." The judge also concluded that the ATA was the solution to deterring juvenile criminal behavior: "It is time for everyone to understand, that those people who choose to take guns to settle disputes are accountable for what they do, be they 12 years old, or 15 years old, or 50 years old." The suggestion was that even a 12-year-old child should be held accountable in adult criminal court.

Legal Cynicism on Trial

When Joseph appeared in court for sentencing, Karen White was finally able to make a brief statement about the social circumstances of the shooting. Karen spoke of her sorrow for the Lawson family and the loss of their son. She then went on to say that her family loved Joseph too, and pleaded for judicial compassion. She explained: "He acted under his perceived notion that he was in mortal danger for his life . . . given the depressed ghetto area in which this situation took place, it is not at all unlikely or unimaginable that a teen would resort to violence with a weapon."

This was the most direct reference to social context in Joseph's trial, and Karen was only able to introduce its significance *after* the guilty verdict was reached. Karen White's statement was an explanation and a plea, not an excuse or a justification. She acknowledged that her son had made a terrible mistake, adding, "And myself, I have made some mistakes, and I know you have to pay consequences for them. But I don't see what [purpose] his life or most of his life behind prison walls can serve." As indicated in Figure 3.2 and discussed further below, the area in which Joseph grew up was exactly the kind of South Side neighborhood of exclusion and containment that is the starting point of our theory of legal cynicism.

Karen White's doubts about the purposes of long sentences for juveniles were already well established in the academic research literature. A 1992 New Jersey study found that the risk of reconviction was lower for youth tried in juvenile than those convicted in adult courts (Fagan and Deschenes 1990). Relatedly, a report by the U.S. Department of Justice concluded: "the bulk of the empirical evidence suggests that transfer laws, as currently implemented, probably have little general deterrent effect on would-be juvenile offenders" (Redding 2010:8).

If Joseph White had been tried in juvenile court, his lawyer would have been allowed an opportunity to explain the social reality of White's life as a 15-year-old, and a more revealing picture would have emerged. It would have exposed the segregated experience of racial exclusion and containment in South Side Chicago neighborhoods. It would have highlighted the failure of schools and the police to provide effective crime prevention and protection, and the role of gangs as substitute sources of protection and identity. Finally, it would have shown that acts like those in the Tilden High shooting are often self-defense responses to these conditions.

The social reality of gangs and guns is that they are accepted among adolescents as a legally cynical but nonetheless normal part of everyday life among socially excluded and racially isolated youth. In the often brutally policed South Side of Chicago, it would not occur to Joseph, or his friends and peers, that the authorities would protect them. Instead, Joseph's abnormal social environment made his minimal, but legally cynical, association with the Mickey Cobras a normative, if not necessary, choice.

To fully comprehend Joseph's circumstances requires understanding the social and racial history of Chicago, its ineffective and violent policing, and the territorial, self-protective dynamics of its youth gangs. Consider the scene of the crime and its place in the history of Chicago's evolving economic and social problems. Tilden High School is located at the intersection of 47th Street and Union Street in the South Side area of Chicago known historically for the Union Stock Yards. The school was once highly ranked in the educational hierarchy of South Chicago, and the area surrounding it is still called "New City"—a hopeful-sounding designation from the 1920s. But by the end of World War II, the Union Stock Yards had closed its gates, and manufacturing jobs had dwindled, including well-paying jobs in the steel industry. As the area descended into long-term economic decline, inevitable tensions mounted in the New City area and in Tilden High School.

As we noted in previous chapters, growing numbers of African Americans settled in the South and later West Sides of Chicago following the Great Migration. Real estate operators steered African Americans who could afford to buy homes into South and West Side neighborhoods, and they simultaneously scared Whites into leaving (Rothstein 2017). In 1971, Joseph White's family moved to their home on West 51st Street, about a mile from Tilden High. When the family moved there, the surrounding area was still overwhelmingly White and only four percent Black. However, as Joseph approached high school in 1990, New City had become less than one-third White, nearly half Black, and about one-quarter Hispanic. Thus, the South Side's economic depression combined with White flight and its impact on real estate values deepened the impoverishment of its residents and contributed to Chicago's legacy as one of the most racially segregated cities in America.

"Gangs, Guns, and Drugs"

Karen White was a supervisor in the accounts department of a large Chicago newspaper when Joseph entered high school. Joseph remembered that his mother left for work at five in the morning and returned at about four in the afternoon. His father worked from nine to nine, six days a week. Soon after moving into their new home, Karen learned about the gang problems in her family's community:

It was the Mickey Cobras that were in the area. I didn't know a lot about gangs; I was never affiliated, but moving into that area and through my kids and their friends, we found out the area we lived in was the Mickey Cobra area.

Apart from the Mickey Cobras, wider territorial claims of other gangs in the area further complicated the lives of South Side residents. Tilden High's low-income "feeder neighborhoods" were each dominated by a different gang. At the time of the shooting, at least six gangs had a significant presence in neighborhoods around Tilden: the Black Gangster Disciples, Mickey Cobras, Black P. Stones, Vice Lords, Latin Kings, and Satan's Disciples. White students also belonged to gangs, including those in RJ and RM Daley's Bridgeport neighborhood.

Tilden High had become a place where gang members could socialize and carry out recruitment and moneymaking activities. A school police officer who worked at Tilden in the early 1990s concluded that the gambling episode that led to the deadly shooting probably followed a tentative truce between the school's Black gangs. Students like Joseph had to negotiate the boundaries of the gangs and the feeder neighborhoods in their movements to and from, as well as within, the school. It was a complicated and constantly changing world in which today's enemies might be tomorrow's allies; and so, for most youth at Tilden, it was difficult if not impossible to avoid gang entanglements completely.

Joseph received good grades in school the year before the shooting, and he won a trophy as the most valuable player on his basketball team. He had hoped to avoid this volatile environment by going outside the neighborhood to South Shore High School, which Michele Robinson Obama attended, but his family was unable to make this happen. By the spring of 1992, Joseph was already at least a passing participant in gang activity, and Karen White felt increasingly powerless to keep him away from this scene.

Joseph White had to come to terms with his environment. The recent recession had technically ended, but the "jobless recovery" left unemployment largely unabated in New City. A teacher described the situation confronting youth at Tilden: "A lot of these kids from blue-collar families, it didn't look like they had much of a future. You know, they had seen their parents laid off left and right." The result was a significant increase in drug crime, gun homicides, and gang violence that peaked along with unemployment in the early 1990s. The levels of homicide for young African American males were devastating, rising among eighteen-year-olds from about twenty to sixty per hundred thousand population (Blumstein and Rosenfeld 1998).

In the late 1980s and early 1990s, Americans, Black and White, became increasingly apprehensive about the movement of guns and gang violence into public schools. Chicago was no exception, and RM Daley made it a central part of his law and order politics. According to a U.S. Department of Justice report (Snyder and Sickmund 1995), in 1992 the rate of violent victimization of juveniles between the ages of twelve and seventeen was nearly three times that for adults, and among youth the rate of victimization was about 20 percent higher for those who were Black compared to those who were White. In 1990, 20 percent of youth in a nationally representative sample of students in grades nine through twelve said they had carried a weapon at least once in the previous month, and between 1983 and 1992 juvenile arrests for weapons violations more than doubled (Snyder and Sickmund 1995). Data from the period also point to an increase in violence in schools. Rates of violent victimization rose in the early 1990s, peaking at about nine incidents per hundred students before falling to less than half that by the end of the decade (National Center for Educational Statistics 2019).

Under these social conditions, Judge Neville's remarks suggesting that Joseph White should have sought protection from his school and the police were either naïve or disingenuous. It was well known on the South Side that when police in New City picked up Black youth whom they could not charge with crimes, they often would drop them off in an area where they were likely to be beaten by local residents. The year of the Tilden shooting, the Chicago Police Board fired two White police officers who had assaulted two African American youth and dropped them off in a White part of New City, where a gang of White youth subsequently assaulted them. A Cook County Criminal Court judge had previously acquitted the officers on charges of official misconduct and battery (Stein 1992).

Such practices had been repeated over the years, dating at least as far back as RJ Daley's youth. The recurring incidents of abuse and corruption confirmed the worst fears of young Black males and their parents about the potential role of the police in their lives. The assumption that the police were a source of protection for Black adolescents was fraught at best (Witt 1985). It was this kind of cynical *dis*belief in the law and its enforcement that led Joseph and other youth to join gangs for self-protection.

Justice on Trial

On the day of the dice game, Joseph reported that he was outsized and outnumbered by his counterparts in the locker room: "This one boy asked me for the money. But he didn't just want the money. He wanted my jacket and a bunch of other stuff. And you got to remember, I was only 5'7" and 140 pounds." In the days that followed, he bought the handgun, misguidedly thinking it was an equalizer; a source of protection that could help him safely get back and forth to school. But at school, on the day of the shooting, he found himself in the hallway between periods, surrounded and under attack. To Joseph, it was entirely a matter of self-defense. He recounted the scene vividly in his trial testimony:

A: There were 7 to 15 guys who were all trying to get a piece of me.

Q: So were you aiming at anyone in particular?

A: No. I fired the gun to get them up off me. And for the gun being an automatic, you squeeze off several shots at one time.

Q: Why didn't you fire the gun at the ground or in the air?

A: Because I was on the ground. And fire into the ceiling or fire into the ground, I wasn't sure. I didn't have time to think.

Q: So, you were just shooting and just happened to hit them?

A: Right. I didn't even have time to consider firing into the floor or firing into the ceiling because, contrary to what a lot of people believe, it wasn't where, you know, they were over, they're over there and I'm right here. It wasn't like that . . . It was literally me being grabbed, held, punched, kicked . . . . So that entire time I was getting assaulted. That entire time I was getting pummeled, I was getting beaten . . . it seemed like forever in my mind, but in real time it . . . [was] playing out, snap, snap, snap.

Judge Neville sentenced Joseph to 45 years in prison on the charge of first-degree, premeditated murder. In 2012 and 2016, the U.S. Supreme Court ruled that automatic life sentences for juveniles were unconstitutional (Hoerner 2019).

Near the end of the trial, Karen White encountered Linda Lawson outside the courtroom and apologized:

I knew there was nothing, absolutely zero, that I could say or do that could minimize her loss or bring her son back. I was trying to talk to her to let her know that in no way did I condone this action . . . if I could do anything in the world to change things, I would. I also let her know that Joey would, because Joey told me, 'Mamma, I didn't want to kill that boy, I killed somebody' . . . . Not only did he take a life, he destroyed all our lives in that single miscalculation.

At that point, Joseph White had already lost a year of his life, but he would lose many more. At sixteen, he was sent to Menard Maximum Security Prison in downstate Illinois to begin serving his term among adults. Over the years, Menard's inmates had ranged from John Wayne Gacy, a serial child killer, to Fred Hampton, the Black Power activist who, as we described in Chapter One, was later assassinated in his sleep by the team of Chicago police officers and FBI agents acting with the assistance of Cook County State's Attorney Edward Hanrahan. Opened in 1878, Menard Prison was 300 hundred miles south of Joseph's Chicago home. A six-hour drive through the Land of Lincoln provided those who visited Joseph plenty of time to wonder: Was this the rule of law? Or was it a legal exercise tainted by legal cynicism?

4
Shut Out, Locked Up, and Foreclosed

With Andrea Cann Chandrasekher

A Paradox?

Patrick Carr and colleagues (2007, hereafter Carr) reported an apparent paradox in interviews with 150 adolescents in high-crime Philadelphia neighborhoods: these youth were upset by their experiences with police, yet their anger was transitory and they also called for "more cops, tougher laws/stricter penalties, and tougher drug interdiction" (463). If this support for the police reflected the thinking of most residents of high-crime neighborhoods, it would turn our exclusion-containment theory on its head, allying these residents with punitive policing. This chapter reports evidence to the contrary.

The provocative title of Carr's Philadelphia study—"We Never Call the Cops and Here is the Reason Why"—raises the question: If these respondents believed in punitive policing, why wouldn't they "call the cops"? Studies have found that residents of high-crime neighborhoods actually *do* call police. According to Moskos (2008), 911 calls are the primary contact of police with citizens, and several studies have found that 911 calls are especially common in hyper-segregated neighborhoods, despite doubts that the police will respond appropriately (Desmond, Papachristos, and Kirk 2016; Desmond and Valdez 2013). Bell (2016) examined Washington D.C. mothers' use of the police by calling for help when other solutions were unavailable. As Bell (2019:205) noted, this strategic, "semi-agentic engagement" is not a "*natural* response" but reflects the harsh reality of people's limited options in disadvantaged communities. Thus, people may call the police, even when they do not trust or are hostile to them, because of the limited options for safety and security in these neighborhoods.

Carr and Bell agreed that encounters with police can generate legal cynicism, but they disagreed beyond this. Carr argued that this cynicism is "attenuated" by overriding cultural support for "pro-social" criminal justice policies, while Bell (2017) linked this cynicism to ongoing "legal estrangement." This difference is especially relevant to our exclusion-containment theory.

Legal Cynicism, Procedural Injustice, and Legal Estrangement

Our exclusion-containment theory of legal cynicism links American crime problems to hyper-segregation and to residents' deep skepticism about police protection and crime prevention. We argue that legal cynicism is *persistently* linked to operational policies of exclusion and containment. This persistence follows from what Bell (2017) calls "legal estrangement" and what we call the exclusion-containment process.

Carr's cultural attenuation argument derives from Tom Tyler's (2017) procedural justice theory. This theory maintains that people's perceptions of the police are grounded in their interactions with them, and that people will view the police positively and cooperate with them if they believe that the police have treated them respectfully and fairly. According to Carr, "youth are negatively disposed toward police because they have experienced procedural injustice . . . [but] their opposition is temporary" (2007:469). This use of procedural justice theory involves two problematic assumptions: (a) that hostility toward police is transient, and (b) that police can readily be trained to work well with youth, and others, when enforcing the law.

Carr argued that negative experiences with police can be superseded by a "largely untapped potential of young people to actively contribute to community-based crime reduction" (2007: 471). We maintain that negative perceptions of police are not transitory, and that the confidence placed in police "fairness" and "trust" by this theory is misleading. We turn instead to Bell's (2017) expansion of legal cynicism theory to include legal estrangement: "I introduce the concept of *legal estrangement* to capture both legal cynicism . . . and the objective structural conditions (including officer behaviors and substantive criminal law) that give birth to this subjective orientation" (2066). The structural rootedness of Bell's approach anticipates lasting negative citizen interactions with police.

Bell (2017) drew on an interview with Shawna, a woman from Baltimore, to illustrate how police actions contribute to legal cynicism and its long-lasting effects. As Bell (2017:2091) described it, Shawna's perspective on the police was "complex, but largely distrustful." As a child, Shawna wanted to become a police officer, but this changed, in part because of neighborhood stories of crimes by police (e.g., rapes, shootings), the police killing of Freddy Gray, the police treatment of those who protested his death, and her observations of disrespectful security guards. Bell described Shawna as someone who never had a serious encounter with the police, wanted to trust them, and was a general law follower, but who was "convinced that the police are not trustworthy for people like her" (2099). Shawna's experiences revealed "a cleavage, or estrangement, from the enforcers of the law" (2099).

Bell's analysis suggests that legal cynicism is a point of lasting inflection in life course development. The feelings of *symbolic* exclusion Bell introduced through Shawna's description of how police see her—as a potential thug rather than a citizen—have social and structural origins, as well as subjective and objective consequences. In subsequent work, Bell (2019) underscored that although people's feelings about the police and their trust in them are not trivial, the more salient issue is how members of disadvantaged groups cope with daily reminders of the ways various institutions, including the police, view and treat them.

In Chapter One, we argued that Chicago's housing projects were a fateful source of social exclusion during Richard J. Daley's tenure as mayor. We describe in greater detail below how RJ and then RM Daley used public and private funds to build structures that separated the Loop and downtown Chicago business districts from the city's South and West Side neighborhoods, shutting out and containing residents within hyper-segregated neighborhoods. These policies are central to our exclusion-containment theory and connect the structural and social dimensions of this exclusion.

Blocking off downtown Chicago excluded minority residents from its economic and cultural capital, concentrating socio-economic disadvantage in separately contained spaces. Later, mass incarceration further intensified the city's hyper-segregation and its concentration of disadvantage. The "iron fist" of incarceration grew with the construction of hi-rise public housing—and rose further during its deconstruction—intensifying neighborhood exclusion and containment. In turn, home repossessions and foreclosures further intensified this process during the financial crisis, broadening RM Daley's imposition of what Bell (2017) calls symbolic exclusion. RJ and RM Daley's dual dynasty persistently reshaped the landscape of Chicago.

In the first half of this chapter, we describe how this reshaping of the city took form in a variety of structural and symbolic ways. In the second half of the chapter, we analyze the consequences of this reshaping of Chicago's urban environment for the already fraught relationship between minority citizens and police. These citizens often urgently need preventive and protective services that police too seldom provide—despite the hopes of Carr's Philadelphia study.

Structural Symbolism and Entrenchment of Social Exclusion

When most Americans think about downtown Chicago, they think of its iconic landmarks stretching along Michigan Avenue, Lake Shore Drive, and north along the shores of Lake Michigan. This panoramic front lawn of the city stretches north from Grant and Millennium Parks and the Art Institute, through the Loop and across the Chicago river to Michigan Avenue and the Magnificent Mile—with its iconic Tribune Tower, the Water Tower Mall, and the John Hancock Building—before reaching still farther north to Lincoln Park and its free public zoo. Chicago's architectural landscape—with its parks and buildings—designed by visionaries such as Daniel Burnham, Ludwig Mies van der Rohe, and most recently Jeanne Gang—fix the eyes of the city and its visitors on an enticing stretch of the Chicago imagination.

RJ and RM wanted Chicagoans to see a "city of neighborhoods" in this urban landscape; a vista that promised a transformational trajectory of globally inspired economic growth. But to see only this is to miss the accompanying story of the city's segregated and economically disadvantaged neighborhoods. This city's urban landscape combines the promise of inclusion with the reality of its social exclusion and containment, which were built systematically around a series of interconnected and unwelcoming structural barriers.

The result divides Chicago into opposing spaces (see Chapter Two Figure 2.2). Its structural barriers form a semi-circular arc that extends from the south to the north buffering Chicago's lakefront Gold Coast and leading to the gentrifying neighborhoods of Lakeview, Uptown, and Edgewater. These structural barriers protect the prosperity of the city's downtown business districts and north lakefront from the city's economically disadvantaged South and West Sides, although these parts of the city—especially the south and west loop—also include islands of gentrification accompanied by their own problems as well as opportunities.

The physical markers and barriers that separate the centrally included downtown from the peripherally excluded South and West Sides of Chicago consist of overlapping, interwoven, massive structures with forbidding symbolic meanings. The exclusion is social in its deliberate concentration and separation of groups, and it is structural in its use of imposing natural and manmade forms to demarcate its less-than-subtle boundaries. These structures include multi-lane expressways, the citywide El and Metra rail systems, large public and privately planned residential developments, expanding educational institutions, as well as the twists and turns of the Chicago River.

Building a Divided City

The structures we describe are interwoven to channel and control public access. They mark boundaries of group separation and political entitlement. These structures influence everyday movement, not only by imposing barriers but also by signaling to groups—especially those situated outside the cordoned off city center—that they do not belong and are not wanted inside the downtown business districts. Aside, that is, from the essential work "outsiders" do in the city's sizable service sector and in other low-paying jobs.

Descriptions of these structural barriers typically ignore race and class, in ways similar to the absence of these realities in day-to-day American conversational discourse. Yet their positioning communicates much about race and class. Thus Hirsch (1983), in *The Making of the Second Ghetto*, aptly characterized Chicago's public housing as a "domestic containment policy." The high-rise housing projects are only part of the story and today have mostly been torn down; but, together with the city's expressways and other enduring structural impediments, they remain powerful and unforgotten reminders of the lasting historical divisions that still define the symbolic boundaries of Chicago's day-to-day life.

From the Expressways to the Projects

Built in the 1950s to connect O'Hare Airport to the city center, the construction of the Kennedy Expressway was an important sign of the scale of things to come. The city's

African American population was approaching 25 percent. In response to a dramatic housing shortage, Black residents were increasingly funneled into the newly built high-rise projects, such as the massive Henry Horner Homes with its 15 floor buildings, located west of downtown. Work was already underway on Henry Horner when RJ Daley was elected mayor in 1955. The next mega-project, Robert Taylor Homes, was even more imposing, consisting of 28 high-rise, 16-story buildings. Completed in 1962, this development stretched several miles into Chicago's South Side (see Figure 4.1).

Two factors made this public housing development especially noteworthy. First, its imposing buildings marked an important border of Chicago's growing South Side Black neighborhoods, just to the east of RJ's family home in Irish Bridgeport. Second, it was immediately south of three additional African American populated projects: Harold Ickes Homes, Dearborn Homes, and Stateway Gardens.

Together, these public housing projects stretched more than four miles. Their imposing architecture extended the State Street Corridor into the heart of the South Side and constituted the largest concentration of public housing in the nation. It was a huge and densely populated expression of the harsh side of what Nelson Algren (1951) called this *City on the Make*. As Venkatesh (2000) later explained in his powerful description of the *American Project*, Robert Taylor Homes (as well as many other public housing projects) would be targeted for destruction less than a half-century after it was built, and its residents would be removed with little care or provision for their alternative housing.

In RJ Daley's Bridgeport neighborhood, residents had long viewed the expanding South Side Black Belt as a threat, and the new projects were regarded as an insufficient solution. So, RJ created another formidable structural barrier, this time using federal interstate highway funds to link the Kennedy Expressway with the new Dan Ryan Expressway. The Dan Ryan was purposefully designed to run immediately alongside the hi-rise projects.

The Dan Ryan was unprecedented, with its seven lanes flowing in each direction, creating a combined 14 lanes of fast-moving traffic. It was located on the Bridgeport side of Taylor Homes, making the tall project buildings an overbearing east-facing border. The buildings massively reinforced an intimidating message that Blacks were not welcome to cross this forbidding arterial divide or otherwise cross over into the Bridgeport neighborhood (see Figure 4.2).

Not in MY Backyard

Cohen and Taylor (2000:188) explained that RJ Daley closely monitored plans for the Ryan Expressway. The plans initially called for the Dan Ryan to head south, close to the Daley family home. However, "when the final plans were announced, the Dan Ryan had been 'realigned.'" In deference to Daley's wishes, it "now made two sharp

Figure 4.1 Notable Chicago Public Housing Projects, circa 1965

curves in a short space, but the new route turned the Dan Ryan into a classic racial barrier between the Black and White south sides."

The addition of the elevated Red Line El tracks, which run down the middle of the Dan Ryan Expressway, increased the Ryan's significance as a formidable barrier. The Red Line took most of its riders into the Loop and on to the north side commercial

Figure 4.2 Chicago Public Housing Projects and the Dan Ryan Expressway

and residential districts. This provided access to the center of the city but, as we explain below, it did not convey a sense of symbolic belonging.

The Black and Latinx populations of Chicago continued to spread west—despite RJ's best efforts—but leaving the Bridgeport neighborhood as a place apart and intact. RJ had successfully made the point that Chicago would grow in ways that separated racial and ethnic groups. Even when these barriers were circumvented, their symbolic messages of not belonging were easily recognized.

A lasting display of how this exclusion still plays out today is apparent at the State and Chicago Red Line stop. This classic El stop, just a few blocks west of Michigan Avenue, is the location of a MacDonald's Restaurant that serves as a kind of meeting place for arrivals and departures to the South Side. If this restaurant were located at the government border crossing of two nation states, it might be called a "Rest Station"—but it is not a restful setting.

This MacDonald's is more like a closely monitored checkpoint. It is a reminder of Malcolm X's observation that "The South" is everything below the Canadian border. The hardness of a frequent police presence delivers a message, with officers in their puffed-out protective vests and armed with conspicuous weaponry. Hardened blue and white SUVs frequently are on standby nearby. The terms of engagement are often armed, wary, and tense.

As the 1960s progressed, RJ Daley combined massive investments in public housing and transportation with federal funding that added an educational component to his vision of a defensible downtown. This involved the creation of a University of Illinois Chicago campus and plans for the largest convention center in the country, McCormick Place. The campus would help address White Chicagoan's fears of Henry Horner Homes and other West Side projects, while the convention center would help further seal off the city's South Side.

Building a Convention Center and a University Campus

In its 1958 *Development Plan for the Central Area of Chicago*, the Department of Public Planning called for the construction of the massive convention center. The center—named for Colonel Robert McCormick, the former editor-publisher of the *Chicago Tribune*—was built alongside the planned intersection of the Stevenson Expressway and Lake Shore Drive. Erected on top of rail lines entering the city from the south, the convention center was opened in 1960, while the Stevenson was completed in 1964.

The Stevenson expressway significantly bisected the city and connected Lake Shore Drive with the Dan Ryan and Kennedy expressways. In this way, the Stevenson formed another barrier, symbolizing the northern end of the South Side and connecting passing cars to the Dan Ryan. Together, the Stevenson Expressway and the McCormick Convention Center "boxed in" the city's South Side development, pushing its continued expansion to the south rather than the north.

The 1958 plan also called for a University of Illinois Chicago campus. The campus would serve the growing number of high school graduates whom the more elite downstate Champaign-Urbana campus did not admit, or who could better afford a commuter school made accessible with city bus routes. It was a timely idea, but it also created conflicts between at least one neighborhood that wanted the campus—Garfield Park—and another that did not—Harrison-Halsted (Cohen and Taylor 2000).

Garfield Park feared a rapidly increasing White flight, and residents hoped a new campus could avert this. To the east, Harrison-Halsted was a multi-ethnic neighborhood and home of the near century-old Hull House and its surrounding buildings developed by Jane Adams. The plans for the new university campus required that Hull House be broken into parts and relocated, with the breakup making a further statement about the city's priorities. The city also designated the area as a redevelopment site, qualifying it for government urban renewal funding.

It was clear that neighborhood wishes were not the priority when the city chose Harrison-Halsted. Cohen and Taylor (2000:228) explained how powerful interests and racial fear predicted this choice:

The Harrison-Halsted site was a few blocks west of the Loop .... It was close enough to serve as the kind of 'anchor' for the Loop that downtown business leaders were looking for. And it would serve as a racial barrier . . . between the Loop and another nearby concentration of poor blacks.

The latter reference was to two of the largest public housing complexes on the West Side: the Jane Adams Houses and the Robert Brooks Homes. Like most of the high-rise public housing projects, they were torn down in the early 2000s, resulting in major dislocation for the residents. It was a signal of more dislocation to follow.

Public-Private Partnerships and "Middle Class" Housing

By the end of the 1960s, federal funding was ending for public housing, expressways, and convention centers. At the same time, the postwar baby boomers were entering their high delinquency and crime-prone adolescence, heightening Chicagoans' fears. This and associated concerns about White flight to the suburbs especially concerned city hall (Wilson 1987). Between 1960 and 1980, the White population in two communities, West Town and the Near West Side, dropped by nearly half.

Both RJ, and subsequently RM Daley were drawn to a new plan for public-private housing development that responded to concerns about White flight. The plan involved a powerful private sector group called the Central Chicago Area Committee [CCAC]. The CCAC included the CEOs of Sears Roebuck, Illinois National Bank and Trust, and Commonwealth Edison. In the early 1970s, CCAC proposed a joint venture to create new "close in" barriers to protect and promote commercial and residential development in the city center.

In 1973, the city and CCAC released the Chicago 21 (1973:1) plan "to restore the historic role of the center city and to preserve what is unique about Chicago." Predictably, this plan had less to do with historic architecture than with the marketing of "middle class" housing and commercial development.

The plan called for privatization of new residential housing development. It gained momentum and support in the 1980s by focusing on younger homebuyers. According to Austen (2018:135), "the anti-urban impulse that had sent middle-class families to the suburbs had reversed itself, and young professionals—the decade's Yuppies—wanted to live . . . in city centers near their jobs and one another." The Chicago 21 plan was based on the belief that these young urbanites would move downtown if they could be persuaded they would be safe and protected.

Chicago 21 and the Coalition to Stop It

"Carl Sandberg Village" was a forerunner of the housing the Chicago 21 plan favored. The village was proposed by Arthur Rubloff, an unapologetic powerhouse private for-profit downtown developer who secured RJ's support. Rubloff wanted to create a large strip of middle-class (i.e., White) housing to buffer the Gold Coast and the "Magnificent Mile" from incursions of Black residents living in the Cabrini-Green housing project.

Rubloff (see Rast 2002:31) actually spelled out, in capital "B-L-A-C-K" letters, the perceived threat and growing fears that the nearby Cabrini-Green housing project posed in the minds of Michigan Avenue shop owners and Lake Shore Drive condo dwellers. Opened in 1942, Cabrini-Green originally was populated by 586 two-story row houses in low-rise buildings. In the late 1950s, it added 1,925 units in 15 mid- and high-rise buildings, and in the early 1960s, 1,096 units were added. The speed and scale of this expansion scared the residents of the nearby Magnificent Mile area.

RJ responded by giving Rubloff a green light to create Carl Sandberg Village, a half-mile stretch of apartment buildings on LaSalle Avenue between Clark and Division Streets. "The city now had its barrier," Andrew Diamond (2017:228) wrote, "protect-ing the Gold Coast from the Cabrini-Green housing project." Rubloff was accurately giving voice to how much White Chicagoans were fearfully seeking protection from minorities and crime.

Ben Austen (2018) explained how the "shutting out" of Cabrini-Green from up-scale Lincoln Park took shape: "North Avenue, the boulevard separating the housing project from Lincoln Park, was widened . . . [and] facades were remade so that entrances opened onto opposite-end courtyards, and roads were turned into cul-de-sacs" (60). The newly conceived residential barriers communicated a symbolic message, even though they did not fully block all access to the downtown shops and lakefront beaches. A person could actually still walk little more than a mile south from Cabrini-Green along Oak Street to Michigan Avenue and arrive in the heart of the Magnificent Mile.

However, bringing a conspicuous new addition of middle-class housing into the area further distanced Cabrini-Green's residents—socially and economically— from the Magnificent Mile shopping area. And that, as much as the structural divide of bricks and mortar, was what RJ Daley and Rubloff set out to do. The eventual destruction of Cabrini-Green and plans for commercial and residential redevelopment of the surrounding and nearby North and Clybourne area were set in motion. Today all that remains of Cabrini-Green are several sections of the original row housing.

Basing its plans on Rubloff's success in gaining support from city hall, CCAC's Chicago 2 extended its planning to the South Loop. David Ranney (2003) noted that the planners followed the same logic, making prospective residents feel "well pro-tected" from the South Side. Chicago 21 called for redeveloping 600 acres of aban-doned railyards into a community of 100,000 people. It took until 1986 to scale up the development—which included Central Station—and RM Daley signaled its ul-timate success when he and his wife moved from Bridgeport to live in the area in the mid-1990s.

The South Loop development was a major financial success for its homeowners, the city, and new businesses in the area. But it also provoked a social movement, the Coalition to Stop Chicago 21, organized to oppose the city's new public–private development ethos. In *At Home in the Loop*, Lois Wille (1997:93) recalled how Stop Chicago 21 saw the plan as a "[W]hite-only fortress." Architects had replicated the ethos of Sandberg Village: the buildings faced inward and, in a nod to London's prized "residential gardens," new park areas were fenced off and restricted to residents.

The citywide alliance of Black and Latinx groups opposed to Chicago 21 helped elect Harold Washington mayor in 1983. Yet the alliance could not stop or dramatically alter the growing momentum of Chicago 21. As seen in the previous chapter, the effect of this symbolic and structural exclusion was to increase feelings of legal cynicism, including what Bell (2017) called legal estrangement, and more broadly a sense of not belonging. All of this contributed to the opposition RM Daley experienced in the hyper-segregated South Side census tracts leading up to the 2003 election we discussed in Chapter Two.

The symbolic and structural exclusion we have described reinforced the protective and punitive turn of the 1980s, as described in previous chapters and as led by the ascent of the city's new Mayor RM Daley. RM received extensive voter support from the predominately White lakefront and north neighborhoods of the city, and, as mayor, he drew on his experience as Cook County state's attorney to further tighten the screws of criminal and civil law enforcement.

From Mass Incarceration to Foreclosures

An early indication of the tightened criminal justice system was the escalation in the 1980s in imprisonment (Clear 2007; Raphael and Stoll 2013; Western 2006). There was some support in Black neighborhoods for criminal justice policies that contributed to mass incarceration (Forman 2017); however, these neighborhoods were more deeply concerned about government failure to address structural causes of crime. Police responses to resident complaints typically combined hyper-enforcement practices such as stop and frisk and a focus on minor drug, property, and civil order offenses (e.g., trespassing) with unresponsiveness to resident 911 calls for assistance (Bell 2019; Forman 2017; Fortner 2015). "Mass incarceration" was the predominant result (Western 2006).

In Figure 4.3, we present a map of incarceration for 2006–2008. We measured incarceration with data developed by Cooper and Lugalia-Hollon (n.d.) to identify Chicago's "Million Dollar Blocks" (based on the estimated cost of incarcerating residents). These data reflect counts of the number of people per census tract who received a custodial sentence (i.e., jail, boot camp, or prison). As this map shows, census tracts in the highest quartile of incarceration were disproportionately located in minority neighborhoods, particularly on Chicago's South and West Sides (see Figure 2.2, Chapter 2). We further disaggregated tracts in the fourth quartile to draw attention to the neighborhoods where incarceration was particularly intense, involving more

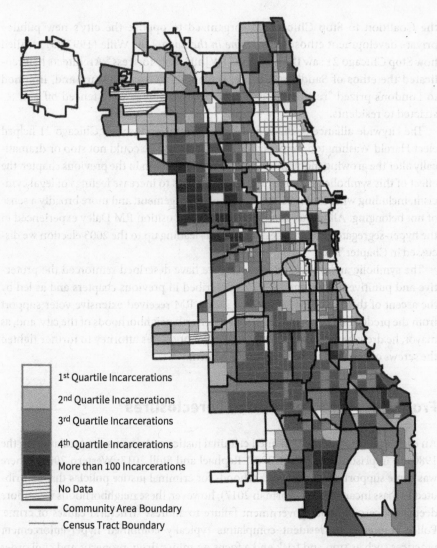

Figure 4.3 Average Number of Incarcerations in Chicago Neighborhoods 2006–2008

than 100 residents per tract. These tracts were, as our exclusion-containment approach predicts, concentrated in Black neighborhoods.

On the civil side of law enforcement, another sign of a tightening justice system was the concentration of home foreclosures in Black and Latinx neighborhoods (Hall, Crowder, and Spring 2015). The increase in foreclosures started after the escalation in imprisonment and involved what James Baldwin (2010) would have called "Negro removal" from home ownership, again in neighborhoods cordoned off from the downtown business districts. In Figure 4.4, we provide a map of 2006–2008 foreclosures, by quintiles, by census tract (we use quintiles to show the large number of tracts at

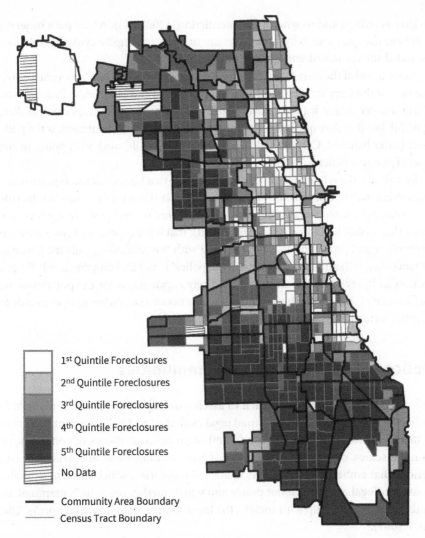

Figure 4.4 Foreclosures in Chicago Neighborhoods 2006–2008

Legend:
- 1st Quintile Foreclosures
- 2nd Quintile Foreclosures
- 3rd Quintile Foreclosures
- 4th Quintile Foreclosures
- 5th Quintile Foreclosures
- No Data
- Community Area Boundary
- Census Tract Boundary

the upper end of the distribution). Our measure of residential foreclosures was gathered by a private company, Record Information Services. We had information for all single-family 2006–2008 foreclosure repossessions. High-foreclosure tracts were disproportionately in neighborhoods excluded by the protective arc of barriers that increasingly shielded downtown Chicago.

The remainder of this chapter focuses on how racial isolation and exclusion intensified police containment on the South and West Sides in response to 911 calls for police assistance. As we have noted, although Carr found youth in high-crime areas were initially hostile toward police, they also argued that this was transitory, with most youth soon endorsing punitive policies that included "more cops, tougher laws/

stricter penalties, and tougher drug interdiction" (2007:263). As we have observed, this begs the question: Why would racially isolated and legally cynical residents in excluded and contained settings ever call the police at all?

As we noted at the start of this chapter, this question is especially provocative given the title of the Carr article: "We Never Call the Cops and Here is the Reason Why." Carr's answer is that legally cynical youth felt the police were impolite and disrespectful, but that they quickly got over their anger at their mistreatment: if the police were better behaved, Carr argued, even more youth would work with police in support of punitive policies.

In contrast, the remainder of this chapter argues that legal cynicism is persistent in high-crime neighborhoods (i.e., not transient); that this legal cynicism results from the perceived ineffectiveness of police crime prevention and protection efforts (i.e., more than police impoliteness and disrespect); that it is the persistent need for crime prevention and protection that is associated with the continuing calls for police assistance (i.e., rather than "we never call the police"); and that ongoing needs for protection and prevention are therefore the likely explanations for the prevalence and persistence of 911 calls in high-crime neighborhoods (i.e., rather than demands for tougher/stricter policing).

Police 911 Calls in Minority Communities

We used a neighborhood approach to assess our explanation of citizens' calls for police assistance. Our analysis joined legal cynicism, and Bell's concept of legal estrangement, with Stephen Vaisey's (2009) "dual process" theory of conscious and non-conscious cognition. The origins of legal estrangement are structural conditions that embed non-conscious historical memories, which in turn generate a conscious legal cynicism about police and which further result in "a marginal and ambivalent relationship with society, the law and predominant social norms" (Bell 2017:2081).

In the mid-1990s, 30 to 40 percent of Chicagoans said their police did not do a good job of preventing crime or maintaining order (Kirk and Papachristos 2011). We hypothesize that neighborhood exclusion and containment increased this legal cynicism about police prevention and protection, while further intensifying urgent calls for this prevention and protection.

Legal estrangement is a less explicitly conscious cognitive process than legal cynicism. According to Bell (2017:2017), "legal estrangement is a cultural and systemic mechanism . . . beyond individual perceptions." Vaisey's dual process theory anticipated this kind of less conscious estrangement combined with a more conscious legal cynicism. Drawing on Vaisey's dual process theory, Harding and Hepburn (2014) emphasized that neighborhood narrative accounts unconsciously stimulate residents' actions. We similarly argue that Vaisey's dual process approach points to a combined conscious and non-conscious process that leads to decisions to call 911, despite low expectations about police delivery of urgently needed prevention and protection.

As we noted in Chapter Two, Sampson and Bartusch (1998) introduced legal cynicism to explain why African Americans—especially in racially isolated neighborhoods—simultaneously distrust the legal system and condemn adolescent deviance. In this chapter, we suggest that when framed within Vaisey's (2009) dual process model, legal cynicism theory additionally anticipates that neighborhood residents will react to criminal behavior with a resigned willingness to call police when prevention and protection are urgently needed (see also Kennedy 1997).

Our argument has four parts. First, we further summarize Vaisey's (2009) dual process model. Second, we link Vaisey's theory with the neighborhood-level cultural schema of legal cynicism. This cynicism is intensified in racially excluded and contained communities and coincides with urgent calls for police assistance, in the absence of alternative solutions.

Third, we consider the use of procedural justice theory to explain crime reporting. As proposed by Tyler (2017) and adopted by Carr, this theory posits that residents' positive interactions with the police contribute to favorable assessments about the legitimacy of police and builds trust and confidence in them; these in turn presumably elevate residents' reporting of crime to police. Yet, as Sampson and colleagues (2018) noted, micro-level phenomena (i.e., such as trust and confidence) are inadequate to explain macro-level neighborhood crime reporting. We argue that neighborhood-level legal cynicism—which arises from police failures to prevent crime and thus protect minority neighborhoods—influences crime reporting at the same time that it explains the persistence of troubled police–community relations in these neighborhoods.

Fourth, we examine how crises of social and structural exclusion—from hyper-segregation to mass incarceration and home foreclosures—mediate connections between legal cynicism and responses to crime in structurally excluded and contained minority neighborhoods.

We explored these ideas with the macro-, meso-, and micro-level data collected in Chicago and introduced in Chapter Two. We show how structural forces combine with legal cynicism to contribute to neighborhood variation in 911 calls for help. Our results suggest that police failures to prevent crime and provide protection—more than concerns about procedural legitimacy—are necessary to explain America's racially troubled police–community relations.

Elaborating the Dual Process

Vaisey's (2009) dual process model was inspired by research demonstrating that thoughts and decision-making move along two distinct cognitive tracks: "one fast, automatic, and largely unconscious, and one slow and deliberate, and largely conscious"

(1704; also see Kahneman 2011). He noted that when respondents are interviewed, their narratives are often contradictory, suggesting conflicting conscious and unconscious processes. Vaisey argued that survey data can unravel discrepancies in people's explanations of their actions, and he uses them to explain narrative inconsistencies. For example, he found that adolescents are "profoundly influenced by cultural forces in ways that they are largely unaware of and unable to articulate but that nevertheless shape their moral judgements and choices" (2009:1704). The implication is that the same is true for adults.

Vaisey's work showed how survey questions can explain apparent paradoxes by identifying "enduring, internalized cultural schemas" (1699). He demonstrated that survey questions "tend (probabilistically) to produce a choice consistent with the underlying schema, even if the person does not understand why the choice is the most desirable" (1691–2).

We contend that conscious as well as less conscious forms of cognition both contribute to relevant cultural frames, schemas, and narratives. Harding and Hepburn (2014:19) noted that although people may express an array of narratives, they are most influenced unconsciously by, and then consciously embrace, narratives that resonate with their own experiences and those of valued others.

Such framings may reveal key features of neighborhoods (e.g., Small 2004). Thus, according to Vaisey (2009:1687), actions like calling police involve "schematic associations" solidified through cumulative experiences, both unconscious and conscious. The former schemas may be so deeply entrenched that they are unrecognized. Our hypothesis is that in the United States, cultural frames have historical and residentially segregated contours that are defined by structural variation in neighborhood racial/ethnic exclusion and containment.

The Role of Legal Cynicism

Sampson and Bartusch (1998:786) used legal cynicism to explain how rules of law can lose their capacity to constrain non-normative behavior. Kirk and Papachristos (2011:16) emphasized that this cultural frame develops, in part, because people view the police as ineffectual in providing safety and security. Elaborated in this way, legal cynicism highlights the failure of law and its agents—the police—to both prevent unlawful behavior and provide protection from this behavior. Legal cynicism operates both at the individual and neighborhood levels. While Sampson (2012) and Kirk and Papachristos (2011) used it to understand neighborhood variation in violence, we believe it can also be used to explain neighborhood-level differences in community engagement with (e.g., 911 calls) as well as estrangement from police.

Legal cynicism is high among African Americans and in African American neighborhoods (Sampson 2012), as are 911 calls (Desmond and Valdez 2013). This is likely because, even though legal cynicism involves skepticism about police, residents have little choice but to call police and other first responders. Thus, even though Black residents are more likely than Whites to have conscious and non-conscious negative thoughts and feelings about the police, because of their own and others' mistreatment, these do not preclude their calling police for help when there is no one else available.

The responses are familiar: if your house is on fire, you call the fire department; if someone is dying, you call an ambulance; and if a crime threatens your own or others' security, you call the police. Residents summon police hoping for preventive and protective results, even in the face of past disappointments. Thus, Bobo and Thompson (2006) found that 93 percent of African Americans surveyed said they would call police if their home was burglarized, even though only 35 percent thought the police would respond appropriately.

Historical Dimensions of Exclusion, Containment, and Legal Cynicism

The process by which cultural schemas such as legal cynicism come to operate unconsciously as well as consciously in association with hyper-segregated neighborhood exclusion and containment has deep historical roots. Bell (2017:2106) described how lasting collective memories are based not only on personal experience, but also by:

> . . . observing and hearing about the experiences of others, passing accumulated wisdom from parent to child, observing interactions in public space, seeing (or not seeing) murals and other forms of public commemoration, watching television, scrolling through social media, and sharing all of these personal and vicarious experiences in the community.

Bell noted that scholars too seldom tap into what she calls these "cultural emergences."

Among African Americans, background experiences that have given rise to these emergences include slavery, lynching, segregation, and the Jim Crow laws that preceded the 20th-century Great Migration. Wilson (1987) and Massey and Denton (1993) traced the legacy of this cumulative experience to the 1970s and 1980s and to the resulting residential concentration of poverty in racially isolated neighborhoods. Wilson (also Sampson and Wilson 1995) drew particular attention to how this concentration increased as well-paying manufacturing jobs and upwardly mobile families moved out of inner-city neighborhoods.

Of course, the history of race and crime in America did not end in the 1970s and 1980s. Beckett and Western (2001) have shown that the 1990s saw mass incarceration that involved historic increases in concentrated imprisonment of minority men and women, along with a simultaneous reduction in government welfare support (see also Garland 2001; Raphael and Stoll 2013; Western 2006). In Chicago, the correlation between neighborhood economic disadvantage and incarceration rates reached extremely high levels (~.8; Sampson 2012).

In turn, an ensuing housing crisis further culminated in the Great Recession. Thus, the 2000s marked a new historical assault on minority neighborhoods: foreclosure repossessions (Bocian, Li, and Ernst 2008) and evictions (Desmond 2016). In the United States, an estimated 2.5 million foreclosures occurred between 2007 and 2009, disproportionately among African American and other minority families (Bocian et al. 2008; Hall et al. 2015; Rugh, Albright, and Massey 2015). Foreclosures also intensified racial segregation and isolation (Hall et al. 2015). This represented a new peak in the patterns of exclusion and containment we have earlier described. European scholars and policymakers (e.g., Walker and Walker 1997) use the concept of "social exclusion" to refer to the disaffiliation and disconnection that results from being "shut out" of conventional institutions, such as affordable housing, while Western (2006:105) conceptualizes the peaking high levels of incarceration of minority men in the early 2000s as "profound social exclusion."

However, as Vaisey suggested, most residents do not cognitively identify the convergence of such problems in the specific ways articulated in the social scientific formulations of Western and others. Instead, responses in affected neighborhoods may often take the form of a more practical, reflexive, and generalized awareness that is a non-conscious cognitive response.

For example, Bell (2016) noted that the loss of welfare protections and mass incarceration removed many men from families. This left many mothers with few options but to summon the police strategically in response to threats to their households' safety and security; however, Bell argued that her respondents' narratives did not always or clearly articulate this motivational backdrop to calling 911 for police assistance.

Incarceration and foreclosure repossessions constituted successive sources of systemic exclusion that disproportionately removed minority men, women, and children from their families and their homes. We expect that this removal increased problems in minority neighborhoods and thus led to more 911 calls for help. Yet, research is inconclusive about the relationships between incarceration, foreclosures, and police crime reports (Cui and Walsh 2015; Kirk and Hyra 2012).

Concentrated imprisonments and foreclosures are products of deliberate policy choices. They reflect state-enabled investment and financial policies (Hagan 2010; Hagan et al. 2015; Hinton 2016) and, in this sense, they have deliberately and repressively intensified concentrated disadvantage in Black communities. Again, the processes have often been obscure, defying conscious understanding, and producing collective estrangement. As a result, these processes have become sources of less consciously articulated—but nonetheless practically sought—resident demands for crime prevention and police protection.

Procedural Justice or Injustice?

Procedural justice theory seeks to improve resident–police relations (Meares 2014; Skogan, Van Craen, and Hennessy 2015; Sunshine and Tyler 2003; Tyler and Huo

2002; Thibaut and Walker 1975; Tyler and Jackson 2013). According to Sunshine and Tyler (2003), reformed policies and training that foster "procedural sensitivity" would enhance police legitimacy and result in increased trust, confidence, cooperation, and reporting of crimes. They argued that procedurally sensitive training would also insulate police from "societal forces, such as demographics or economic conditions, which shape crime rates but are beyond police control" (Sunshine and Tyler 2003:20). Indeed, based on their analysis of individual-level survey data, Sunshine and Tyler concluded: "regardless of ethnicity, people cooperate with the police when they view the police as legitimate" (20).

In a review of procedural justice theory and research, Nagin and Telep (2017:22) stressed that the individual-level focus of this theory means "larger societal influences are left in the background." The dual process approach that we favor maintains that people do not base their perceptions of police simply on their own experiences; instead, they consciously and unconsciously draw on those of their family, friends, and neighbors. Thus, views about the police can be measured as cultural frames that vary across neighborhoods (Kirk 2016).

Sampson and Wilson (1995) emphasized that contextual factors complicate the relationship between race and crime. Bell (2016, 2017, 2019) further argued that micro-level perceptions of procedural justice are not easily, if ever, effectively freed from their macro-level associations with economic disadvantage and social exclusion. As a result, collective cynicism about macro-level procedural *injustice* likely contributes to police mobilization.

The methods and measures analyzed in procedural justice research also make it vulnerable to the individualistic fallacy. As noted above, Sunshine and Tyler (2003) claimed that "procedurally sensitive" training would "free" police from societal forces. Yet most procedural justice research has not used community-level analyses. Instead, it has analyzed individual-level perceptions of the procedural correctness of police practices in conjunction with the same individuals' self-reports of their cooperativeness with police.

Thus, there is reason to believe the positive relationship posited by procedural justice theory between police procedural sensitivity and resident crime reporting will not hold in community-level samples of disadvantaged minorities. Perceptions of criminal *injustice* (Hagan, Shedd, and Payne 2005) and legal cynicism are more often observed in minority settings where calls for police assistance are most common (Kirk 2016). Skepticism combined with reliance on the police is the apparent paradox with which this chapter began.

Legal Cynicism and Ongoing Structural Change Processes

Mario Small (2018) emphasized the importance of understanding the processes through which individual and collective decisions, such as calling 911, are made. He noted that the kind of macro-level 911 police call data we analyze in this chapter are appropriate for some purposes, including the study of neighborhood-level events; nonetheless, he maintained: "these are data on the outcome (the decision), not the process through which the outcome came about" (8058). Small rightly noted this would be a serious problem if we were grounding our explanation in individual-level mechanisms; however, the starting point in our explanation is not the individual level.

Our starting point is social and structural level processes of exclusion and containment leading to racial/ethnic isolation. We are particularly concerned with changes in social and structural processes of racial/ethnic exclusion. This is why we have focused so extensively on the historical, as well as cross-sectional, processes that led to hyper-segregation in Chicago. This is also why, in the propositions and analyses that follow, we include measurement of the process through which neighborhoods changed over time in the extent of their segregation and, in turn, how these changes are related to subsequent 911 calls. These propositions and analyses are aimed specifically at testing how past and more recent processes of change may be linked (net of crime itself) to pleas for preventive and protective police assistance.

Six Propositions about 911 Calls for Police Assistance During the Daley Years

Our elaboration of Vaisey's (2009) dual process theory at the community level implies that historical and contemporary mistreatment of minorities—particularly their residential segregation, exclusion, and containment—create a conscious and nonconscious residue that generates and perpetuates legal cynicism resulting in urgent calls for police assistance. Vaisey emphasized that cultural schema can have such recurrent resonance and be so repeatedly internalized as to be unconscious; yet, he also argued that these internalized unconscious thoughts can be at least partially revealed through survey measurement. We used this dual process model to examine six propositions about neighborhood variation in residents' 911 calls with the same Chicago census tract data we analyzed in Chapter Two.

We measured 911 calls with the universe of all census tract–level citizen calls for three types of crime in 2006 through 2008: property, drugs, and violence (see Appendix for details on these and other items). We used a yearly average for the three years to limit the effects of annual fluctuations. We expected that the amount of crime in a neighborhood should be the most important determinant of 911 calls, and so in our final equation we included crime-specific police reports for the three types of crimes we examined. This inclusion of police reports helps us isolate the size and significance of relationships between 911 calls and other neighborhood variables, net of the level of police reports of neighborhood crime.

Exclusion-Containment Effects: Our first proposition was that at both nonconscious and conscious cognitive levels, racial social exclusion and containment would have strong, persistent, and significant effects on resident-reported crime, and thus these patterns would be especially pronounced along racial lines.

Results from our first equation indicated strong support for our initial proposition (see Tables, Chapter 4 Table 1). The coefficients for the third and fourth (i.e., most concentrated, hyper-segregated) quartiles of African American tracts were strong, significant—net of significant effects for other structural variables—and evident for all three types of crime.

We used predicted crime counts to illustrate the magnitude of the effects associated with racial segregation and containment (see Figure 4.5). The number of expected yearly property crimes was 159 for tracts in the first quartile. It was more than double that, 346, in the fourth quartile. The disparity was even greater for crimes involving drugs or violence. The yearly averages for these were 45 and 368 for tracts in the first quartile, compared to 263 and 887 for those in the fourth quartile.

Legal Cynicism Effects: Our second proposition was that legal cynicism about police prevention and protection from crime is a key measurable motivational source of discursive insight into resident reporting of crime. We expected this cultural schema to have durable, direct, and indirect mediating effects that reflect and transmit the conscious and non-conscious influences of racial and ethnic structural exclusion and containment on resident-reported crime.

We introduced legal cynicism in our second equation (see Tables, Chapter 4 Table 2). As predicted, legal cynicism was positively and significantly associated with resident 911 calls to report all three types of crime. We modeled these relationships with predicted counts for various levels of legal cynicism (5th to 95th percentile). Predicted counts for 911 calls for tracts at the low and high ends of the distribution for legal cynicism showed notable differences. For property crimes, the counts were

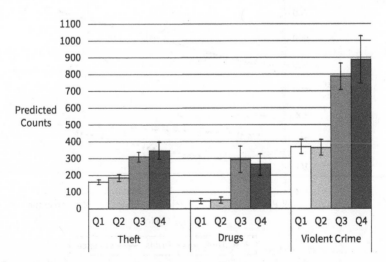

Figure 4.5 Predicted Counts of 911 Calls about Theft, Drugs, and Violent Crime across African American Quartiles of Exclusion-Containment (with 95% Confidence Intervals)

respectively 226 and 267; for drug offenses they were 106 and 257; and for violence they were 498 and 710 (see Figure 4.6).

Adding legal cynicism also reduced the third and fourth quartile African American tract structural exclusion and containment effects from the first equation. Mediation analyses (see Liu et al. 2014) showed that legal cynicism was a significant transmitter for the associations between the concentration of African Americans (i.e., quartiles three and four) and all three types of crime (see Tables, Chapter 4 Table 3). These findings reflected the operation of legal cynicism as a dual conscious and non-conscious mediator of the relationship between racial exclusion-containment and 911 crime reports. The legal cynicism measures were from 1994–1995, while the 911 data were from 2006–2008, indicating that the direct and indirect effects of this legal schema have persisted for over a decade, as anticipated in our second proposition and in our discussion of the enduring, *non*-transitory nature of legal cynicism effects.

Exclusionary Process Effects: Our third proposition was that racial exclusion effects are the product of both continuity and change in levels of structural hyper-segregation, with increases in the neighborhood exclusion and containment of racial/ ethnic minorities resulting in more resident-reported crime, and decreases resulting in less.

Our test of this proposition introduced the measures of change from the last chapter in racial/ethnic exclusion from 1990 to 2000. The results for our third equation (see Tables, Chapter 4 Table 4) indicated that the influence of racial/ethnic exclusion on crime was a continuing *process*: an increase in African American concentration was positively associated with 911 calls about all three crimes, while a

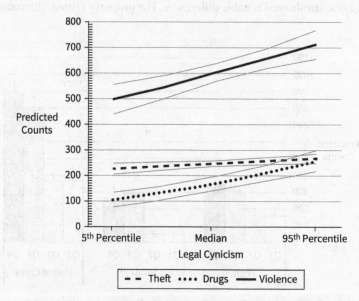

Figure 4.6 Predicted Counts of 911 Calls about Theft, Drugs, and Violent Crime across Legal Cynicism (with 95% Confidence Intervals in gray)

decrease was associated with a drop in them. As predicted, counts indicated increases of 44 (property), 58 (drugs), and 98 (violent) crimes and decreases of 50 (property), 150 (drugs), and 162 (violence). Consistent with our dual process approach, continuity *and* change in racial exclusion-containment accounted for neighborhood variation in 911 calls.

Procedural Justice Effects: Our fourth proposition was that procedural justice theory provided an insufficient explanatory and policy response for understanding the association between neighborhood-level race and reported crime. Procedural justice theory maintains that interactions with the police, and views of those interactions, will independently influence the decision to call 911. We used data from the second Chicago study described in Chapter Two to address this.

We created two census tract measures to assess procedural justice. The first focuses on prior police mistreatment. It is based on a question from the CCAHS Chicago survey (House et al. 2012) that asked respondents if they had ever been "unfairly stopped, searched, questioned, physically threatened or abused by the police." Our second measure is a two-item procedural justice scale created by Kirk (2016). The scale uses the extent of agreement with two statements: "police in your local community can be trusted" and whether "the police are fair to all people regardless of their background"; high scores indicate agreement with the statements. We introduced police mistreatment and procedural justice perceptions, along with two other perceptual variables (i.e., collective efficacy and tolerance for deviance) in our fourth equation (see Tables, Chapter 4 Table 5). The results contrasted with procedural justice theory, but were consistent with our fourth proposition. Net of the other variables, neighborhood variation in prior mistreatment by the police was not significantly associated with 911 calls, and perceived procedural justice had a significant *negative* effect on 911 calls for all three crimes. The implication is that when neighborhood residents *didn't* have confidence and trust in the effectiveness of the police to prevent and protect them from crime, they nonetheless were more likely to call 911 in hope of eliciting this prevention and protection.

Mass Incarceration and Foreclosure Effects: Our fifth proposition considered the influence of state structured and systemic exclusion-containment involving mass incarceration and foreclosed home repossessions. Our expectation was that both forms of structural exclusion-containment would further intensify the relationship between racial/ethnic exclusion and resident-reported crime.

From 2006 to 2008, an average of 29 people, per tract per year, were sentenced to jail or prison (see Figure 4.3). There was an average of 14 incarcerations per year for tracts that were in the first quartile of African American concentration; in the most highly segregated tracts, the average was 47 incarcerations per year. There were two clear foreclosure patterns: (1) they increased over time (from 1,120 in 2006, to 2,705 in 2007 and 4,325 in 2008) and (2) they were concentrated in racial minority neighborhoods (e.g., south and west Chicago). Thus, the average number of yearly foreclosures was nine in census tracts in the first quartile of the distribution of African Americans; it was more than double, 19, in tracts located in the fourth quartile (see

Figure 4.4). In general, incarcerations and foreclosures occurred disproportionately in structurally excluded tracts that contained the poorest neighborhoods and the highest proportions of minority residents.

Results from our fifth equation 5 (see Tables, Chapter 4 Table 6) showed that incarcerations and foreclosures were both positively and significantly associated with 911 calls about each type of crime. Both associations were curvilinear, suggesting that, at high levels, emptying neighborhoods of people—through foreclosures or incarcerations—reduced calls to police.

Predicted margins indicated 911 call counts of 176 for property crimes, 34 for drug offenses, and 333 for violent crimes in communities that had few residents incarcerated. In contrast, neighborhoods with high levels of incarceration had predicted call counts of 311, 304, and 835 for these three crime types (see Figure 4.7).

Communities with few foreclosures also had low predicted call counts for property, drug, and violent crime: 188, 176, and 457 respectively. In high-foreclosure neighborhoods, the predicted 911 call counts were 317 for property crimes, 241 for drug offenses, and 771 for violent crimes (see Figure 4.8).

Including incarceration and foreclosures in our analysis also resulted in notable decreases in the coefficients for African American exclusion. Mediation analyses (see Tables, Chapter 4 Table 7) showed that incarceration and foreclosures were both significant transmitters of the relationships between racial isolation of Black neighborhoods and 911 calls for all three types of crime, with incarceration playing the larger role. Incarceration was also a significant mediator of the relationship between legal cynicism and 911 calls for all three types of crime. These incarceration and foreclosure

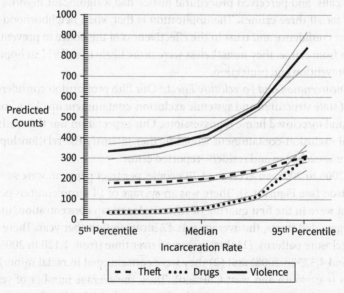

Figure 4.7 Predicted Counts of 911 Calls about Theft, Drugs, and Violent Crime across Incarceration (with 95% Confidence Intervals)

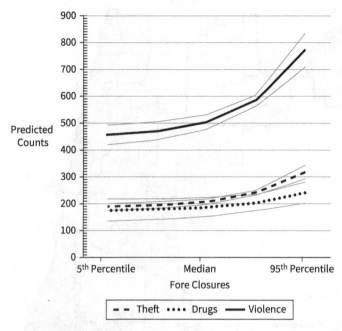

Figure 4.8 Predicted Counts of 911 Calls about Theft, Drugs, and Violent Crime across Foreclosures (with 95% Confidence Intervals in gray)

effects reflected extensions of structural processes in contemporary Chicago. They made explicit the ongoing and disadvantaging links between hyper-segregation and foreclosures and incarceration, processes of exclusion-containment that we have emphasized in our structural-containment theory of legal cynicism. Foreclosures and incarceration also reflected a tightened coupling of the civil and criminal justice systems that we have identified as a key part of RM Daley's regime.

Police and Resident Reports: Our sixth proposition was that while police and resident crime reports overlap, 911 calls more closely reflected residents' concerns. We expected that residents are more sensitive to neighborhood conditions, and changes in them, and that these influence their crime reports *net of police-reported crime.*

We added police reports of crime to our sixth and last equations to assess this final proposition (see Tables, Chapter 4 Table 7). As expected, we again saw a recurring positive step-like quartile increase in the association of African American structural exclusion-containment with 911 calls for crime, now with the police crime reports also included in the prediction equation. We also saw that police reports, reflecting officially recorded occurrence of crime, mediated associations between 911 calls for property crime and African American tract-level hyper-segregation, although not for 911 calls about drug or violent crimes.

A final map of Chicago (Figure 4.9) brings into sharp relief the geospatial patterns suggested by our analysis. This map reflects the distribution of African Americans

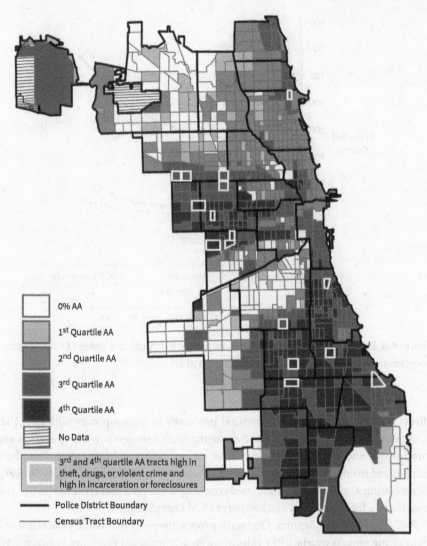

Figure 4.9 Predicted 911 Calls by Police Districts, Exclusion-Containment Quartiles

across census tracts, with darker shading reflecting higher concentrations. It uses thin black lines to demarcate census tracts and heavy black lines to delineate police districts. It uses a white line to distinguish tracts where legal cynicism and incarcerations or foreclosures were high (i.e., above the 90th percentile), as were predicted counts for 911 calls for property, drug, or violent crime (we set other variables to their means).

A number of patterns were immediately apparent. First, there were no white lines for tracts in the first or second quartiles. In contrast, there were eight highlighted tracts from the third quartile and nine from the fourth (some tracts crossed district lines but we counted them only once). Second, these 17 tracts were spread across 12 police districts; only four districts (3, 10, 11, and 25) had more than one highlighted tract. This dispersion suggested that resident reliance on 911 calls for help is common in a number of racially segregated Black communities that had to cope with high levels of foreclosures, incarceration, and crime. These highlighted tracts also struggled with limited economic resources. In 1990, the average unemployment rate across them was 18 percent; 31 percent of families were on social assistance; and 37 percent were officially poor.

The Persistent Effects of Legal Cynicism

In 1972, Congressman Ralph Metcalfe reported on "The Misuse of Police Authority in Chicago." He found "a crisis in police community relations . . . at all levels." Almost 50 years later, in 2016, Mayor Rahm Emanuel received a "Police Accountability Task Force" report indicating police–community relations might even be worse, resulting in an "historic outcry" that "had reached a breaking point with the entire local law enforcement infrastructure."

Procedural justice theory (Tyler 2017) is a currently popular approach to such problems of community–police relations. Carr and colleagues (2007) used this theory to address a paradox in their respondents' narratives: the youth they interviewed said police abuse and the lack of due process are unfair, but their sense of injustice was nonetheless transitory and replaced by "widespread support for pro-criminal justice solutions to crime" (469). The procedural justice theory they used maintains that better training of police in procedural practices would increase trust and confidence and promote cooperation in crime reporting.

However, we did not observe the transitory or procedural justice patterns they expected. To begin, we did not find evidence of low levels of residents reporting crime in Chicago's hyper-segregated neighborhoods; instead, we found high levels of 911 crime calls in these disadvantaged Black communities, especially where there is increased legal cynicism about police crime prevention and protection.

We used an exclusion-containment and dual process perspective on legal cynicism to explain this paradox. Our use of the dual process approach maintains that survey questions can reveal collective motivations of cultural frameworks, such as legal cynicism, and that these frameworks can account for the paradoxical nature of neighborhood narratives associated with summoning the police. These collective motivations include pleas for crime prevention and protection, despite cynicism about the capacity of the law or the police to deliver these outcomes.

The persistent influence of legal cynicism in the hyper-segregated neighborhoods of Chicago is a response to being excluded and contained—that is, shut out and kept away from—the economic and cultural capital of the city. The collective response to this experience is not temporary or transitory, as Carr and colleagues suggest; instead, it reflects a historical conscious and non-conscious accumulation that is central to our exclusion-containment and dual process theory of legal cynicism.

We found expressions of legal cynicism about police effectiveness in Chicago that, paradoxically and enduringly, are persistently associated with heightened calls for police assistance. Legal cynicism is important for not only understanding 911 calls about crime, but also because it is a mechanism that meditates the influence of neighborhood-level racial/ethnic exclusion and containment. Our point is not that all 911 calls should result in criminal charges. Indiscriminate charges heighten and intensify cynicism about police ineffectiveness in crime prevention and protection; instead, our findings clearly indicated the problems of police–community relations in minority neighborhoods where concerns about ineffective prevention and protection predominate. As Bell (2017) emphasized, persistent and pervasive police mistreatment and neglect, along with legal cynicism and the neighborhood structural disadvantages of exclusion and containment, all contribute to "legal estrangement."

The need for community-level research about procedural justice is pressing because policymakers have eagerly embraced it. This theory was the foundation of a frequently cited police training program in Chicago; it was the basis for recommendations by a presidential commission (President's Task Force on 21st Century Policing 2015), and was central to a report by the National Research Council Committee on Proactive Policing (see Nagin and Telep 2017). Yet by embracing the procedural justice framework and neglecting neighborhood-level sources of perceived procedural *injustice*, policymakers have mistakenly ignored important sources of the police–community relations they seek to reform.

We found that problems of policing high crime rate neighborhoods are more complex, entrenched, and cumulative than procedural justice theory suggests. This chapter contributes to understanding of the ongoing troubled state of police–community relations by more fully analyzing resident-reported crime. Emergency 911 calls play a formative role in police–community relations and correlate strongly with police crime reporting—more strongly than other known predictors. These calls for police assistance are far more common in the hyper-segregated neighborhoods of exclusion and containment that are cumulatively shaped by dual conscious and non-conscious cognitive processing of "lived neighborhood experiences" that result in legal cynicism. Feelings of being involuntarily excluded and contained within neighborhoods are a recipe for legal cynicism that is prevalent and persistent.

The cumulative nature of these processes is vividly reflected in our analysis of the persistent influence of the 1990 census tract measure of hyper-segregated Black neighborhoods as a predictor of 911 calls for police assistance and police-reported crime in 2006–2008, as well as by the mediation of this effect of hyper-segregated racial/ethnic exclusion and containment by legal cynicism and, more recently, by heightened levels of incarceration and home foreclosures.

Our findings indicated that the dual impact of conscious and non-conscious cognitive processes was especially strong in the 1990s and in relation to residents' cynical feelings about crime prevention and protection. Legal cynicism's direct effect on 911 calls by people concerned about crime prevention and protection in their neighborhoods was striking in its strength and statistical significance, more than a decade after its measurement in 1994–1995. These 911 calls expressed a persistent desire for crime prevention and protection— notwithstanding past disappointments.

Politicians and policymakers have historically responded to calls for assistance from minority neighborhoods with punitive measures, from stop and frisk policing to mass incarceration. Yet the underlying plea of these calls for prevention and protection persisted. As Hinton, Kohler-Hausmann, and Weaver (2016) noted: "When [B]lacks ask for *better* policing, legislators tend to hear *more* instead." Their observation indicates that minority communities, politicians, and the police see these issues from radically different vantage points.

This chapter began with a paradox expressed in narratives about the police. We have presented evidence for a survey based exclusion-containment and dual process theory of legal cynicism that addresses the paradox of such narratives. Our theory of legal cynicism is anchored in indicators of a focal concept that reflects collectively shared motivational feelings in minority communities: that the police are unable or unwilling to provide preventive and/or protective assistance in a system that can make it seem, especially to endangered adolescents, that "laws are made to be broken." The latter belief contributes to our understanding of both neighborhood reactions to crime and the criminal behavior itself.

Decades of mass incarceration and a later housing crisis that led to widespread home foreclosures and repossessions continue to mediate the effects of legal cynicism in Chicago's disadvantaged minority neighborhoods. Yet the desperate hope persists that calls for police assistance can deliver safety and security and reduce crime, especially by youth at ages when delinquent and criminal behavior is common.

Our analysis of survey and official data gathered over several decades in Chicago has shown that a cultural schema of legal cynicism—operative at both more and less conscious levels—was a crucial component in a cognitive landscape that demands crime prevention and protection. These needs and demands are wide-ranging, long-standing, and deeply entrenched.

5
History is Not the Past

Past Forward

Police misconduct is commonplace in Chicago. It ranges from the indifference about the plight of populations the police are supposed to protect, to the police use of fatal violence against these populations. It also has a long history. Chicago established its first police department in the 1850s. Jeffrey Adler (2007) used police records to show that between 1875 and 1920, Chicago police officers were responsible for one out of every 18 homicides, with a notable escalation in the early 20th century. This made Chicago one of the most violent places in America, and the turn of the century increase in homicides by police was especially large. Black victims constituted more than 20 percent of police killings, while the Black population was about three percent. The police had an explicit shoot-to-kill policy, and African Americans bore its brunt.

Police were also guilty of ignoring violence by White residents. The July 1919 race riot we described in Chapter Two was precipitated by the police's refusal to arrest the man who had killed a Black teenager for swimming at a Whites-only beach. They were also guilty of ignoring attacks by Whites during the riot and, in some cases, participating in attacks against African Americans (Tuttle 1970).

As we saw in Chapter Two, nearly a half-century after the 1919 riot, demonstrations for open housing—including ML King's Chicago Freedom Movement—sparked violence that the Chicago Police Department again refused or failed to safely contain. For more than a century, official reports have documented Chicago's long history of police brutality (Andonova 2017). Reports in 1904 and 1928 described the police as "rotten to the core" (Adler 2007). In 1972, Alderman Ralph Metcalfe authored a report that anticipated later investigations by the U.S. Department of Justice (2017) and Mayor Rahm Emanuel's Police Accountability Task Force (2016). The latter was headed by his successor as mayor, Lori Lightfoot. Police misconduct persists as a seemingly boundless source of scandal in Chicago politics.

And so it continues. Many of the cases of police misconduct are well known from media accounts. For example, in the 1960s, police officer James "Gloves" Davis had a reputation for covering his right hand when he beat suspects. He was also notorious for his involvement in the raid that killed Black Panther activist Fred Hampton (Diamond 2017:184). The torture perpetrated by Police Commander Jon Burge and his "midnight crew" began in the early 1970s in Area 2 and 3 police stations. The torture peaked in the mid-1980s, and it took until 2010 to produce a conviction—but not for torture—and a prison term for Burge (Taylor 2014).

In 2016, the *Guardian* published a series of articles charging that police abuse of suspects did not end with the firing of Jon Burge. According to the *Guardian*, Chicago police "used punches, knee strikes, elbow strikes, slaps, wrist twists, baton blows and Tasers" while interrogating men at its Homan Square Facility (Ackerman 2016). The Chicago police denied that any abuse occurred, but more than four years later, Chicagoans continued to protest against mistreatment at this facility and called for its closure (Hickey 2020).

Routine police abuse was not limited to the interrogation of suspects held at police stations and holding centers. In the spring of 2018, the Cook County State's Attorney's Office announced it would no longer treat as credible the actions of ten Chicago police officers led by supervising Sgt. Ronald Watts (Gonnerman 2018; Rogers 2018). Housing project residents reported these officers planted drugs, framed suspects, and bullied victims into false confessions. Much of this misconduct took place in the neighborhoods located in Chicago Police Districts 2 and 3. The Watts case involved a hundred or more wrongly convicted defendants, with victims stretching from the 1970s to the present. Recent cases of abuse also include the 2014 shooting of Laquan McDonald and the 2019 arrest of Anjanette Young—cases we turn to in our Epilogue. The inescapable conclusion is that Chicago police violence against African Americans continues.

The recurring history—including the actions of officers Watts, Davis, Burge, and many others—raises pressing questions about police misconduct and brutality in Chicago; questions that past studies of this and other cities are beginning to inform. At the city level, the most basic finding that ties past research to our present concerns is the well-documented association between hyper-segregated racial exclusion, spatial containment within neighborhoods, and complaints about police misconduct (e.g., Holmes 2000; Smith and Holmes 2003, 2014). Yet we still know relatively little about the recurring neighborhood-level processes involved (Faber and Kalbfeld 2019), and more specifically about the historical and cultural mechanisms that have mediated these relationships.

Cultural narratives, as we have shown in previous chapters, are essential for understanding historical connections between neighborhood structural conditions and the problems they produce. We focus again in this chapter on the segregation of neighborhoods and legal cynicism, this time in connection with the accumulation of complaints over lengthy periods about police misconduct. We hypothesize that the history of racialized exclusion and containment of hyper-segregated neighborhoods intensifies legal cynicism about police brutality and increases complaints in a recurring pattern about this and other forms of police misconduct.

The case of Joseph White we presented in Chapter Three supports the thesis that legal cynicism about police protection of residents in segregated neighborhoods can lead youth to avoid reporting serious threats to their safety, while instead resorting to self-help (Black 1983) for purposes of self-defense (Kirk and Papachristos 2011). This cynicism helps explain why residents of segregated neighborhoods may often endure rather than complain about police mistreatment (Faber and Kalbfeld 2019).

However, while the Joseph White case study illustrates a tendency toward avoidance of the police, the research reported in Chapter Four on resident crime reporting shows that legal cynicism in hyper-segregated neighborhoods is nonetheless persistently associated with seeking police assistance through 911 calls. A central hypothesis considered in this chapter is that legal cynicism also leads residents to take more consequential steps toward filing formal complaints about police misconduct.

Explaining Complaints about Police Misconduct

In this chapter, we used census tract data to analyze connections between racial segregation, legal cynicism, and complaints about police misconduct. Recent studies have used these data to investigate connections between officers who use excessive force (Ouellet et al. 2019) and to explore the relationship between race and judicial decisions about complaints (Faber and Kalbfeld 2019). In this chapter, we go beyond these studies and analyze the connections between structural and cultural factors and complaints.

Thus, we used a neighborhood approach to explore how racial segregation, ongoing histories of police misconduct, and legal cynicism continue to operate over long periods as sources of complaints about police misconduct. We again used the measure of legal cynicism we introduced in Chapter Two. The data for this measure were propitiously collected in Chicago in the mid-1990s (Sampson et al. 1997), the period following the height of the Burge torture activity and the Watts extortion crimes described earlier. We are particularly interested in how cumulative histories of police misconduct contribute to the creation of continuing cultural narratives of legal cynicism within neighborhoods and lead to recurring complaints about police misconduct.

Our analysis drew from the provocative writings of James Baldwin (2010). Baldwin emphasized that many, if not most, issues studied as "Black problems" are more accurately understood as "White made problems." Jill Lepore (2020a:28) reports that every study of race and urban riots, at least since 1917, has found that White police are sources of the abuse of Black citizens (e.g., Zelizer 2016). This is another way of saying that acts of police misconduct, including torture and brutality, are prototypical examples of what Baldwin called White made problems.

These problems typically have their origins in historical and political contradictions. The contradiction we have emphasized in this book lies at the intersection of the institutional promise made by police departments to serve and protect neighborhood residents, as contrasted with the coercive role that the police persistently play in the exclusion and containment of disadvantaged African American residents in hyper-segregated neighborhoods.

This contradiction symptomatically lies at the heart of an exchange in a 1968 senate confirmation hearing involving Otto Kerner, Chair of the 1968 National Commission on Civil Disorders, about the role of White racism in riots. The southern racist Senator, Strom Thurmond, wanted to know about a central thesis of the Commission Report that Kerner had overseen.

> Thurmond: Why do you say 'white racism' caused these riots?
>
> Kerner: I beg your pardon.
>
> Thurmond: Why do you want to blame the white people ... for this trouble?
>
> Kerner: Because we say this has developed over a period of time, and the people in the Negro ghettoes indicated that the rebellion was against the white establishment.
>
> Thrumond: ... What does that term mean? What did you think it meant when you put it in this report or approved of it?
>
> Kerner: I thought it meant this—that over a period of years the Negro was kept within a certain area economically and geographically and he was not allowed to come out of it (cited in Lepore 2020a:29).

Kerner was essentially articulating the role of what we have called an exclusion-containment theory in explaining legal cynicism and its connection to crime and criminal justice.

As in earlier chapters, we tested whether the association between narratives of legal cynicism and police complaints were independent of other predictors. Some predictors may contribute to both legal cynicism and complaints, making their association spurious, while others may be powerful transmitters leading from racial segregation to complaints. We explored a relationship between legal cynicism in the mid-1990s and contemporary complaints as illustrative of a historically cumulative cultural frame with White institutional origins. Building from Baldwin, our hypothesis is that understanding the role of White-dominated institutional practices in creating neighborhood histories and cultural narratives is crucial to explaining contemporary complaints about police misconduct.

James Baldwin's Long View of History

James Baldwin (2010) noted that history is often wrongly thought of as simply a passing parade of events receding into the past, rather than as ongoing cumulative processes that shape our current and future lives. He insisted: "History is not the past. It is the present" and "we carry our history with us" (154).

Baldwin further described the fearful and contagious consequences for Black Americans of "carrying lived history" into the present, insisting that, "the full story of [W]hite and [B]lack in this country is more vast and shattering than we would like to believe." He used a medical metaphor to emphasize his point: "Like an unhindered infection in the body ... [this history] has the power to make our whole organism sick." This chapter includes evidence that current abuses of White on Black policing are crucially informed by Baldwin's insistence that we acknowledge the cumulative and contagious nature of our infectious history.

The Princeton historian, Eddie Glaude Jr. (2020), observed that Baldwin was nothing less than revolutionary when he insisted that, if we are to ever more fully understand how White American thinking has gone wrong in its conceptualization of what colloquially has often been called the "race problem," we must do nothing less than turn our thoughts about this "burdensome problem" upside down:

> This is Baldwin's revolutionary act: to shift or invert the "[W]hite man's burden." The problem is not us. Instead Americans must understand as best we can, because our lives depend on it, the consequences of this deadly projection. Through this lens, the "[B]lack man's burden" is the brutal behavior of [W]hite people in thrall to a lie (2020:106–107).

This "brutal behavior," we have suggested, prototypically includes the lie of pretending that the police mandate in America is to serve and protect all citizens, when this mandate is more specifically to exclude and contain African Americans in hyper-segregated neighborhoods. As Lepore (2020a:29) concluded: "It was as it has ever been." That is, it continues.

Assuming the latter inference about the police role in the hyper-segregation of African American neighborhoods is correct, what are its consequences? Our hypothesis is that one consequence of collectively "carrying" historical memories of this kind of brutality (and other forms of police misconduct) in hyper-segregated neighborhoods is a readiness to file official complaints about contemporary abuses of police power. Our analysis of police complaints in this chapter further suggests that mobilization and resistance by #BlackLivesMatter and other African American neighborhood movements reflect a rational effort to mobilize and collectively carry forward the cumulative force of these painful memories for purposes of reform.

Racial Segregation and Policing

Baldwin was quick to remind readers that the racial segregation of Chicago (Massey and Tannen 2015) and other American cities had a long, still ongoing, and persistently violent legacy (also Sampson 2012). As we noted at the start of this chapter, the historical roots of Chicago's racial segregation and race-based violence date to at least the early part of the 20th century, when White property owners used assaults, arson, bombings, and other types of violence against African American arrivals from the South, violence typically ignored by the predominantly White Chicago police (Hamilton and Foote 2018; Rothstein 2017). Other factors also isolated African Americans in densely populated, highly segregated neighborhoods, including not only the scale and timing of the first and second Great Migrations, but also the *de facto* effects of the GI Bill, the Fair Housing and Federal Highway Acts, restrictive covenants, school segregation, and bank redlining.

As we noted in the previous chapter, the Chicago Housing Authority constructed nearly three-quarters of its residential projects in poor Black areas that contained and thereby excluded project residents from the city's White neighborhoods (Rothstein 2017). Policing in minority neighborhoods was and is two-faced. In many Black neighborhoods, the presence of the police is episodic (Goffman 2009) and provides little consistent crime prevention or protection (Leovy 2015). Yet, these same communities often experience policing that includes Stop and Frisk (aka SQ&Fs, Terry stops), carding, curfews, and excessive and sometimes fatal violence (Glaser 2014; White and Fradella 2016; Zimring 2017).

Heightened policing in these neighborhoods is associated with high crime rates (Sampson and Lauritsen 1997), while the extent and concentration of racial segregation are independently related to the scale of policing (Carmichael and Kent 2014). The combined result is that African Americans are "watched, questioned, and detained more than others" (Kennedy 1997: x; also see Ekins 2016; Lerman and Weaver 2014).

Lepore (2020b:66) traced contemporary militaristic policing practices to August Vollmer, who, in 1909, became chief of police in Berkeley, California. "After all," she quoted Vollmer as observing, "we're conducting a war, a war against the enemies of society." These were Vollmer's enemies: "Mobsters, bootleggers, socialist agitators, strikers, union organizers, immigrants, and Black people." Khalil Gibran Muhammad (2010) called the latter mistreatment "the Condemnation of Blackness."

Lepore further traced what we have called the fundamental contradiction of modern policing to our still resonant mid-20th century cultural representations on television of what the police predominately do. On the one hand, shows like Dragnet and Adam-12 used 1950s–1960s legal procedurals set in Los Angles to portray modern police work as largely limited to crime solving. On the other hand, this era's non-fictional nightly news reports showed Americans something shockingly different: "Arkansas state troopers barring Black students from entering Little Rock Central High School in 1957; Birmingham police clubbing and arresting some seven hundred Black children protesting segregation in 1963; and Alabama state troopers beating voting-rights marchers in Selma, in 1965" (Lepore 2020b:68). The memories of this contradiction are still with us.

One wonders: did Malcolm X have Chicago more specifically in mind when he said the American South extended to the Canadian border? Chicago has a long history of racialized and abusive policing (Hamilton and Foote 2018: Table 2) that has continued well beyond the crimes we have attributed to Davis, Watts, and Burge. According to an American Civil Liberties Union (2015) report, over a four-month period in 2014, 72 percent of Chicago's SQ&Fs involved Black Americans, who represented only 32 percent of the city's population. Baldwin reminds us that—north, south, east, or west—we need to understand that the history of America's racial contradictions is disproportionately a national White made problem.

Complaints about Police

The filing of official complaints is among the most obvious challenges to the abuse of police power. Resident complaints generally originate from interactions and observations of police misconduct, while disrespect and brutality are the strongest predictors of complaints (Terrill and Ingram 2016). Felstiner, Abel and Sarat (1980/1:631) observe that filing a complaint involves a process by which individuals transform the experience of an injury or insult into a grievance, for example, through a sequence of "naming, blaming, and claiming" police misconduct.

Aggrieved people do not necessarily file complaints. The National Institute of Justice Police-Public Contact Survey found that less than five percent of respondents who reported police improperly interacted with them subsequently filed a complaint (U.S. 2015). Police misconduct in and of itself often contributes to the reluctance to file a complaint. The Department of Justice's (U.S. 2017) investigation of Chicago police documented frequent police intimidation as well as refusals to accept potential complainants.

A *Chicago Tribune* (Gorner and Hing 2015) article reported that a majority of complaints initiated in 2010–2014 were never formalized because the initiator did not provide required details. Complaints in Chicago require the filing of an affidavit, and many people refused to complete the complaint because of fear of police retaliation. This is consistent with Felstiner and colleagues' conclusion that, "too few wrongs are perceived, pursued, and remedied" (1980–81: p. 632).

Several researchers have described the individuals who file complaints and the officers against whom the complaints are filed (McCluskey and Terrill 2005; Terrill and Ingram 2016). Race is a consistent correlate of complainants (Kerstetter, Rasinski, and Heiert 1996), and younger adult males are disproportionate sources. However, some recent research found that complaints were not significantly associated with officer race, net of other factors (Terrill and Ingram 2016).

Studies of the backgrounds of individuals who lodge complaints and officers they complain about are useful for understanding the individual-level dynamics of the complaint process. However, neighborhood analyses use a different approach and focus on links between complaints and area characteristics. As Sampson noted (2012:23), the latter studies take "individuals seriously ... [but] focus on social mechanisms and processes that are supra-individual in nature."

Neighborhood conditions are, in this sense, "socially productive" (Sampson 2012:358). For example, Robert Kane (2002) used an "ecological" approach to show how neighborhoods contributed to police misconduct. Using 1975-1996 precinct-level data on New York City police misconduct, Kane (2002) found positive associations between complaints and concentrated economic disadvantage, residential mobility, and an increase in the proportion of Latinx, but not African American, residents.

The latter finding is perhaps surprising, given that city-level analyses have typically reported a sizable, significant association between percent African Americans and complaints (Holmes 2000; Smith and Holmes 2003, 2014). Although Kane's focus is on neighborhood structural conditions, he considered the role of cultural differences in a subsequent analysis (Kane 2005). There he theorized that legal cynicism may be higher in structurally disadvantaged neighborhoods. However, Kane did not elaborate on this thesis nor empirically explore it. We address this point in this chapter.

Legal Cynicism as a Cultural Frame

As noted in earlier chapters, legal cynicism is a cultural narrative that involves perceptions of the law as illegitimate and of the police as disinterested in, unresponsive to, or ill equipped to address residents' concerns about crime. A cultural narrative can be a historically enduring account reflecting collective expectations, information sharing, and community understandings. And it can operate at both micro-individual and macro-neighborhood levels (Eisner and Nivette 2013).

As we have seen in earlier chapters, legal cynicism is higher at both the individual and neighborhood levels among Blacks, Hispanics, and other racial minorities. In this chapter, we focus on the connection between racial segregation and neighborhood legal cynicism, net of other variables, and their relationships with current, as well as, prior experiences of police misconduct. The latter reflects Baldwin's insistence that historical experiences often "carry forward" in a process of cumulative influence.

Sampson (2012:59) emphasized that a macro-level community focus on places, rather than people, provides important insights into the ways enduring cultural frames are part of "the perceptual (or cognitive) social organization" that emerges in neighborhoods. His point is that macro-level cultural narratives vary across neighborhoods and are distinct from individual micro-level dispositions and the characteristics of people living there (see also Harding and Hepburn 2014).

Neighborhood cultural narratives may be particularly important in poor, inner city, Black communities where mobility and outside contact are low. Sharkey (2013) found nearly three of four Black families living in the poorest, most racially isolated communities in the early 2000s lived in these same neighborhoods in the 1970s. In these communities, children can inherit their parents' neighborhood environment and "all that goes with them" (Sharkey 2013:45), including historically influenced cultural frames such as legal cynicism.

Research has consistently shown that African Americans disproportionately view the police negatively (e.g., Hagan and Albonetti 1982; Hagan et al. 2005; Weitzer and Tuch 2006). A comprehensive review of 92 studies documented that, in general, Black Americans report less confidence in police and are more dissatisfied, mistrustful, and suspicious of them (Peck 2015). In a study of 12 large U.S. cities, Chicago residents' confidence in the police was second to last (Skogan 2006); it was especially low in Black, economically disadvantaged communities, and this has continued into the present (Skogan 2006; also see Shedd 2015; Van Cleve 2016).

Like Baldwin, Geoff Ward's (2016) "microclimate" approach emphasized that cultural frames are grounded in specific geographical spaces with distinct histories. He noted that local as well as more general histories of racism, discrimination, and socio-political exclusion shape contemporary cultural frames, and that trans-generational traumatic experiences of violent police victimization are endemic to the history of these Black communities. African Americans arriving in early 20th century Chicago brought with them historical memories of lynching and other racial violence.

Laurence Ralph (2013) has documented ways in which a history of police misconduct and views about the police have become part of the cultural fabric of Chicago neighborhoods. He described legal cynicism as a cultural frame that involves, "a kind of socially and politically charged remembering through which people transform experiences of pain into collective narratives" (112). In focus groups and interviews, Ralph found that African American residents living in segregated neighborhoods routinely recalled Jon Burge's use of torture techniques that occurred decades earlier. In 2009, Ralph (2017) attended a meeting where 35 families met to discuss a police fatal shooting of a local boy; 21 of the families specifically referred to Burge or the victims he and his officers tortured. Consistent with Baldwin's insistence that "history is not the past," these families described contemporary police mistreatment by using Burge's name as a verb, calling it being "Burged" (2017: 263). According to Ralph (2020:179), almost everyone he spoke with knew "what the term means."

As we noted in Chapter One, the Jon Burge case illustrates the immunity commonly granted police misconduct. Although Burge began torturing suspects in the early 1970s, he was not fired by the Chicago Police Department until 1993, and he was not convicted of a crime until 2010. Ralph's (2013) ethnographic research has emphasized the ways that interaction among neighborhood residents can foster and embed legal cynicism in a community's culture, thereby representing "a quality of neighborhoods, and not simply the views of a particular individual" (Kirk, Papachristos, Fagan, and Tyler 2012:84).

Is Legal Cynicism a Neighborhood Deficit or Asset?

In earlier chapters, we noted that much research on legal cynicism focuses on its relationship with crime. Studies have reported links between legal cynicism and self-reported minor offenses (Reisig, Wolfe, and Holtfreter 2011), intimate partner violence (Emery, Jolley, and Wu 2011), and other violent crimes (Corsaro, Frank, and Ozer 2015), including homicides (Kirk and Papachristos 2011). Some of these studies have used what Hunter and Robinson (2016) observed is a common perception in research on poor, urban, Black, neighborhoods: that neighborhood attributes like legal cynicism are "deficits."

This perspective suggests that people in these communities see little value in complaining about police mistreatment because they see authorities as disinterested, dismissive, hostile, or racist—and as unresponsive to complaints about this mistreatment. Analyses of complaints against Chicago police have shown that, compared to Whites, African Americans, particularly those in predominantly Black and high crime neighborhoods, are less likely to have their complaints validated by authorities (Faber and Kalbfeld 2019). Residents may be further discouraged from filing grievances if they believe police will punish them for doing so (Lerman and Weaver 2014). This logic suggests that, all else equal, neighborhood legal cynicism should be negatively associated with complaints about the police.

But we find an alternative perspective more persuasive. It suggests that legal cynicism does not consistently lead to legal disengagement. As noted in earlier chapters, Bell's (2016) research in high crime minority neighborhoods of Washington D.C. found that Black mothers had major misgivings about the police that were reflective of legal cynicism; yet, these mothers still called 911 when they thought it could be strategically helpful. For example, they would call police if they thought the person whom they were calling about would get needed therapeutic treatment, rather than being arrested.

Other research similarly has demonstrated that people who actively distrust the police will engage them when they believe it can be beneficial (Bobo and Thompson 2006). In Chicago, Skogan (2006) reported that more than half of Black respondents said they had contacted the police. Moreover, about 60 percent of people who had been stopped by police said they nonetheless would contact them if they felt they needed them.

Many African Americans also actively support police reforms (Weitzer and Tuch 2006), and while they are critical of police, they do not differ significantly from others in the punishments they recommend for police misconduct (Seron, Pereira, and Kovath 2006; see also Skogan 2006). These findings suggest that Black communities want what other communities also expect from policing: fair, just, and lawful treatment, effective protection, and sustained efforts to reduce serious crime (Ekins 2016; Weitzer and Tuch 2006).

Hunter and Robinson (2016) concluded from such studies that there is a belief in Black neighborhoods that holding the police accountable by filing complaints can be beneficial, and therefore that doing so can be a neighborhood "asset." Felstiner and colleagues (1980/1:644) argued that support in one's community—"[the] reaction of a wide social network"— is an important predictor of whether people will transform personal grievances into legal grievances using complaint processes. Complaints are, from this perspective, potentially productive: an avenue for protesting police mistreatment, illegal practices, and abuses of power.

As we saw in Chapter Two, legal cynicism is positively associated with concentration of Blacks in racially segregated neighborhoods (also Kirk and Matsuda 2011), and our analysis in Chapter Three showed that race and legal cynicism predict 911 calls for police assistance. Likewise, Desmond, Papachristos, and Kirk (2016; 2020) report a positive neighborhood-level association in Milwaukee between percent Black and 911 calls (also see Schaible and Hughes 2012), although recent and severe police brutality can interrupt this pattern. These studies suggest neighborhood legal cynicism is positively associated with filing complaints about the police. And, given its heightened levels in African American communities, legal cynicism may also mediate the association between racial segregation and complaints.

Mass Incarceration, Home Foreclosures, and Other Cultural and Structural Factors

Mass incarceration and home foreclosures and evictions are of particular interest to us, because of their concentration in racially segregated, disadvantaged communities. Mass incarceration, especially when it involves police pursuit of people wanted on warrants (Brayne 2020; Goffman 2014) as well as home foreclosures, particularly when police are involved in resident removals, often provoke conflicts between police and residents and increase complaints. However, these relationships may be curvilinear. At high levels, incarceration may leave behind fewer people who have a high likelihood of interacting with police. Foreclosures and evictions may increase abandoned properties, and neighborhoods may have so many foreclosures that police presence decreases.

Several cultural narratives described in previous chapters may also influence complaints: perceptions of procedural justice, collective efficacy, and tolerance of deviance. As noted in the previous chapter, Tyler (2017) argued that perceptions of procedural justice involve people's assessments of how the police have treated them and the fairness of their decision making. In contrast, legal cynicism focuses on broader evaluations of law and police enforcement, as well as local and historical factors. Perceptions of procedural justice are assumed to be more narrowly grounded in people's recent interactions with police.

As we noted in Chapter Four, most descriptions of perceptions of procedural justice have focused on individual-level, psychological phenomena (Mazerolle et al. 2013; Tyler 2017). Yet, we maintain that relationships between perceived procedural justice and police complaints rise above the micro level (Nagin and Telep 2017). People share their experiences and evaluations of police directly and increasingly through social media. These can coalesce into neighborhood cultural narratives (Kirk 2016).

Collective efficacy and tolerance of deviance may also influence police complaints. People in neighborhoods with high collective efficacy may see reporting police misconduct as a commitment to their community or as a civic duty. Tolerance of deviance also varies across neighborhoods. Yet acceptance of adolescent misbehavior probably does not translate into tolerance for police misconduct.

While our earlier discussions of neighborhood structural attributes focused mainly on racial segregation, a broader literature also considers neighborhood-level economic disadvantage, immigrant concentration, and residential instability (Kane

2002). We took these additional factors into account in analyzing complaints about police misconduct.

Four Predictions about Police Complaints

We have drawn on the writings of James Baldwin to make the point that the long history of police mistreatment of Black Chicagoans living in this city's segregated communities "is not the past." Instead, this history is culturally remembered, exercises a lasting influence that is reflected in expressions of legal cynicism, and continues to unfold in response to citizen complaints about new forms of police misconduct such as mass incarceration and home foreclosures. Our discussion therefore leads to four predictions. First, the influence of legal cynicism is long-lasting and thus extends over long periods of time. Second, the relationship between legal cynicism and complaints is positive, not negative. Third, legal cynicism is an observable mediator of relationships between racialized neighborhood exclusion-containment and resident complaints about police misconduct. And fourth, the association between legal cynicism and these complaints is independent of other cultural and structural conditions that are known to influence them.

Counting Complaints and Their Correlates

Our analysis used data described in earlier chapters, as well as data from the 2010–2014 American Community Surveys and additional sources described next (see also Appendix A). Our outcome variable used Chicago police records on 7,087 misconduct complaints filed in 2012–2014. In 2014, the Illinois Supreme Court ruled the public should have access to these misconduct records. This ruling was a response to persistent complaints by Diane Bond and the lobbying of Jamie Kalven, a journalist and human rights/activist, and others. Kalven and the *Invisible Institute* posted the data online.

We used additional data from the *Invisible Institute* to measure the historical legacy of accumulated grievances. These include 21,748 tract-level cases for 1980–1994. Demonstration of the effect of this neighborhood-level historical variable—net of other factors—would support Baldwin's thesis that "history is not the past" but rather a recurring "lived experience."

Most complaints about police misconduct arise from interactions with police, most often from officers' investigations of people and places they believe are linked to criminal activity. We expected that, all else equal, complaints would have been higher in neighborhoods where these interactions were routine, and less common in communities where they were unusual. We used tract-level police-reported crime as a proxy measure of these interactions. These yearly crime data come from Chicago police records for 2012–2104.

We applied the same measures of racial/ethnic segregation and legal cynicism as in earlier chapters. Our expectation was that racial/ethnic segregation is a source of the historical legacy Baldwin identifies, and that legal cynicism in turn mediated and transmitted the effect of this legacy.

We also included the structural and cultural control variables discussed in Chapters Two and Three. We did this to make sure we did not overlook other sources of associations between complaints and racial segregation, legal cynicism, and complaint histories. We also controlled for change in neighborhood structural characteristics, as we did in Chapter Four, although here the change is between the 1990 census and American Community Survey averages for 2009–2014.

Our outcome was a count variable modeled with negative binomial regression (Cameron and Trivedi 2013). The first equation included a historical measure of prior police complaints (1980–1994) emphasized by Baldwin's approach, along with racial segregation and other 1990 census measures. The second equation added legal cynicism as a key mediator of effects of historical and racial measures. The third equation included the other variables described in Chapters Two and Three.

Analyzing Complaints about Police Misconduct

Descriptive data indicated the most common complaints about police misconduct were first amendment speech violations (34 percent), personnel/operations violations (31 percent), arrest or lockup abuses (19 percent), search infringements (10 percent), or verbal abuse (3 percent). As expected, complaints were more common in Black neighborhoods, with approximately 1.9 and 1.6 in the lower quartiles for percent Black compared to 5.2 and 5.7 in the higher quartiles. As noted in earlier chapters, legal cynicism was on average lowest among census tracts in the first quartile, and increasing in a step-like gradient in remaining quartiles.

Bivariate associations between complaints provided initial evidence of the key relationships hypothesized in our analysis (see Tables, Chapter 5 Table 1). That is, the number of complaints was positively and significantly associated with African American exclusion-containment, an increase in neighborhood proportion of African Americans, legal cynicism, incarceration, and residential foreclosures. Complaints were negatively associated with Hispanic concentration, as well as with decreasing neighborhood proportions of Blacks and Hispanics.

Our multivariate analysis started with 1990 racial segregation, 1980–1994 police complaint histories, and structural census measures (see Tables, Chapter 5 Table 2). In this first equation, the earlier complaint histories and racial segregation measures had the influences that Baldwin would predict: that is, both higher 1990 African American quartile tracts and higher 1980–1994 police complaints were positively related to complaints years later, in 2012–2014. Complaints also increased with concentrated disadvantage (and number of residents, and residential stability).

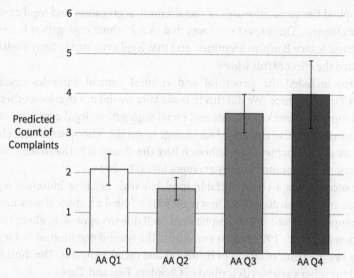

Figure 5.1 Predicted Counts of Complaints across African American Quartiles, with 95 Percent Confidence Intervals

We used predicted counts of complaints to demonstrate the magnitude of these associations (see Figure 5.1). The number of expected yearly complaints was just over 2.5 for tracts in the first quartile; and double that (5) for tracts in the fourth quartile. A comparison between two communities with the same number of census tracts (12), Portage Park and Woodlawn, indicated that the predicted number of complaints per year in Portage Park would be approximately 30, whereas in Woodlawn it would be 56. In 1990, 10 of Portage Park's 12 tracts were in the first quartile for percent African American (i.e., less than one percent), and the remaining two were in the second quartile (i.e., less than 13 percent). In contrast, seven of Woodlawn's tracts were in the third quartile (between 13 and 97 percent Black) and the other five were in the fourth (more than 97 percent Black).

Our results indicated that the number of predicted complaints in 2012–2014 in tracts that had had a limited history of police complaints was just under two and half complaints, whereas those that had a higher history of complaints have a predicted count of four complaints, about two-thirds more (see Figure 5.2). For concentrated disadvantage, tracts that had a lower level would have expected more than three complaints per tract, whereas tracts that have a high level of disadvantage would have had more than four complaints (see Figure 5.2).

We introduced legal cynicism into the analysis in our second equation (see Tables, Chapter 5 Table 2). Consistent with our thesis, legal cynicism was positively and significantly associated with complaints about police behavior in 2012–2014, apart from prior complaints, racial segregation, and other neighborhood attributes (concentrated disadvantage and other structural characteristics). The results suggest that the predicted number of complaints was just over 2.5 for tracts that had low levels of legal

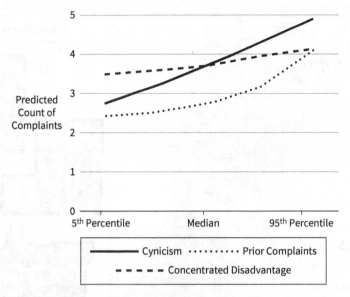

Figure 5.2 Predicted Counts of Complaints across Values of Prior Complaints, Legal Cynicism, Prior Complaints, and Concentrated Disadvantage

cynicism and almost double at just under 5.0 for tracts that had high levels (see Figure 5.2). Including legal cynicism also improved the overall fit of the model and reduced associations between complaints and several variables, including Black segregation, prior complaints, and concentrated disadvantage. Mediation analyses confirmed legal cynicism's role in the transmission of the effects of these variables on complaints (see Tables, Chapter 5 Table 3).

We introduced all of our control variables in our last estimated equation (see Tables, Chapter 5 Table 2). Including these variables reduced the association between legal cynicism and complaints, *but it remained significant*. Only one of the variables we added in this equation was significantly associated with complaints net of other factors: there was an expected positive association between complaints and police reports of crime.

The persistent and strong effect of past police complaints on more recent police complaints—with recent police reports of crime controlled—supports the Baldwin thesis that "carrying" the ongoing lived narratives of the history of policing problems in these neighborhoods has led to continuing complaints about police misconduct.

Mapping Police Complaints in Chicago

A map (Figure 5.3) of Chicago's census tracts (using thin lines) and police districts (with heavy black lines) locates the historical microclimates of reported police

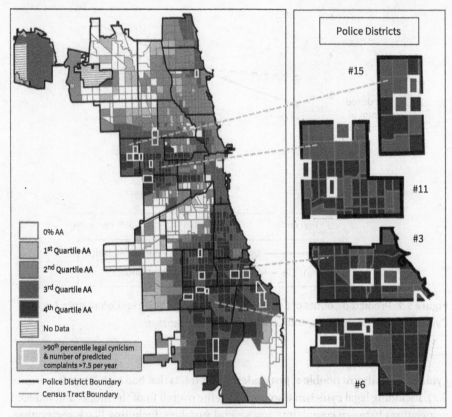

Figure 5.3 Predicted Complaints by Police Districts, Exclusion-Containment Quartiles

misconduct emphasized in the works of Baldwin (2010), Ward (2016), Ralph (2013), and Sampson (2012). The map uses a heavy white line to distinguish tracts where legal cynicism and predicted police complaints were both high (i.e., above the 90th percentile) and in the top two quartiles of percent African American residents. There were 16 tracts high in both variables in the third quartile, and 15 tracts in the fourth (we counted tracts spread across district lines only once). Moreover, there were five tracts that were above average in all three years (two in the 3rd and three in the 4th quartiles).

Although there was notable variation in cynicism and complaints across tracts and the districts in which they were located, five police districts had an especially large number of tracts in which legal cynicism and predicted complaints scores were both high. These were districts 3 (including portions of Woodlawn, South Shore, and Greater Grand Crossing on the south side); 5 (not magnified; including portions of Pullman, West Pullman, Roseland, and Riverdale on the far south side); 6 (including Auburn Gresham on the far southwest side); 11 (including East and West Garfield Park and portions of Humboldt Park on the west side); and 15 (including the southern portion of Austin also on the west side). Recall that 911 calls about crime were also high in tracts in three of these districts: 3, 11, and 15 (see Chapter Three).

Many of these districts became nearly exclusively African American during the second phase of the Great Migration that began during World War I and increased dramatically after World War II. After the Supreme Court imposed an end to postwar restrictive covenants in 1948, several Chicago neighborhoods experienced major changes. The result was an expansion of Chicago's historic Black Belt to include a number of previously "protected" neighborhoods: Woodlawn, North Lawndale, Auburn Gresham, and Austin. Each of these neighborhoods had its own history and trajectory, but they shared the strains of segregation, racial isolation, and the entrenchment of legal cynicism central to the local historical consciousness formed during and after the Great Migration to Chicago.

Members of the Chicago Police Department reacted to this period of change in ways that also characterized other large American cities. More experienced officers used their seniority to obtain assignments to patrols in more stable areas, while less experienced officers were sent to more segregated, racially isolated neighborhoods (Fan 2016). These are areas in Chicago, and in other cities, where African American complaints about police misconduct and abuse of power continue to abound.

Police Complaints and Citizen Activism

In 2013, three women—Alicia Garza, Patrisse Cullors, and Opal Tometi—started #BlackLivesMatter (BLM) in response to George Zimmerman's acquittal for killing Trayvon Martin (BlackLivesMatter 2018a; Khan-Cullors and bandele 2017). In 2014, BLM's prominence escalated, in part, because of its role in the protests over the police shooting of Michael Brown in Ferguson, Missouri (Taylor 2016). In Chicago, residents similarly came together through the BLM movement to protest police violence against African American individuals and communities, including the 16 shots police fired in the killing of Laquan McDonald (BlackLivesMatter 2018b).

The right to protection from police misconduct is a cornerstone of American constitutional democracy. A hallmark of the BLM movement is its skepticism about the constitutional protection this right provides, especially from racially targeted police misconduct. Although originally focused on fatal vigilante and police violence, BLM grew out of and into a broader critique of racially targeted police misconduct. In their BLM memoir, Patrisse Khan-Cullors and asha bandele (2017) described routine police abuses and micro-aggressions, emphasizing the humiliation and silencing they cause.

They noted that, in their neighborhoods, "law enforcement had nothing to do with protecting and serving, but [was about] controlling and containment" (28). This silencing is consistent with Mathew Desmond and colleagues' (2016, 2020) finding in Milwaukee that the particularly gruesome police abuse of a local man, Frank Jude, was followed by a reduction in the reporting of crime incidents. It likely also explains

why one of BLM's early demands was for more community control over police law enforcement (Khan-Cullors and bandele 2017; Taylor 2016).

Two prominent assumptions about organized protest and resistance characterize
the BLM movement. The first is that organized collective action and demands for the
enforcement of constitutionally embedded fair treatment and due process guarantees
can change the behavior of the police and other state agencies toward Black communities. The second is that communities will work together to change the police and the
legal system, even communities where hostility toward the police and the legal system
are pronounced. In these communities, it is widely believed that the police, and the
criminal justice system more broadly, are disinterested in solving crime problems.
This skepticism is particularly high in the most racially isolated African American
neighborhoods. For these reasons, the pursuit of complaints about police abuses of
power by residents of these neighborhoods is uncertain and not taken for granted.

Geoff Ward (2016) argued that understanding racial violence requires a close examination of the microclimates where it takes place. Chicago's hyper-segregated
neighborhoods illustrate Ward's argument. Police abuse and complaints about mistreatment vary widely in their frequency and nature across neighborhoods. However,
they are most prominent in the excluded and contained racially isolated Black neighborhoods where, as Laurence Ralph's (2013; 2020) research revealed, accounts of police mistreatment have become part of neighborhood historical consciousness.

In these communities, cynicism about the police, and the legal system more
broadly, have developed into a cultural framework or narrative that provides residents with a lens through which to make sense of their neighborhoods' histories and
the events that are experienced, witnessed, and shared by friends and neighbors. This
cultural frame is durable and enduring: it reflects a collective memory, a historical
consciousness, and a communal knowledge (Ralph 2013) that are located in a particular microclimate or geographical space (Ward 2016).

Robert Sampson (2012:367) underscored the connection between cultural narratives and places. He argued legal cynicism is but one example of "culture structures"
that involve the production and reproduction of knowledge and understanding within
communities. Our research shows that legal cynicism predicts neighborhood variation in the extent to which people file legal complaints about police misconduct—
complaints that are, to some degree, acts of protest and resistance against police
abuses of power. Ignoring these spatial effects risks committing an individualistic fallacy (Sampson and Wilson 1995), as does attributing poor police relations solely to
the attributes and actions of individual complainants and police officers.

Our analysis builds on an auspiciously timed, mid-1990s measure of legal cynicism
that is predictive of complaints about police abuses more than a decade later in 2012–
2014. Data on legal cynicism were collected in the context of at least a half-century of
highly publicized police abuse noted earlier. This abuse included the widely reported
James "Gloves" Davis beatings dating from the 1960s; the jointly organized Chicago
police and FBI action resulting in the death of Fred Hampton in 1969; the Jon Burge

torture squad activities from the 1970s to the 1990s; and the ongoing Ronald Watts extortion scandal that began in the 1990s.

Some studies have found that legal cynicism is negatively associated with contacting the police (Kirk and Papachristos 2011); however, we find that this pattern does not apply to the filing of police misconduct complaints. Instead, we find a long-term positive impact of legal cynicism in racially segregated and isolated Black Chicago neighborhoods on contemporary complaints, net of other sources. Drawing on Hunter and Robinson (2016), our research suggests that legal cynicism is, in this sense, not a neighborhood deficit but instead an asset that benefits communities. Our results raise the possibility that complaints are a form of neighborhood resistance undertaken in protest and defense of others who experience police abuse—responses that are consistent with the assumptions and collective actions identified above as motivating the activism of BLM.

Our research provides new support for the claim that legal cynicism is a communal, historically conscious, cultural framing with deep, long-lasting significance for police–community relations. It underscores the need for more research on connections between policing, cultural narratives, and the long history of racial segregation. Reflecting on the use of state-sponsored violence to maintain segregation, Richard Rothstein (2017:151) asked, "How long do the memories of such events last? How long do they continue to intimidate?" James Baldwin (2010:154) provided a troubling but incisive answer: "history is not the past. It is the present. We carry our history with us. We *are* our history. If we pretend otherwise, to put it very brutally, we literally are criminals."

6
Prolonging the Thirty-Year Cover-Up

In the previous chapters, we explored connections between racial segregation, legal cynicism and estrangement, and the politics of policing in Chicago. We examined how this city's Black communities responded to daunting problems of police mistreatment and abuse associated with the politics of Mayor Richard M. Daley's thirty-year law and order regime. In this and the following chapter, we return to this regime's torture scandal. As we noted in Chapter Two, Jon Burge was never charged for the torture he, and officers under his command, committed in the 1970s, 80s, and 90s. Indeed, it was not until 2010 that Burge finally faced any meaningful consequences for his actions. In that year, Burge was convicted of obstruction of justice and perjury.

In this chapter, we examine how a special investigation prolonged the protection of Jon Burge from prosecution in the criminal courts from 2002 to 2006. The *Invisible Institute* posted the investigation's report, the depositions it gathered, as well as other relevant documents on the web (Hunt n.d. Special Prosecutor. Reports and Evidence; to enhance readability we refer to the speaker and page numbers when citing these documents).

This investigation of Burge and his officers was conducted by a Cook County "special state's attorney" at a cost of seven million dollars. It enabled veterans of the Daley political machine to protect Jon Burge, as well as his officers and his superiors, including RM Daley, by extending the cover-up that, by 2002, was entering its third decade.

Jon Burge, RM Daley, and the Special State's Attorney

It took until the new millennium to build sufficient pressure to generate a new investigation of the tortured confessions of Andrew Wilson and the other African American victims of Jon Burge. In 2002, the Cook County Bar Association, the Justice Coalition of Chicago, and more than sixty other groups petitioned for a review of the allegations against Burge. The investigation was handled by a special prosecutor and his assistant who were both veterans of Daley machine politics.

The special prosecutor, retired Illinois appellate court justice Edward Egan, could count nine family members who were Chicago police officers, and he had written an important court decision denying an appeal by Andrew Wilson. Egan's assistant, former assistant state's attorney Robert Boyle, was chief of the criminal division under Edward Hanrahan during the police killing of the Black Panther activist Fred Hampton. Activists complained that appointing these men made it likely that "the dice were loaded." It would take four years and repeated delays for the prosecutor to even issue a report. In the end, the report only added to growing legal cynicism about police misconduct and torture in Chicago. Many people, especially activists from Chicago's South and West Sides, saw the report as a cover-up.

There were further reasons for suspicion. While the prosecution took sworn depositions from four leading public officials, including the currently serving Mayor RM Daley, only a summary of an "interview" was included with the former Mayor Jane Byrne. Yet Byrne was a major player in Andrew Wilson's arrest and interrogation. The prosecution summarized her unsworn interview in a cursory three-page statement.

This contrasted with a 99-page sworn deposition from Richard Brzeczek, the police superintendent of the Chicago Police Department appointed by Byrne. We will show that Brzeczek's deposition foretold the direction Egan and Boyle would take the inquiry.

Egan and Boyle conducted three additional sworn depositions. The first was with William Kunkel, Daley's chief deputy in the state's attorney's office and the lead prosecutor of Andrew Wilson. If asked the right questions, this deposition could have proven an important starting point. As lead prosecutor in the Wilson case, Kunkel was a potential source of previously unreported and therefore unknown information.

The second deposition involved RM Daley, who was accompanied and coached by two city corporate counsel. *This is the most significant publicly revealed and sworn deposition ever given by Daley in the Burge case.* Another unreleased deposition was taken from Daley in 2018 (Taylor 2019:495); however, it is likely unrevealing, given Daley's advanced age, health problems, and propensity for obfuscation, including an "I don't recall" defense. Daley's earlier deposition leaned heavily on this defense. Yet this 2006 deposition nonetheless provides revealing insights into the ways in which Daley was inclined—and selectively encouraged by his corporate counsel—to strategically avoid answering questions.

The last deposition was with Richard (Dick) Devine. Devine served under the first mayor RJ Daley and became RM Daley's first assistant in the state's attorney's office. Devine was later elected state's attorney after RM was elected mayor. He was still serving in this role and continuing to cover RM's tracks during the special prosecutor's investigation.

Egan and Boyle's depositions recorded the covering accounts given by key actors in the Wilson case. These were made publicly available by the *Invisible Institute* (Hunt n.d.). Three of the depositions were sworn statements and therefore liable to prosecution for perjury. The depositions by Daley and his aides provide insights into how Daley and his team carefully evaded responsibility for the torture scandal. Our analysis suggests that these depositions, as well as the Byrne interview, while not necessarily probative, are reflective of the special prosecutor's strategy to protect some, but not all, of the officials involved in the Wilson case.

This stage of the cover-up proceeded in several parts. The first part involved identifying Police Superintendent Richard Brzeczek as a participant and the eventual lone scapegoat in the special prosecutor's report. The second part cursorily pursued and thereby obscured the involvement of former Mayor Jane Byrne in the scandal, while in the process helping to strategically set up Brzeczek as a scapegoat. The third part revealed how the three top-level figures—Kunkle, Devine, and Daley—crafted mutually supportive accounts of their roles in the scandal.

The mechanics of this cover-up included three recurring assertions made by the key actors: claims that they were not directly involved in the events; attributions of responsibility to lower level figures; and claims that they could not remember—"I don't recall"—crucial details and events. We review the Brzeczek testimony first because it was the initial sworn deposition. *Ten long months later*, the special prosecution conducted its unsworn interview with Mayor Byrne. We then turn to the sworn depositions of the key players from the state's attorney's office: Kunkle, Daley, and Devine.

The Brzeczek–Daley Backstory

Investigations of highly organized crimes often build from lower- to higher-level suspects, hoping to gain cooperation and information to hold highly placed participants accountable. This could have been the special prosecution's logic for first interviewing Police Superintendent Richard Brzeczek in March 2005. However, as we explain next, a backstory better accounts for the decision to focus first on Brzeczek. This backstory involved a unique rivalry between Brzeczek and RM Daley.

Brzeczek was the working-class son of Polish immigrants. He joined the Chicago Police Department after graduating with a bachelor's degree from Chicago's Loyola University. Brzeczek continued to work in the police department while earning a public administration degree at the Illinois Institute of Technology, followed by a law degree from John Marshall Law School. He was ambitious, perhaps excessively so. He became the first police officer to rise from within the department to become its general legal counsel. And he was appointed by Mayor Jane Byrne as the youngest-ever Chicago police superintendent.

RM's political emergence was traced in Chapter Two. He graduated with a bachelor's degree from DePaul University and, following in his father's footsteps, earned his law degree there as well. He was taking early steps among a rising class of Irish Chicagoans finding their way upward through the city's growing law and law enforcement bureaucracy. In 1972, at the age of 30, RM was elected to the Illinois state senate, where he served for eight years. In 1980, he was elected Cook County state's attorney, where he also served for eight years; 1980 was the same year that Brzeczek was named police superintendent.

Daley and Brzeczek were both staunch law and order advocates, and they emerged nearly simultaneously as closely watched and rival rising stars in Chicago law and politics. Yet, Brzeczek was ultimately less successful than RM, and along the way he collected powerful enemies as well as supporters. He was close to Jane Byrne. He made the unusual choice to do a television commercial, as police superintendent, supporting her 1983 campaign for re-election as mayor. This was the same year RM decided to challenge Byrne by running against her for the Democratic nomination.

However, this was also the year Harold Washington became Chicago's first Black mayor by first defeating both Byrne and Daley in the all-important Democratic primary. Daley subsequently decided to run in the general election as an "independent Democrat," but Washington won handily. Along the way, Brzeczek had indiscreetly attacked Washington for failing to pay several years of past income taxes. It was an attack Mayor Washington would neither forgive nor forget.

RM Daley accepted his defeat by Washington in the mayoral election and was re-elected as state's attorney. In contrast, Brzeczek had to resign as police superintendent to avoid being fired by Washington. He later acknowledged that his problem might have been that he was "never a team player." But that was hardly the full story—a story that was told in an unlikely book he co-authored several years later with his wife Elizabeth (Brzeczek, Brzeczek, and DeVita 1989).

The story gained speed early in Brzeczek's tenure as police superintendent, when he emerged as a media star and popular figure in Chicago. His law degree, good looks, and youthful appearance encouraged speculation about his national ambitions, for example, to become head of the FBI. He traveled extensively during this period for meetings and speeches—to testify in Washington, to speak at Harvard University, and beyond.

Life changed for Brzeczek when on a flight to New York to appear on *Good Morning America* he met a flight attendant with whom he began a torrid affair. He was also becoming a heavy drinker and reckless risk taker. Still, throughout his three years as police superintendent, he insisted (to himself and his wife) that his life and work were totally under control.

It was obvious to Brzeczek's wife that something was going wrong, but he managed to conceal his heavy drinking and adultery from the press and public. He was still held in high regard. The city staged a large sendoff party when he left the police department, with some three thousand guests attending. The party was a worrisome signal of things to come. In their book, Brzeczek recalled that he drank too much at the party and seemed even more despondent than usual; although surrounded by friends and family, he "sat with his head in his hands, crying, for most of the evening" (Brzeczek et al. 1989:29).

Soon after resigning from the police department, Brzeczek went to work at an elite LaSalle Street law firm, Levey and Erens. He was living with his wife and family but continuing the extramarital affair, and his life was beginning to spin more quickly out of control. Yet he was still able to conceal his personal problems from the public and, remarkably, Republicans began talking about him as a potential candidate for state's attorney, running against the incumbent Democrat RM Daley.

The pressure to run was national as well as local, including from the Republican National Committee Chairman, who had seen polls showing that Brzeczek was more popular than Daley in Chicago. The Republicans saw Brzeczek as an opportunity to overturn the Daley dynasty. Brzeczek's firm promised to pay his full salary during the campaign and guaranteed him a spot if he later wanted to return. He persisted in saying no to the idea of running against Daley—until the day he finally said yes—announcing simultaneously to the public and his shell-shocked wife that he was running for state's attorney (Brzeczek et al. 1989:32).

Brzeczek was now drinking more and more heavily. He was drunk on the evening of the formal announcement of his candidacy. Three days later, he confessed to his wife that he was having not just one but two affairs. Miraculously, despite a succession of crises and throughout the campaign, he continued to live with his wife and family. And they eventually wrote the book noted above, calling it *Addicted to Adultery* (Brzeczek et al. 1989; see also Lavin 1989).

Brzeczek had been far ahead in the polls when the campaign began, but it ended disastrously: he received less than a quarter of the vote, and RM won in a landslide. Adding insult to injury, despite having promised earlier to guarantee his salary and position, his law firm now severed its ties to Brzeczek.

Brzeczek's near yearlong campaign was an unremitting descent into drunkenness and despair. Two news stories finally hastened the nonstop decline: one speculated that the Brzeczeks were divorcing, while the other revealed that the state's attorney's office was investigating a police contingency fund that Brzeczek had used and reimbursed for travel expenses while superintendent. But the story wasn't over. Although U.S. Attorney Daley publicly declined to prosecute the case, his state's attorney's office persisted and charged Brzeczek with twenty-four counts of theft and official misconduct. It looked suspiciously like revenge for challenging Daley's election. Deep in depression and mental decline, Brzeczek checked into a psychiatric hospital.

The high-security hospital was designed for suicidal patients. The irony of being locked up was not lost on Brzeczek.

I had spent most of my life locking other people up, but now *I* was locked up. As miserable as I felt, I couldn't help thinking about the similarities between being arrested and being admitted to a psychiatric ward. Both places strip you of your personal possessions, your identity, and your dignity. It was a humbling and humiliating experience (Brzeczek et al. 1989:81).

A further irony was that just a few years earlier, RM Daley had chaired a state senate committee that passed mental health reform legislation (Koeneman 2013:65–67).

This reform work did not soften RM's thoughts about prosecuting Brzeczek, even though Brzeczek had reconciled with his wife, who now helped him launch a new solo law practice. The theft charges involved two checks for just over 1,200 dollars. Brzeczek had controlled a police department budget of over 400 million dollars. The discrepancy of only 1,200 dollars was an odd confirmation that he had mostly held things together professionally during his descent into mental illness and adultery.

There were embarrassing problems in the state attorney's office handling of the case, despite RM having recused himself from official involvement. When the prosecution called two witnesses from the police financial department, both wound up admitting they had altered department records. The judge called them "bureaucratic forgers" (Myers 1987), and the state's principal witness—the flight attendant—impeached herself with inaccurate statements (Brzeczek et al. 1989:213–214).

The judge gave the most damning statement about the prosecutors when he publically concluded: "there's a very clear pattern of disclosure to the press on the part of the Chicago Police Department and the state's attorney office . . . " (cited in Brzeczek et al. 1989:217). The judge further observed: "There is a *real question of selective prosecution, vendetta, et cetera*' regarding the state's case against Mr. Brzeczek." The obvious implication was that the prosecution was politically driven by Daley. For his own part, Brzeczek said, "A lot of people, myself included, think Richie Daley indicted me just to make sure I would never be a political threat to him again" (Brzeczek et al. 1989:219).

Finally, in May 1987, the court acquitted Brzeczek on all counts. It is an understatement to say that his and RM Daley's relationship was unusual. When Brzeczek ran for state's attorney against RM, he said, "I didn't have anything personal against the state's attorney . . . I just didn't think he was particularly good at his job, but it wasn't *personal*" (Brzeczek et al. 1989:49). Brzeczek later concluded it was *more* than personal, saying, "Daley set out to destroy me politically, personally and professionally" (Lavin 1989). The enmity between these individuals likely had something to do with why the special prosecutor in the torture investigation, with his long-term ties to the Daley Democratic machine, selected this Republican enemy of Daley and the Democratic machine for the first deposition.

A Scapegoat Waiting to Happen: Richard Brzeczek

There were three other interconnected actors besides Brzeczek in the first phase of the torture scandal: Mayor Jane Byrne, Deputy Police Superintendent Joseph McCarthy, and Detective Jon Burge. Mayor Byrne and Officer McCarthy were important for reasons introduced in Chapter One. Byrne had handpicked Joseph McCarthy to lead the largest manhunt in the city's history for the killers of police officers Michael Fahey and Thomas O'Brien. She met with Area 2 officers repeatedly, telling them to use "all means necessary" to solve the killings (Taylor 2019:38), and Byrne ultimately passed on a tip that led the manhunt to the killers, Andrew and Jackie Wilson. Nonetheless, the depositions began with Brzeczek and not with Byrne.

For reasons that would gradually become apparent, the questioning of Brzeczek prominently focused on a controversial meeting with his command staff. In his deposition, Brzeczek said he called a meeting of his staff leaders immediately after receiving a letter from Dr. Raba, the director of medical services at the jail, about the injuries and suspected torture of Andrew Wilson. Special Prosecutor Egan asked Brzeczek directly about the meeting: "Is it correct when you got the letter of Dr. Raba, you called a group of command personnel, which included two deputy superintendents and you asked them, how could something like this happen in Detective Area 2?" [This and following quotes are from the first deposition (Brzeczek 41)].

Brzeczek's answer implicitly adopted the defense of "attributing responsibility to lower level figures," implying that commanders below him were responsible for Wilson's injuries. He said that he got no response from his commanders, which suggested they were invoking a code of silence.

> A. I'm visualizing that meeting, you know, I'm getting a lot of blank faces ... and no responses.
> Q. Can you elaborate on that for me? When you say you couldn't get an answer to that, can you tell us what was actually said by anybody?
> A. ... I'm saying, this is the biggest manhunt. The whole world is watching ... And I still didn't get any response. It's, like, get out of here. I was angry at them because they were there. They were all there, and this still happened. How can it happen? That's what I wanted to know (42–45).

Egan asked which officers attended this meeting, and Brzeczek responded: "I know that [deputy superintendents] Lyons and McCarthy were in that group of staff" (48). Egan then challenged Brzeczek's account:

> "I have to tell you this ... A long time ago we contacted McCarthy, and he has records to show that he was at Mayo at that time" (48). Brzeczek responded by modifying his answer,
> A. McCarthy's at Mayo?
> Q. Right.
> A. Could very well be.
> Q. You mean it's possible you're mistaken that McCarthy was present?
> A. My recollection was of Lyons, McCarthy, and other command personnel being there. I can't be specific and be absolutely certain (49).

Egan then returned to Dr. Raba's letter, pressing Brzeczek about his interactions with his command personnel.

> Q. I personally don't think you're the type of individual as a superintendent would stop at asking a bunch of command personnel how this could happen ... I can't understand why, knowing you, that, you wouldn't say, wait a minute. I want to know the names of everybody that had any custody of Andrew Wilson, and I want somebody to interview them and to question them and have them explain in detail as to how this happened (49–50).

Brzeczek again answered with a "denial by distance" defense, which he explained was built into office procedures governing complaints about police misconduct. This procedure organizationally removed him from the responsibility that Egan's question implied.

> A. Well . . . but that's what I had [Frank] Nolan for, to do that as head of OPS [Office of Professional Standards]. I wouldn't conduct the investigation myself (50).

The special prosecutor would eventually challenge this kind of answer as amounting to a dereliction of Brzeczek's duties as superintendent.

When the prosecutors again asked about his response to Dr. Raba, the answer Brzeczek gave did not necessarily help. Brzeczek repeated that he did two things: called the meeting of his command personal and initiated the investigation through the department's OPS. Brzeczek had office evidence that the investigation had indeed been initiated. But beyond this, he could only say that the head of the office, Frank Nolan, was in charge, and that he (i.e., Brzeczek) had responded to the letter from Raba by talking only to Nolan:

> A. I think the only person I may have shared that with when I first got the letter was Nolan.
> Q. And he's dead.
> A. Yeah . . . (77).

Nolan would obviously not be available for further questions.

About half way through the Brzeczek deposition, Egan and Boyle began to ask about the events leading up to the torture of Andrew Wilson. Brzeczek's answers revealed that Officer Joseph McCarthy had played a large role in the Wilson brothers' case. Brzeczek recalled:

> A. My phone rang. I answered it . . . and it was McCarthy. And he said the mayor [Jane Byrne] had called [to tell] him to handle the press conference on the arrest of the Wilson brothers. I said, the mayor wants you to handle it, handle it. That's why I didn't go out there. Because if I went out there, the press would have wanted to talk to me, not to McCarthy
> Q. But he did participate in the arrest, didn't he?
> A. He did . . .
> Q. . . . why did she want him [McCarthy] out front?
> A. She liked him.
> Q. . . . That's a dangling participle.
> A. There's a whole sidebar to that whole issue right there (51–53).

Speculation about the "Sidebar"

There is no further discussion in the deposition as to what this "whole sidebar" referred to, but it seems reasonable to ask whether this was a juncture in the deposition where issues involving personal relationships were placed "off the record." Perhaps most notably, this might have been a moment in which Brzeczek wanted to make clear that he did not now want to go back to the collapse of his life a decade and a half earlier. He likely did not want to discuss his marital problems, his failed bid to unseat RM Daley as state's attorney, the charges placed against him by Daley's state's attorney's office, and the hostilities that characterized his relationship with Daley. Brzeczek's reference to a "sidebar" shut off such questions for the moment, but Egan later returned to the topic by asking, "When you had to deal with him [Daley] in a professional way . . . Was it a good working relationship?" Brzeczek simply answered, "I didn't have a relationship with him" (57). It seemed a shorthand way of saying he did not want to talk about it.

The Brzeczek Deposition Resumes

In Chapter One, we noted that Mayor Byrne oversaw the South Side of Chicago manhunt for the Wilson brothers. She had chosen Officer Joseph McCarthy, who was known for leading a group called the "ghetto raiders," to direct the "house to house" search for suspects. We also pointed out that Howard Safford, the President of the Afro-American Police League, had told a reporter, "McCarthy responds directly to the mayor. No one can touch him" (Cruz 1982). Joseph McCarthy worked with Jon Burge in the South Side manhunt, with both actively participating in Andrew Wilson's arrest, after which Jon Burge took Wilson for questioning. Mayor Byrne indicated she had relied on McCarthy to keep her informed about the manhunt and the interrogation of the Wilsons that followed.

Byrne likely knew that the two officers Andrew Wilson was suspected of killing—Fahey and O'Brien—worked under McCarthy in the Gang Crimes Unit. McCarthy worked more closely with these officers than Brzeczek. Furthermore, officers in McCarthy's Gang Crimes Unit were known to have participated in Area 2 torture of suspects (Taylor 2019:133).

All of this made Mayor Byrne at least as appropriate a subject for a sworn disposition as Brzeczek; instead, prosecutors limited their investigation of Byrne to an unsworn interview they conducted ten months later. It may be noteworthy that Special Prosecutor Egan quickly steered the Brzeczek deposition away from Byrne when her close tie to McCarthy was revealed. Egan now changed the focus of the deposition to the letter Brzeczek sent to State's Attorney Daley, along with the letter from Dr. Raba insisting on an investigation of Wilson's injuries.

As noted earlier, Brzeczek referred Raba's letter to the police department's Office of Professional Standards [OPS], which resulted in the matter receiving "a CR number which docketed the complaint" (72). Brzeczek reported that he then decided to send his own letter through the mail to Daley, with Raba's letter attached. He informed Daley he had opened an OPS investigation and, given the importance of the case, he asked for direction as to how he should proceed.

Eagan, in turn, asked if Daley responded to the letter and whether Brzeczek discussed it with Mayor Byrne, which evoked another version of the "I don't recall" defense. Beyond his indication that Daley had not responded to him, Brzeczek said he remembered little else.

A. I don't know what I was thinking back at that time, but I did not follow up.

Q. Did you tell Mayor Byrne about sending Daley this letter?

A. I do not recall any discussion I may have had with Byrne about either the letter from Dr. Raba or the letter I sent to Daley. I just do not have any recollection (59–60).

The questions turned next to a topic Brzeczek was less likely to have forgotten. This was "A Unit Commendation to Detective Area 2," issued under his name, with Jon Burge indicated among the recipients.

Q. You believed that somebody in Detective Area 2 had brutalized Andrew Wilson, and yet you issued a commendation to every officer in Detective Area 2 for their work in the Andrew Wilson case.

A. Okay.

Q. Can you tell me why?

A. There was a tremendous amount of good police work that went into the investigation of the killings of Officers Fahey and O'Brien. And not trying to put my thinking into the Awards Committee, but I think [it was] based upon that collective team effort, that's why the award was presented to everyone there . . . I don't think that there was any specific individual identified.

Q. Oh, there are—the one I saw has I don't know how many names.

A. I know what you're saying. Everybody who got the award is identified.

Q. Including Burge?

A. Everybody who got the award is identified, okay? What I'm saying is, in terms of the abuse of the prisoner, I think at the time that the award was issued, there was no specific individual at Area 2 who was or may have been identified as being the one causing the abuse to the prisoner (60–61).

Egan's later questions turned back to the letter from Brzeczek to Daley. This time he more successfully elicited speculation about Daley's response—actually his non-response—to Brzeczek's letter.

Q. Did you make any inquiry after the letter was sent?

A. No.

Q. Did you expect a response within some period of time?

A. I expected some type of response, even from someone who would be first chair [i.e., Kunkle as the lead prosecutor] on the case. But I got no response . . .

Q. Can you share with us why you thought you would not get a response?

A. I think that the situation was potentially volatile over at the state's attorney's office.

Q. You mean in classic politics, not because of—you mean a [B]lack/[W]hite thing or a candidate-against-candidate kind of thing?

A. No, not candidate versus candidate, but, you know, people focused on political careers, making decisions today realizing that five, ten, 15 years . . .

Q. Oh, you're talking about Byrne/Daley.

A. I'm sorry?

Q. . . . You're talking about Byrne/Daley. That kind of politics?

A. Yeah, that kind—that type of thing, yeah (79–82).

This exchange suggested that the Andrew Wilson "heater crime" killing of Officers Fahey and O'Brien confronted both Byrne and Daley with short- and long-term political problems that we mentioned in Chapter One. In the short term, they were locked in a looming primary battle in which winning White voters seemed essential. A confession could speed up the process and thus the chances of a quick conviction and sentencing. Yet, in the coming general election, and probably in the long term, they both would also need to attract Black as well as White voters.

Both appeared to "solve" this problem by pushing the torture of Andrew Wilson out of public view. Brzeczek, officially serving under Byrne's direction, accomplished this by referring Raba's letter to the police department's OPS and sending a copy of the letter to Daley asking for direction. In turn, Daley handed off the Brzeczek and Raba letters to a reliable subordinate in the state's attorney's office of special prosecutions, Frank DeBoni.

DeBoni later closed the investigation of Wilson's torture, explaining that Andrew Wilson would not cooperate with prosecutors. Brzeczek's OPS did much the same, using the justification that Brzeczek had not received a response to his letter from Daley or anyone else. However, DeBoni's central role in closing the investigation of Wilson's injuries and suspected torture would re-emerge in the deposition of Mayor Daley reported below.

As noted above, Byrne and Brzeczek left their respective elected and appointed positions after Harold Washington won the 1983 mayoral election. However, Daley continued as state's attorney and then mayor, and he was now potentially implicated in a cover-up of torture with consequences that would follow him for the rest of his political career. We return below to the suspiciousness of the connections of RM Daley and Frank DeBoni in relation to the suspected cover-up.

The deposition of Brzeczek presented one more occasion for him to note the prominent roles of Byrne and McCarthy, along with Burge, in the early stages of the torture scandal. The prosecution introduced the question in the context of the "heater crime" that had convulsed the city:

> Q. . . . you were the superintendent. Who was, well, did you call the shots as to who was in charge once it became a very public quest? . . . We all remember the unfortunate pressure that the police department was under.
>
> A. Well, we had multiple activities going on at the same time, some consistent, some inconsistent . . . One of the problems we encountered was that the special operation people under McCarthy decided that they're going door to door and kick doors in . . . So we had those problems, you know, with some clamor from the community about the Gestapo tactics that were taking place, and that was the gang crimes people and special operations people (87–88).

Brzeczek's answer brought the focus of attention back to Mayor Byrne and her early activities with McCarthy and Burge in directing the aggressive manhunt and interrogation of Andrew Wilson. However, Egan now shifted attention away from McCarthy with a question that elicited a one-word answer from Brzeczek. Egan asked: "Would it have been more likely that [deputy superintendent] Tom Lyons would have been involved relative to questioning at 11th Street that maybe was beginning to ripen than McCarthy would have been involved?" (91). Brzeczek simply answered, "Yes."

Shortly thereafter, Egan asked Brzeczek to further clarify his claim that he had followed official protocol in dealing with Raba's letter.

> Q. In answer to a question, you said, "But what I did here was took Dr. Raba's letter and implemented the mechanism that had been established to investigate these allegations." What does that mean? What mechanism were you talking about?
>
> A. To docket the complaint, get the CR investigation started (98).

Later, Egan and Boyle would conclude Brzeczek should have done more. It therefore seems reasonable to ask: Were Brzeczek's problems with Daley interwoven with his distanced and pro forma fulfillment of his responsibilities during this period? Were these errors of professional omission rather than commission? Did making Brzeczek into a scapegoat for the cover-up depend on turning the portrayal of these omissions into commissions? Were Byrne, McCarthy, and Burge—rather than or in addition to Brzeczek alone—major players in the collective origins of the torture cover-up? And, why did it take ten months to follow up on Brzeczek's sworn deposition with an unsworn subsequent interview with Mayor Byrne?

The Tiny Imperfect Mayor: Jane Byrne

Keith Koeneman (2013), RM Daley's biographer, offered a thumbnail sketch of Jane Byrne and her relationship with RJ and ultimately RM Daley.

> When Dick Daley first met five-foot-three-inch Jane Byrne . . . she was a thirty-one-year-old Irish Catholic cutie. Daley, mayor of Chicago, who had the rounded face and sturdy girth of his sixty-two years—immediately liked her and invited Byrne to come see him at city hall. Daley and Byrne—both of whom combined political toughness with warmth and charisma—would quickly develop a lasting emotional bond . . . Three years after the death of Daley, Byrne—a high-energy campaigner and political free spirit—would become the first female mayor of Chicago, a position for which she was temperamentally ill-suited (2013:36).

Koeneman went on to observe that RM competed with Byrne for his father's attention, which Koeneman suggested led to a long-lasting jealousy.

Byrne's temperament might have been reason enough for Egan and Boyle's cautiousness about engaging this unusual politician—on record or at length. The interview with Byrne is summarized with thirteen bullet points and eight concluding paragraphs. Egan did not attend the interview that Boyle conducted, which also made it unusual. Byrne's partner and daughter accompanied her to the interview.

The interview confirmed that Jane Byrne had met Jon Burge on the first of three visits to Area 2 leading up to the arrest of Andrew Wilson. On each of the two following visits, she also met and talked with Burge. She further confirmed the extent of her contact with Deputy Superintendent Joseph Murphy, who she described as her "direct appointment." She reported that all of her communications during the investigation were through McCarthy rather than Brzeczek. McCarthy and Burge were apparently Byrne's primary, if not exclusive, contacts regarding the Wilson killings of Fahey and O'Brien.

Byrne's involvement in the apprehension and interrogation of Andrew Wilson was pivotal. Byrne, rather than Brzeczek, gave Burge and McCarthy instructions about how to conduct their work. She said she believed in "direct" (i.e., house to house) police work as "her way of doing things," and that this was necessary to catch the killer. She indicated her awareness that this way of conducting the manhunt resulted in "community problems" on the South Side.

Beyond conceding responsibility for the aggressive methods used in the manhunt for the killer of Fahey and O'Brien, Byrne revealed little knowledge of the various components of the investigation and interrogation. She said that she knew next to nothing or could not recall anything about all of the following:

- The letter sent by mail from Brzeczek to Daley with Raba's letter insisting on an investigation of Andrew Wilson's injuries

- Any conversation with Brzeczek concerning brutality in Area 2 under the supervision of Jon Burge
- Any indication from Brzeczek, after receiving the letter from Raba, that he believed physical abuse of detainees had occurred at Area 2 under Burge's supervision
- The awarding by Brzeczek of a commendation to Area 2 personnel and Jon Burge after the Wilson arrests
- A meeting by Brzeczek with his command personnel after receiving the letter from Raba, with Brzeczek asking, "How could this occur at Area 2?"

The information summarized from the interview with Byrne conveyed a sense that she had little, if any, contact with Brzeczek about the killing of the two officers. However, Byrne did report that she had Brzeczek, Lyons, and McCarthy to dinner to communicate her gratitude for the department's efforts in arresting the Wilson brothers.

The second to last paragraph of the summary of the Byrne interview returned to the matter of Brzeczek's reported meeting with his command personnel after receiving Dr. Raba's letter. *This paragraph concluded with Boyle reporting, "I then told her [Byrne] that two Deputy Superintendents, Lyons and McCarthy, as well as the commander of the entire Detective Division at Area 2, Commander Milton Deas, had stated that they had never attended such a meeting* (emphasis added)."

Had Brzeczek misreported the meeting of this group? The statement unequivocally reports that all three command personnel indicated "they had never attended such a meeting." Was this a truthful report, or did it simply repeat a dubious code of silence claim?

The special prosecutor seemed to be building a case with Brzeczek as the scapegoat. Brzeczek's claims to have responded appropriately to the letter from Dr. Raba about Andrew Wilson's injuries included three specific assertions: (1) he had held a meeting with his command personnel asking what had happened; (2) he had initiated an OPS Investigation with Frank Nolan in charge; and (3) he had sent a letter through the mail to State's Attorney RM Daley asking for direction. The special prosecutors used the unsworn interview with Byrne to repeat that top command personnel claimed they were not at the meeting that Brzeczek said he called, and that Frank Nolan was dead and therefore could not substantiate departmental efforts to investigate Andrew Wilson's injuries.

Why was Byrne's interview not a sworn deposition, and why was it summarized rather than transcribed and with Special Prosecutor Egan absent? Assistant Special Prosecutor Boyle's summary was left to speak for itself, while attention turned next to the top level of the chain of command and responsibility in Daley's state's attorney office—the suspected heart of the thirty-year cover-up.

The Mayor and His Men

RM Daley's leadership team consisted of three men: William Kunkle, who served as Daley's chief deputy; Richard (Dick) Devine, who served as Daley's first assistant; and then Daley himself. The depositions we consider next clearly established these three men as the top level of command in the state's attorney's office.

Their role is important because if they had fully investigated the handling of Brzeczek's letter, the role of Jon Burge and his "midnight crew" in the torture of Andrew Wilson, and a hundred or more other Black suspects before and after Wilson, might have been exposed and stopped. Daley—as the state's attorney and recipient of the letter—was at the center of this controversial issue. The three signs of cover-up we identified previously in this chapter are abundantly evident in the depositions of the men in Daley' leadership circle. They include claims of *deniable distance* from the implementation of the cover-up. The depositions further identify attributions of *responsibility to others* at lower levels in the chain of command for the cover-up. And, they copiously illustrate how classical claims of fallible and faulty memory—the "*I don't recall*" defense—were used by each of the top-level actors to cast doubt on their own possible criminal responsibility for involvement in the cover-up.

In each of the depositions, we see how special prosecutors Egan and Boyle led the three leadership witnesses through their accounts of the torture scandal. The sequence of the depositions was likely purposeful in allowing Kunkle to go first in recounting events that were in need of explanation. Daley was deposed next. For the first time—nearly a quarter-century after the scandal began—Daley was finally brought directly into the investigation and asked to answer questions that were, in part, identified in Kunkle's prior testimony.

The special prosecutors then asked Devine to fill in details and answer questions raised by the previous testimonies. The delay of nearly 25 years in staging these depositions and the special prosecutors' investigation gave the Daley team distinct advantages. Unlike the rapid and tightly coupled investigation of the Wilsons' "heater case" in 1982, the special prosecutor's investigation was an exercise of "law in very slow motion."

First Chair: William Kunkle

William Kunkle was deposed in May of 2006. As the first deposed and third-ranking official in the chain of command in the Daley state's attorney's office, Kunkle was asked to explain how the office was organized.

A. There are three persons in the state's attorney office who have some authority or a line of authority, however you want to look at it, over the entire office without division, and those are the elected state's attorney, the first assistant, and the chief deputy (Kunkle 7).

Kunkle was chief deputy at the time of the Wilson brothers' case. and he personally assumed the role of "first chair" in prosecuting them.

Kunkle would later represent Jon Burge in two trials, as well as four other members of the accused torture squad. Along with Dick Devine, Kunkle earned large fees for this work. And in the process, Kunkle also became a state court judge. He was serving as a judge when he was finally deposed by Special Prosecutor Egan and his assistant Boyle, nearly a quarter-century after the Wilson arrests.

The first substantively important issue prosecutors raised with Kunkle involved the failure of Larry Hyman, as chief of felony review, to follow official procedure in taking Wilson's confession statement. For obvious reasons, official procedure required Hyman to ask Wilson about the voluntariness and therefore the absence of coercion of his statement. As chief of felony review, Hyman clearly knew this. So, Kunkle was asked who would have noticed that this essential step by the chief of felony review did not happen.

Kunkle's answer evoked all three of the standard elements we have associated with this cover-up: deniable distance, responsibility of others, and the "I don't recall" defense:

> I don't remember. He [Larry Hyman] would have been telling a lot of people what was going on. He would have been telling Ginex [the chief of the criminal division]. He would have been telling the chief of municipal. He would have been telling Angarola [supervisor of felony trial courtrooms]. He might have been telling me. Now, did he every 10 minutes call all four or five of us? And he might have been talking to Devine [immediately above Kunkle], but did he do that every ten minutes? No (Kunkle 14).

Pressed further, Kunkle answered, "Do I have a specific recollection of any particular conversation? No" (15).

Later in the deposition, the role of Hyman and the unasked question about coercion of Andrew Wilson's confession again came up. Assistant Special Prosecutor Boyle asked Kunkle:

> Q. You would clearly have talked to Hyman?
> A. Correct.
> Q. About what went on out there?
> A. At some point, absolutely ... But primarily [assistant prosecutor] Angarola was talking to Hyman, and then Angarola was talking to me (60).

This was a blind alley: Angarola had died in the intervening years.

At no time did Kunkle take any responsibility for Hyman's not asking Wilson about his confession's voluntariness. To Kunkle, it was simply a forgotten "detail": "I don't know. I have no idea. It's a long time ago . . . [I don't remember] these kinds of details."

The deposition then turned to a common explanation given for the photographs of Wilson's injuries: that the injuries occurred after, and not before, the confession taken by Larry Hyman. Kunkle, among other explanations, suggested the perpetrators of Wilson's injuries were two "wagon men"—Officers Mulvaney and Ferro—who transported Wilson after his interrogation.

Q. And you were of a mind that they were the ones that had injured Andrew, Mulvaney and Ferro?

A. Not all of his injuries but some of them, yes.

Q. But you were convinced that Mulvaney and Ferro had, in fact, mistreated him?

A. No question about that.

Q. Did it dawn on you or occur to you that they had committed a crime?

A. Sure.

Q. Well, what did you do about that?

A. Told Special Prosecutions to handle it.

Q. You told, who would that be, DeBoni [i.e., RM Daley's trusted person in Special Prosecutions]?

A. Well I'm not sure if I did or if the state's attorney and the first assistant did, but someone did (22).

The details again escaped Kunkle.

But Kunkle did obviously remember that when Wilson appealed his initial conviction, the Illinois Supreme Court held, as stated in the deposition, that "there was a presumption . . . that Wilson had suffered injuries while he was in police custody" (29). Kunkle argued that the Illinois Supreme Court was presuming too much, "Which I personally regarded as new law. Others do not" (30).

During several criminal and civil trials involving the torture of Andrew Wilson, Kunkle maintained that the injuries could be explained in three different ways (49). He was unclear about which explanation was correct. The wagon-men explanation was the most frequently repeated explanation. However, Kunkle was unable to explain why this was not fully investigated by the special prosecutions unit in the state's attorney's office—a unit ostensibly established to address such matters.

This brings us to the central matter in the mayor and the midnight crew saga: whether the special prosecutions unit also had followed up on the letter from Police Superintendent Richard Brzeczek about Wilson's injuries. Kunkle answered, as before, invoking all three standard legal cover-up defenses: deniable distance, I can't recall, and responsibility of others. These defenses emerged as he responded to the question: "What happened with the Brzeczek letter?"

Kunkle (35) answered: "In that instance, again, a very vague recollection [of] mine is that Daley received the letter, read the letter, either showed it to me or gave me a copy or discussed it with me, and my response was to give to Special Prosecutions." This appeared to confirm that Daley had received and read the letter.

From this point on, the most explicit answer to the question, "What happened to the letter" would be that from Daley's perspective, the matter had been properly passed to his Special Prosecutions unit, and from Kunkle's perspective, that he could not intervene with the work of this unit because, as prosecutor of the Wilson case, he had a conflict of interest.

Did this mean Kunkle had no further engagement with the letter and its allegations? Not quite. The special prosecutors' questions continued:

Q. So you said to him [Daley] or you decided on your own to give it to
   Special Pros?
A. Right.
Q. Did you ever follow up on it?
A. Meaning?
Q. Did you ever check with Special Pros?
A. Oh, Special Pros—DeBoni or other people from Special Pros would occa-
   sionally talk to me about what's going on with the case.
Q. And do you remember what they told you?
A. I didn't get into what they were doing. That's the whole point of having a
   separate unit.
Q. Do you know who you sound like when you say that? [Police Superintendent]
   Brzeczek . . . So your answer is then that you did not talk to DeBoni and ask
   him what he had done after you turned that over to him?
A. No (57–58).

The indication that the special prosecutions unit handled the "wagon men" allegation and the investigation of the Brzeczek letter led to further questions. Assistant
Special Prosecutor Boyle asked about a paper trail that would indicate how the office
responded to Brzeczek's letter.

Q. What's your recollection as to a paper trail?
A. It might be none.
Q. So it might be done orally?
A. *Oh, absolutely . . . You both [Egan and Boyle] know 26th Street [the location
   of the state's attorney's office]. It's about as under papered as lawyering can
   get, which is sometimes a good thing and sometimes not good* (58–59; emphasis added).

Kunkle did not elaborate—and Egan and Boyle did not ask—how the "under
papering" might have been a good or bad thing.

The deposition was now winding down, and Kunkle took the opportunity to offer
a final framing statement about the "I don't recall" and "under papering" responses
that had left major gaps in his answers to crucial questions. His framing statement
came after a question about an argument known to have developed between Hyman
and another lawyer in the state's attorney's office. Special Prosecutor Egan asked, "Did
anyone ever tell you that the argument was because of a dispute over the procedures
to be followed in taking the statements that day?"

A. Well I don't have any recollection of it, but it's possible. I'm going to be 65
   in September. And just to mention—
Q. That doesn't impress us, Judge. Consider our age, will you?

A. Prosecutor Egan said something earlier that I've sort of been wanting to respond to and that's, yes, I can give you quotes from some of the Gacy witnesses [the John Wayne Gacy trial over which Kunkle presided]. I can remember dates and names and specific things from trial, but there are huge things that I don't remember from the same trials. F. Lee Bailey wrote a book ... and ... he talks about the bathtub brain drain. When you give your closing argument, you can remember every word, but the minute the jury comes back, adios.

Corporate Counsel and the Mayor: Richard M. Daley

Former State's Attorney and now Mayor RM Daley was deposed a month after Kunkle, in June 2006. A perk of being mayor was that RM could bring two of the city's corporate counsel to parry questions. RM maintained that, although he was state's attorney and this was a "heater case," he had distanced himself from the prosecution of the Wilson brothers, could not recall much about it, and had relied on others to manage this as well as other cases. *These are, again, the recurring defenses of distancing, recall, and responsibility of others.*

Recall was a problem from the outset, when RM was asked about the day of Andrew Wilson's arrest.

Q. Do you have a recollection of whether you were informed that the shooter had been picked up?
A. No, I don't recall.
Q. Do you have a recollection of being informed as to what was going on at Area 2 while your office was there when this shooter was in custody?
A. No, I don't recall anything (12).

This was despite RM previously indicating, "There was quite a bit of publicity on it [the "heater case"] ... in regards to the police department" (10), and Kunkle's deposition statements that, "There were a lot of assistant state's attorneys that stuck their nose in at Area 2 ... " (32) and that Area 2 was a "honey pot for a bunch of flies" (59).

The deposition then turned to the role of Larry Hyman. Boyle (14) began by rhetorically observing, "the very fact that he's [Andrew Wilson] supposed to have given an oral statement, and it's approximately eight hours later that the state's attorney [Hyman] decides to take a written statement from him." Boyle wanted to know what led to the eight-hour period before the confession was taken and why Wilson was not asked about his treatment by the police. *Boyle significantly noted that Hyman's "testimony is the only time [as head of Felony Review] that he failed to ask that question"*(emphasis added).

Boyle also asked, "Was that ever brought to your attention, either at that time or perhaps later in the case?" RM answered, "No, I don't recall." He also did not recall hearing that Wilson complained to Hyman in an earlier oral statement of being beaten. Boyle followed by noting that, "Mr. Kunkle has said on the record . . . he believed that those wagon men had committed a crime" (i.e., *after* the police took the confession statement). RM answered, "No, I hadn't heard anything. I don't recall" (14–16).

Boyle next inquired about the letter received from Police Superintendent Brzeczek. This was a sensitive question for RM, since it could connect him directly—and in an ongoing way—to knowledge about police mistreatment of Wilson. RM's corporate counsel clearly understood the import of the question and intervened.

> Q. Do you actually remember receiving this in the mail? That's really my
>   question.
> A. I would have to receive it, so I would have to say . . .
> MS. GEORGES [corporate counsel]: Just if you remember.
> A. I don't remember today (21).

Corporate counsel repeatedly cautioned and prompted RM before he answered questions.

The special prosecutors then asked about what, if any, action was taken in response to the Brzeczek letter. Boyle explained that, as the special prosecutors of the Burge investigation, they had actually "misunderstood" the leadership of the Chicago police special prosecutions unit to which the Brzeczek letter had been referred. Previously they believed Frank DeBoni was in charge of this unit. Boyle reported: "We have now come to learn that Jeff Kent was head of special prosecutions" (23). Kent had been hired from the U.S. Attorney's office to head this important unit.

Boyle had contacted Kent after receiving a call from him complaining about press reports of his involvement. He explained: "I asked Jeff Kent if he knew anything about Andrew Wilson and this letter . . . and he said he didn't recall anything about it" (23). Given the importance of the Brzeczek letter and Andrew Wilson's injuries on the day of his confession, the question remained: Why was the head of the special prosecution's unit not involved—especially given that this was a "heater case?"

> Q. Would there be anything unusual in Mr. Kunkle giving it to DeBoni and
>   not processing it through Kent? And I just ask that because it's kind of, one
>   would say administratively, it should have gone to Kent and not DeBoni
>   and let Kent assign it . . . Why did it go to DeBoni?
> MS. GEORGES [corporate counsel]: If you know.
> A. I don't know (24).

Boyle then asked similar questions about investigating the wagon men, to whom Kunkle attributed Wilson's injuries. RM's answer was again, "I don't recall . . . " (24).

Boyle tried another tack, referencing the Illinois Supreme Court decision that concluded Wilson was beaten while in police custody and before the confession statement. He asked: "Do you recall anybody talking to you about the opinion, you having any questions about . . . " but RM interrupted saying, "No, I don't recall a conversation like that" (26).

Although Boyle was unsuccessful in gaining much information from RM, Special Prosecutor Egan persisted in revisiting some of the same issues, and the mayor's corporate counsel again intervened. Most significantly, Egan returned to the letter RM received from Brzeczek.

> Q. Anyway, now, to get back to Jeff Kent, Kunkle mentioned Jeff Kent to us, but we had been operating always on the supposition that DeBoni was the person. And I share Bob's concern, or puzzlement, about why Kent wasn't given this letter instead of DeBoni. So, the only conclusion I could—one of the conclusions we drew, that somebody just decided to go around Jeff Kent. Could that be?
> MS. GEORGES: There could have been so many reasons.
> A. I wouldn't know.

Egan ended this line of inquiry by asking whether Larry Hyman had left the state's attorney's office and the felony review position shortly after Frank DeBoni reportedly received the letter about the injuries and confession of Wilson. RM responded, "I don't know when he left."

The deposition of RM closed by revisiting the issue around which questions had circled from the beginning: Larry Hyman's failure to ask Andrew Wilson about his treatment by police at Area 2 before taking his confession statement. Egan connected this issue to the dismissal of Jon Burge.

> Q. Are you aware of the civil service proceedings against Burge where there were people who disagreed with the decision that Larry Hyman had made? Are you aware of that?
> A. No, I'm not.
> Q. Are you aware of the fact that there are some people who have had experience in the State's Attorney's office that feel that Larry Hyman made a very, very, poor decision?
> A. I've never heard of that.
> Q. Never heard of that?
> A. No (44).

Egan tried one more time:

> Q. Do you know that the handbook that's used by prosecutors . . . specifically provides that the questioner, that is, the assistant state's attorney, shall make sure that in the statement is the question asking the prisoner if he's been treated okay by the police? Are you familiar with that?

> A. If it's in the booklet, it's in the booklet.
> Q. Would you feel that when you were state's attorney, if an assistant state's attorney didn't follow that direction, that certainly it should be called to his attention that he had violated the policy of the office?
> A. No one ever mentioned he violated any policy.

Egan finally tried to elicit a reaction to the extraordinariness of Hyman's failure to ask about police treatment by asking how this related to the involvement and responsibility of the state's attorney:

> Q. Are you aware that there are some first assistant state's attorneys and state's attorneys in the past that would have wanted to know every single thing that was going on at Detective Area 2 on the 14th [the day the confession statement was taken]?
> A. I wouldn't know that at all (47).

Egan had no further questions.

Daley's Defender: Richard (Dick) Devine

The last of the three leadership figures deposed from the state's attorney's office during the first trial of Andrew Wilson was Daley's first assistant, Dick Devine. The questions that Egan and Boyle asked Devine are themselves an apt illustration of the three roles that distance, the "I don't recall" defense, and the attribution of responsibility to others can play in covering up processes extending all the way to the top of an organization.

Early in the deposition, Devine offered an anticipatory version of the "I don't recall" defense:

> Given what happens to someone who gets into his 60s and talking about events from 24 years ago, I do have some specific recollections and I have some general impressions, yes.

Devine nonetheless acknowledged that he knew Wilson was arrested and in custody "relatively soon after it took place" (19).

In the course of taking Devine's deposition, it became apparent that the Brzeczek letter had been in the hands of at least four people, and that Devine himself became aware of the letter "soon after it was received" (31). *Devine was clearly in a position to know something about what happened with this letter.*

Devine began by explaining Frank DeBoni's role in doing little to respond to the Brzeczek letter.

> He [DeBoni] had reached out to the defense attorney for Andrew Wilson . . . and was told that there is a criminal prosecution pending, we're not going to say anything

at this stage.... So, at that stage, Frank believed he did not have a basis for doing anything.

Throughout their questioning, Boyle and Egan were solicitous of Devine, who was now serving as state's attorney himself. Much as the city's corporate counsel had done for Daley, Boyle helped Devine by raising the possibility that he could not remember important details.

> Q. Do you know or do you a have a recollection of the specific method that DeBoni used? Did he make a phone call? Did he talk to somebody? Or maybe you don't have a recollection of that.
> A. Well I don't know that I ever did. I don't know—there was contact. I don't know if it was in person, I don't know if it was a phone call . . .
> Q. Mr. Kunkle told us that it was he who talked [to] the public defender who represented Andrew Wilson . . . Dale Coventry (49–50).

Boyle noted that Dale Coventry denied having contact with William Kunkle and claimed there was considerable "confusion" at the time. The special prosecutor and his assistant then tried to clarify exactly what had happened; a course of action that took on features of the classic Abbott and Costello skit, "Who's on first?" Assistant Boyle began by noting that Kunkle said he had initiated the conversation at issue in the "well" of the court.

> Q. [Kunkle indicated] that it was he who asked Mr. Coventry to contact Mr. DeBoni, that he asked him in, in effect, the well of the courtroom in some pre-trial proceeding. And the fact is that there apparently was never a contact between Coventry and DeBoni, and Coventry has said that Kunkle never asked him to contact DeBoni.
> Mr. Boyle: Is that accurate, Ed [Egan]?
> Mr. Egan: Well, not exactly.
> Mr. Boyle: That he does not recall?
> Mr. Egan: Well, there was an initial—and I wanted to go into this because I think it is very confusing . . . there's mix-up about who said what to whom and when. In the previous statement, I think you said something about Frank DeBoni contacted the attorney for Andrew Wilson. And I was going to ask you [Dick Devine] who told you that Frank DeBoni contacted Coventry, because—I don't want to trap you on anything (50–51).

Egan now seemed—like Boyle before him—to be taking the role earlier assumed for Daley by the city corporate counsel, with Devine expressing his gratitude, saying, "No, No, I appreciate that" (51).

Egan explained that DeBoni had given a deposition in which he said, "I never called Coventry. I waited for him to call me, and he never did call me" (51). Egan went on to say that they were confused about Kunkle's role and discussed this with

Kunkle "to some extent" (52). Egan then seemed to acknowledge some contradiction between what Kunkle had told them, perhaps to the effect that he had *not* contacted Coventry, which led Kunkle to alter his account:

> Mr. Egan: ... And then the next day he said he had refreshed his recollection, called Bob [Mr. Boyle] up and said something about he remembers now that he importuned—
>
> Mr. Boyle: Coventry.
>
> Mr. Egan: Dale Coventry to get in touch with DeBoni. And he said DeBoni is earnest about this and he's serious about this. And then he . . . he eventually sent us an affidavit [at Egan's insistence] that—well what I'm getting at is, after we got this affidavit, and I talked to Coventry and Coventry denied—oh, that's what it was. He said that he importuned Coventry to please call. Coventry said, "That's absolutely false about him calling—talking to me and getting me—trying to importune me to talk to these people."

Boyle now briefly intervened to establish that Kunkle had asked Coventry to call DeBoni in a passing exchange, apparently in "the well" of the court.

> Mr. Boyle: Did Coventry, though, say that Kunkle had talked to him and asked him to call him [DeBoni].
>
> Mr. Egan: ... And then what else did Kunkle say? Oh, I talked to DeBoni again. And I said, "Did this happen." And he said, well, he has no recollection of it, but he can't say it never happened. But all I can say is, if that happened, that's contrary to what DeBoni said in his deposition.

Egan subsequently brought this portion of the deposition to a confusing conclusion with this summary statement: "All I can say is that Coventry said that is absolutely false. And I know that it is not in the depositions of DeBoni in which Kunkle represented him (52–55)."

This portion of Devine's deposition leaves considerable doubt and uncertainty as to whether anybody in the state's attorney's office actually did anything to follow up on Brzeczek's letter about the evidence that Andrew Wilson had been tortured by police detectives, and that this torture led to a forced confession.

DeBoni had apparently done little if anything with the Brzeczek letter which Daley had directed to him, and DeBoni's superior in the special prosecutions unit, Jeff Kent, had indicated that he was left out of the loop on this important matter. There also was little or no investigation by this unit of the role of the "wagon men" in continuing the abuse of Wilson apparently initiated by Area 2 detectives under the supervision of Jon Burge. And all of this, to use Kunkle's earlier characterization, was "under papered" in terms of an office paper trail.

The Special Prosecutor's Report and a Shadow Response

Finally, a month after the deposition of State's Attorney Devine, the special prosecutor went public with his report. In the weeks before, the *Chicago Reader* featured several pieces by their intrepid reporter John Conroy (e.g., 2006). Conroy expected little from the report, in part because he had heard that Larry Hyman had refused to testify—despite a supreme court order—claiming 5th amendment protection against self-incrimination and trying, through the Illinois Supreme Court, to block publication of the special prosecutor's report.

Conroy and Flint Taylor both suspected that Hyman's actions directly or indirectly involved others, such as Daley, Devine, and Kunkle. Even Daley had volunteered that the Wilson case was a "heater crime," and Conroy and Taylor reasoned that the pressure in the state's attorney's office to obtain a confession must have been intense. Their thinking was that Hyman had consulted directly or indirectly with Daley or his advisors in deciding not to ask Wilson about police mistreatment when he took his confession.

U.S. Attorney Patrick Fitzgerald (see Conroy 2006) was quoted in the *Reader* as saying that even if the report revealed little that was not already known, it "may provide the pry bar needed to get new trials. It may also lead to federal prosecutions for civil rights violations, violations of the RICO statute, and possibly perjury." This reference to the RICO statute—given its focus on conspiracy, corruption, and racketeering—was consistent with suspicions of a cover-up involving Hyman's taking the 5th and the elusive answers by Daley, Devine, and Kunkle in their depositions. Notably, all three possibilities—civil rights violations, RICO, and perjury—represented avenues that Fitzgerald had the authority to pursue as U.S. Attorney for the Northern District Court of Illinois. Fitzgerald's statement was a voice of optimism in the midst of a pervasive mood of legal cynicism about the nature of the coming report.

When the report finally appeared—seven million dollars and more than four years after the investigation began—it read more like a defense of Daley's law and order regime than a condemnation. While the investigation looked into as many as two hundred complaints of police brutality, it found plausible grounds for indicting only Jon Burge and four other officers.

The report broadly framed its conclusion this way: "While not all the officers named by all the claimants were guilty of prisoner abuse, it is our judgment that the commander of the Violent Crimes section of Detective Areas 2 and 3, Jon Burge, was guilty of such abuse." However, even this conclusion was presented as a dead end. Egan and Boyle (16) insisted: "We have considered every possible legal theory that would permit us to avoid the effect of the statute of limitations on any prosecution; regrettably, we have considered that the statute of limitations would bar any prosecution of any offenses our investigation has disclosed."

Probably anticipating that Fitzgerald's first step in pursuing Jon Burge and others would be through perjury charges in a federal prosecution, Egan and Boyle (16) warned: "We have also concluded that the use of the immunity statute to compel testimony and possible contempt citations or perjury prosecutions, under the evidence available to us, would constitute an impermissible procedure identified as a 'perjury trap.'" Invoking the notion of a perjury trap to describe the prosecution of false or contradictory statements by Jon Burge in officially sworn statements was legal cynicism of a unique kind.

Perhaps the most remarkable aspect of the report was that the only person beyond Burge to whom it assigned leadership responsibility was neither Richard M. Daley nor Jane Byrne but Police Superintendent Brzeczek. The report concluded:

> The evidence supports the conclusion that Superintendent Brzeczek was guilty of a 'dereliction of duty' and did not act in good faith in the investigation of the claim of Andrew Wilson. Despite the fact that Brzeczek believed that officers in the Violent Crimes Unit of Detective Area 2 had tortured Andrew Wilson he kept that belief to himself for over twenty years. He also kept Burge in command of Area 2 and issued a letter of commendation to all the detectives at Area 2 (Egan and Boyle: 17).

This suspiciously tidy conclusion ignored Byrne's initiation of the "door to door" manhunt by McCarthy and Burge that led to the torture of Andrew Wilson, the unanswered letter from Brzeczek asking Daley for guidance about investigating Wilson's torture, and the obfuscation about how the letter was handled in the state's attorney's office. The special prosecutor identified just the one new leadership culprit, concluding, "There is insufficient evidence of wrongdoing by any member of the State's Attorney's Office, except one person." And, that one person was Richard Brzeczek (Egan and Boyle 17).

Was this conclusion preconceived and grounded in the rivalry between Brzeczek and Daley that dated to their parallel rise to prominence in the early 1980s, culminating in Brzeczek's decision to mount a Republican challenge to the Democratic machine and Daley's re-election to a second term as state's attorney? Did the special prosecutor conclude that the abundant evidence of torture combined with a disinclination to charge Jon Burge—not to mention Kunkle, Devine, and Daley—required the special prosecutor to identify a scapegoat? Did Brzeczek's inglorious and highly publicized fall from grace involving alcohol, marital infidelity, and psychiatric problems simply make him a target too easy to pass up? And, was this outcome simply preordained by Democratic machine politics?

The report, to say the least, was not well received by the group Flint Taylor (2019) had been working with to expose the breadth and depth of the Chicago "torture machine." As a result, the following year, Taylor joined with a collection of scholars, activists, and advocates to issue a "shadow report" on "The Failure of Special Prosecutors Edward J. Egan and Robert D. Boyle to Fairly Investigate Systemic Police Torture in Chicago."

The shadow report reached a number of conclusions, two of which are of special interest for this volume. These are that the report:

- Ignored the failure of the former Cook County State's Attorney Richard M. Daley, State's Attorney Richard A. Devine, and various other high-ranking officials to investigate and prosecute police officers who engaged in a documented pattern of torture and wrongful prosecution of torture victims.

And, furthermore it,

- Ignored a wealth of evidence establishing that that there was a widespread and continuing cover-up of the torture scandal—a conspiracy of silence—implicating high officials of the City of Chicago, the Chicago Police Department, and the Cook County State's Attorney Office.

The shadow report called for a more probing prosecutorial investigation of police torture and other prosecutorial abuses of power in Chicago criminal law enforcement.

The shadow report was an energizing response to the special prosecutor's report and promised to be the kind of "pry bar" that U.S. Attorney Fitzgerald had envisioned as leading to federal prosecutions. Moving forward, Fitzgerald and the authors of the Shadow Report at least appeared to be marching to the beat of the same drum. But, as we show next, it was not the shadow report alone that captured the attention of Chicagoans.

7

Call It by Its Name

Legal Cynicism and Racist Torture in the Quintessential City

Legal cynicism is a top-down phenomenon. Powerful politicians and law enforcers play prominent roles, stimulating and facilitating policies and practices that breed legal cynicism in affected populations. Understanding how this happens is essential in explaining legal cynicism and its consequences.

In the preceding chapter, we focused on the Cook County special prosecutor's investigation of Jon Burge, his midnight crew, and the torture of Black men in Chicago Police Area 2. We saw how Daley-era elite politicians used tactics of distancing, downward attributions of responsibility, and failures to remember (i.e., "I don't recall") to cover-up their responsibility for policies and practices that generate and perpetuate legal cynicism. In this chapter, we focus on courtroom decisions and sworn testimony from the prosecution of Jon Burge—in arguably the most important trial of the second Daley era—to demonstrate how law can perpetuate a code of silence, in this case enabling racist torture. The *Invisible Institute* posted the transcripts and other relevant documents from the Jon Burge criminal trial on the web (Hunt n.d. U.S. V Burge; to enhance readability we refer to the speaker and page numbers when citing these documents, we do not include a date to distinguish them from other sources).

We also analyze the transcriptions of important courtroom interactions that occurred beyond the hearing of jurors. These interactions involved lawyers' sidebar discussions with Judge Joan Lefkow, the judge responsible for interpreting and ruling on the legal issues raised in this trial. We demonstrate how the judge's rulings about the charges in this case narrowed the prosecution's ability to expose the code of silence that enabled and help perpetuate racist torture by Jon Burge and others. Our analysis in prior chapters revealed the long-term historical consequences of legal cynicism resulting from such processes.

"Do We Care?"

Our analysis of how the top-down process of legal cynicism unfolded during RM Daley's years as state's attorney and mayor in Chicago benefitted from the work of two of the most important writers about police torture in this city: John Conroy and Flint Taylor. Each wrote a landmark book: Conroy's (2000) *Unspeakable Acts,*

Ordinary People, and Taylor's (2019) *The Torture Machine*. There are many similarities in Conroy's and Taylor's analysis; yet they do not fully agree about why the prosecution of police torture in Chicago took so long to even begin.

In 2006, Conroy and Taylor, along with David Bates, a victim of Chicago police torture, discussed the Burge case on Amy Goodman's national activist news show, *Democracy Now!* The episode focused on the 2006 special prosecutor's report that was scheduled for imminent release. This report was newsworthy not only because it was so long delayed, but also because a maneuver by two Chicago lawyers, Joey Mogul and Susan Gzesh, helped to get it released. Mogul and Gzesh had appealed to the United Nations High Commission on Human Rights' (OHCHR) Committee Against Torture (CAT) and traveled to Geneva in May 2006 to appear before it.

Louise Arbour was the UN high commissioner in 2006. She was previously the chief prosecutor at the tribunal for the former Yugoslavia and made history by indicting the first sitting head of state, Slobodan Milosovic. As high commissioner, Arbour authorized simultaneous CAT investigations of torture by soldiers in Iraq and police officers in Chicago. The pairing of these investigations was a bold move. Its logic was that the United States had used torture in both locations and, in both places, the victims were specifically targeted racial/ethnic groups.

In Iraq, the torture was mostly of Sunni suspects (Hagan, Kaiser, and Hanson 2015), while in Chicago it was African American detainees. Using a process called Universal Periodic Review, the committee asked the United States, as a UN member state, to account for its use of torture in Iraq and to complete its four-year torture investigation by the special prosecutor in Chicago. The CAT instructed that the United States "should promptly, thoroughly and impartially investigate all allegation of acts of torture by law enforcement personnel and bring perpetrators to justice" (United Nations, 2006).

Democracy Now!'s Amy Goodman asked Conroy and Taylor to discuss the background and pending implications of the Geneva case. She began by noting the unusual and provocative connection between Abu Ghraib Prison and the South Side of Chicago:

> Extraordinary rendition. Overseas prisons. Abu Ghraib. Guantanamo Bay. Practices and places that have become synonymous with the abuse of detainees in US custody are getting renewed attention at the United Nations this week, where the UN Committee against Torture is holding hearings... But there is one name expected to arise this week that few people in this country will have heard about... It's called Area 2. And for nearly two decades beginning in 1971, it was the epicenter for what has been described as the systematic torture of dozens of African American males by Chicago police officers... To date, not one Chicago police officer has been charged with any crime.

Conroy and Taylor agreed that Goodman had her facts straight, but as they spoke, a difference in their views about the prosecution of torture cases became apparent.

Goodman asked why the Area 2 story was not more widely known and had not already been addressed. To answer, Conroy drew from his book:

... the reason why it's dragged on—I differ with the estimable Mr. Taylor here on this—is that there is no community outrage. People don't care. ... It's African American men, most of them with criminal records. And they're just beyond the pale of our compassion. We just don't care.

Conroy's logic was that, just as the ruling Shia in Iraq didn't care about torture of their fellow Sunni, most White Chicagoans didn't care about the torture of African Americans.

Taylor was more optimistic. He suggested the litigation involving Andrew Wilson—combined with the anticipated special prosecutors' report and the intervention by the CAT—could produce a new sense of public outrage. Taylor explained: "John and I disagree . . . The public outrage reaches certain proportions at different times. We're at one of those key points again today."

Conroy acknowledged the present moment seemed promising, yet he also urged caution:

How significant the international attention will be remains to be seen. ... I think, for those of us . . . to see [Chicago] finally raise to the level of being mentioned in a phrase with Abu Ghraib and Guantanamo is quite thrilling. But whether this will just be one of those media—you know, where the media comes in for a day or two and then leaves remains to be seen.

In his book's final chapter, which he titled "Bystanders," Conroy (2000:256) observed, "only a tiny fraction of working torturers will ever be punished, and those who are can expect their punishment to be slight compared to their crime." He concluded that torture is the near-perfect crime: "There are exceptions, yes, but in the vast majority of cases, only the victim pays."

We agree with Conroy that it is the victims of torture who pay most dearly; nonetheless, there is, in Taylor's more optimistic perspective, an interesting analysis of why this is so and how law could be used to deter torture. Anticipating that the report of the special prosecutors would be disappointing, Taylor shifted his hopes from the state to the federal courts and U.S. Attorney Patrick Fitzgerald.

There are continuing criminal violations here, and if the special prosecutor won't do anything about them, then Fitzgerald, who is the U.S. Attorney here and who, of course, has made his name in the Valerie Plame case and has already indicted Daley's people in a wide-ranging truck scandal, he has to open his investigation into federal RICO or racketeering charges, as well as the obstruction of justice and perjury charges (cited in Taylor, 2019:339–340).

Taylor insisted that to have Chicago grouped with Abu Ghraib should "wake up the U.S. Attorney's Office." Whether this wakeup call would be sufficient to stimulate RICO and racketeering charges would prove a different matter.

Within three days of the televised *Democracy Now!* discussion, a Chicago judge held hearings about the undisclosed special prosecutor's report, and within the week, under further pressure from local activists, the judge ordered the report be made public. The report was a disappointment, but bringing the case back in view and linking it to torture in Iraq was consequential. The torture scandal was now in Fitzgerald's hands and impossible to ignore.

Taylor's allusion to RICO and the possibility of making the Chicago torture scandal into a racketeering and corruption case raised hopes that the investigation would include high-level figures. Fitzgerald had the challenging task of being the first prosecutor, after several decades of cover-up, to take on this issue. However, he ultimately chose to prosecute only Jon Burge, and not for racist torture but for the more opaque charges of perjury and obstruction of justice.

Jon Burge on Trial

Jury selection for the Burge trial began in May 2010. Although Burge was fired by the police department in 1993, he had not been charged with any crimes, much less racist torture. A thirty-year cover-up allowed the five-year statute of limitations to run out the clock on potential torture prosecutions. Fitzgerald's perjury and obstruction charges focused instead on Burge's having lied in 2003 about torturing several victims, including Andrew Wilson, Anthony Holmes, Shadeed Mu'min, Gregory Banks, and Melvin Jones. This required Fitzgerald to establish both the torture and Burge's lies about it. The trial therefore began with the testimony of the torture victims, whom the defense depicted as "lying criminals" at every opportunity.

The defense further alleged that the torture claims resulted from a conspiracy organized by a Chicago gang, Black Gangster Disciples, while they were in prison. This assertion underscored the prosecution's need to introduce corroborating testimony for the victims' claims, ideally from justice system personnel. This required that the prosecution find breaches in the pervasive police code of silence, as well as to work around the judge's pretrial instructions that the *lawyers not raise issues of race, even though race was obviously central to the case.*

The testimonies of two key witnesses, detective Michael McDermott and court reporter Michael Hartnett, would illuminate how policies and practices in the state's attorney's office and in the Chicago South Side Area 2 police station secreted the three-decade cover-up of torture. However, this could only be addressed after the foundation of the prosecution's case was established.

Hearing from the Victims

Anthony Holmes' case began in 1973; it highlighted both the scandal's length and its connection to South Side legal cynicism. As a Black man on the South Side, Holmes' testified: "Maybe you kind of expect to get beat up by police, but you don't expect to get electrocuted" (Walecka:2). The harrowing accounts of three other Black men—Shadeed Mu'min, Gregory Banks, and Melvin Jones—followed and were equally disturbing. But the case most dramatically unfolded around Andrew Wilson.

Andrew Wilson died in 2007, so his testimony came from beyond the grave and was based on his court appearances during his criminal and civil trials. A White special agent read Wilson's answers to questions reenacted by the prosecution's Betsey Biffl. It was compelling testimony. It began with Wilson's recollection of Jon Burge entering the room where he was being held and Burge telling officers that if he were them, "he wouldn't leave marks on Wilson" (Walecka:8); but the marks proved impossible to hide. The prosecution presented photographs showing Wilson's injuries at the hands of Burge's "midnight crew." Wilson's public defender, Dale Coventry, had presented the photos at Wilson's first court appearance. The photos showed marks on Wilson's ears from alligator clips, signature signs of electroshocks applied under Burge's supervision.

Wilson's testimony further recalled the role of Assistant State's Attorney Lawrence Hyman in taking his confession. As noted in previous chapters, Wilson disrupted an early-morning first attempt to take his statement, saying to Hyman, "You want me to make a statement after they been torturin' me?" Hyman angrily told the detective who brought Wilson to "get this jag-off out of here" (Walecka:10). Although Hyman would later refuse to testify and claimed the 5th Amendment protection against self-incrimination, this set the foundation for later testimony by court reporter Michael Hartnett about taking Wilson's confession eleven hours after this first encounter.

Evidence of Wilson's torture was reinforced by testimony of Dr. John Raba, director of the prison medical center. He reported that Wilson's injuries matched his description of his torture (Raba:1382–1383). Raba then wrote a letter to police superintendent Brzeczek insisting on an investigation.

A Sidebar with the Judge

During Dr. Raba's testimony, the prosecution asked the judge for the first of many following sidebars. These were included in the court transcript—but unheard by the jury—and provided key data for this chapter. The prosecution request for a sidebar signaled its concern about a code of silence. This code was central to the cover-up efforts of rank and file police officers, as well as those by high-ranking authorities, and ultimately RM Daley. Prosecutor Betsy Biffl explained:

> Your Honor, I guess we'll front this so we don't end up back here. After I ask him [Dr. Raba] about the letter, I'll ask if he got a response from the superintendent, and the answer is going to be no . . . However, he did get a call from the president of the Cook County Board [of Commisioners, George Dunne; the board is the governing and legislative body of the county] who said: 'Doc, what are you doing? Why did

you send the letter?'... *I think it is relevant because it goes to the fact that there was this chilling effect on everybody who tried to address this issue.... I think it is relevant to this case and the fact that so many people kept quiet and why they may have done that* (Raba:1378–1379; emphasis added)

Defense lawyer Marc Martin objected that Jon Burge was the defendant, not George Dunne: "We object to George Dunn's statement on hearsay grounds. There's no conspiracy charged here. He's [Burge] not a member of a conspiracy" (1379).

The judge overruled, allowing introduction of the phone call from the Cook County board president. However, testimony admitted in this trial *should have included much broader evidence of a code of silence* involving the police and higher level authorities. What the prosecution in this sidebar called the, "chilling effect on everybody who tried to address this issue," and furthermore that, "so many people kept quiet and why they may have done that," were key references to the code of silence that allowed the racist torture regime led by Jon Burge to have gone unpunished for so long.

Two Black Police Officers Speak Out

The prosecution next called two Black police officers from Area 2: Doris Byrd and Sam Lacey. Byrd testified that Burge worked predominately with the A Team, ". . . a nickname that some of us had given a group of detectives who handled mostly all the homicides and heater cases, cases that had high publicity" (Byrd:86). In contrast, officers on the B team were typically assigned "cold cases" that were hard to solve and resulted in few arrests (Ralph 2020).

The prosecutor asked Byrd to describe Burge's interactions with the A Team.

> A: Well, there seemed to be a camaraderie between them.
> Q: When you say there seemed to be a camaraderie, can you tell us what objective reasons or observations you made to reach that conclusion?
> A: Well you would hear conversations of them socializing after working hours when joining him on his boat (86).

Burge had named his boat the *Vigilante*, a term loaded with extra-legal implications.

Another Sidebar

Prosecutor David Weisman now asked for a sidebar in connection with the instructions Judge Lefkow had given earlier not to ask questions involving racial bias. Weisman was concerned the defense would do so indirectly by questioning Sergeant Byrd's competence—implicitly because she was Black.

Judge, in your pretrial you said no racial bias as far as in the workplace. . . . Ms. Byrd has a lot to say about that. We didn't inquire. But if Mr. Gamboney [for the defense] is now going to get into the fact that she—so—she didn't get homicide investigations assigned to her, then I don't think it is fair for us to have to sit there in our seats and not be able to draw out the fact that one, he [Burge] didn't assign [B]lacks homicide investigations; and, two, when they went to a commander to complain, the commander reported it to Burge, and he chewed them out (Byrd:95).

Burge's treatment of Black officers was essential to understanding this case, given the role of race in police torture and it being obscured by the presumed racial neutrality of the perjury charge.

In the sidebar, prosecutor Weisman began to work around this obstacle by introducing the high rate of confession that Burge's "A Team" obtained compared to the rate for Byrd and others:

Here is a woman who didn't even get tough cases, and she barely got written confessions from people. And how are people committing murders getting written confessions? That's the inference we'll draw in closing (Weisman:1483).

Weisman was giving notice that he would be pursuing this line of questioning with his next African American officer, Sam Lacey.

Sam Lacey Implicitly Challenges the Code of Silence

Sam Lacey began work with the Chicago Police Department as a patrol officer, rising to detective before finishing a law degree and leaving the force to start a private practice. He had the confidence of an experienced lawyer and was unintimidated by aggressive questions from defense counsel. Along with Doris Byrd, he worked under the supervision of Jon Burge.

Lacey identified several key members of the "midnight crew"—John Yucaitis, Pete Dignan, and Jack Byrne—along with other members of the A Team. Lacey described Burge's role in Area 2 as, "like the boss. He ran things" (Lacy:170). Lacey highlighted Burge's control in his description of the investigation of the "heater crime" killings of Officers Fahey and O'Brian discussed in Chapter One.

Well, I—particularly one occasion I can recall, we were working on the Fahey and O'Brian homicides, and there was some suspects that had been taken in. And the commander, Commander Deas, and myself was ordered to go down to the Chief of detective's office . . . while the investigation was being taken care of (1559).

Like the Wilson brothers, Deas and Lacey were both Black. The implication was they were to be kept away from the torture scene.

Lacey's involvement in the Wilson case began when he went to the Area 2 station to see if he could help in the search for those who had killed his fellow officers. Burge declined his offer, dismissed a lead he had about possible suspects (who, it later turned out, were the Wilson brothers), and assigned Lacey to duty miles away from the station house (Ralph 2020). In his testimony, Lacey described stopping at the Area 2 office on his way to church on the Sunday Wilson was arrested.

> Q. Now you were there, and you got out of the car. Your family was in the car. Did you hear anything unusual?
>
> A: Yes, I could hear some—someone screaming like for help or something, I don't know . . . It sounded like they were in deep distress.

He described going to the second floor and seeing a handcuffed suspect.

> Q. All right, when you saw that person, did you know who he was?
>
> A. . . . I thought he was one of the Wilsons . . .
>
> Q. . . . did he appear to have any emotion . . . ?
>
> A. Somewhat shocked or dismayed or something like that, but—
>
> Q. . . . Did he have any blood coming from him?
>
> A. . . . No, he was just sitting on the floor.
>
> Q. . . . And when you saw him later that day on the television . . .
>
> A. He looked somewhat haggard and a big bandage around his head, and there was blood on the front of it, the bandage.

These details about Wilson's change in appearance following his interrogation were consistent with the reports of others.

The prosecution then turned Lacey's attention to his own methods and success in investigating cases compared to those of the A Team.

> Q: Did you obtain oral statements from some people?
>
> A: Yes, I did.
>
> Q: How many of those did you get?
>
> A: Several . . .
>
> Q: . . . When you interviewed people, what interview techniques did you use to gain statements from people?
>
> A: . . . I would try to make them feel sad and remorseful and give up some information . . .
>
> Q: Did you notice a trend as to who was obtaining written statements?
>
> A: Basically the guys that worked the A Team, they got a lot of written statements . . .
>
> Q: Did they get more than other detectives in Area 2?
>
> A: Yes, they did (1570–1572).

This pattern of A Team success in obtaining written statements likely resulted from their use of torture, although no one explicitly made this point in court testimony. Ralph (2020) observed that excluding Black officers from high-profile cases also reduced the likelihood that they would directly witness and could testify about the use of torture by officers on the A Team.

Reference to a racial pattern of White (police) on Black (victim) torture, anticipated in the earlier sidebar and disallowed for discussion by the judge in her pretrial instructions, soon reemerged. The prosecution raised it here in response to defense attorney questions about Officer Lacey's earlier report that Andrew Wilson did not look injured when he saw him in the morning of February 14, but looked seriously abused later that day.

> Mr. Beuke [for the defense]: Sir, you in your mind determined that something had obviously happened to Andrew Wilson at Area 2, correct? ... And you immediately went to your supervisor, Commander Deas, and told him that you had seen Mr. Wilson at around 8:30 or 9:00 o'clock in the morning and he was fine, and then you saw him on the 10 o'clock news and he had a big bandage around his head, correct? (1570–1571).

Anticipating where this questioning might lead, the prosecution immediately asked for a sidebar.

> Mr. Weisman: Judge, look, he [defense attorney, Mr. Beuke] can ask those questions if he's trying to show some type of—you know, that he [Officer Lacey] failed to do something. But if he does, he's opening the door to what the court has asked us to keep out, which is that this witness, along with Ms. Byrd, complained about how they were being treated in Area 2 ... it is fine if he wants to ask, but I think—I just want to warn that I think it is then relevant to say if he had reported it, he would have faced the same consequences ... If he wants to withdraw the question on the record, then I will close the door. But if he wants to pursue it, I will consider the door open.
> Mr. Beuke: Just for the record, Judge, I'll do that, but for the record we completely disagree with your Honor's ruling, completely (1623–1625).

The prosecution and the defense had effectively "agreed to disagree." As a result, the door was again closed on the prosecution's attempt to make the point that the torture underlying this case was racially targeted in such an extreme way that the torturers from the A Team were White, whereas the victims were Black. Both sides likely realized that the prosecution was going to convict Burge of perjury and obstruction when this case was finished; however, the prosecution was not going to be able to expose the departmental code of silence that allowed Burge to lead a racist torture squad that victimized more than a hundred Black men.

A White Police Officer Involuntarily Breaks the Code of Silence

The prosecution ideally wanted a White police officer to break the code of silence by providing eyewitness testimony about Jon Burge's torture. This was challenging. The prosecution wound up calling former police officer Michael McDermott, who now worked in the state's attorney's office.

McDermott had previously testified at a grand jury hearing, but now the prosecution asked the judge to treat Officer McDermott as a hostile witness. Speaking for the prosecution, April Perry explained: "His testimony is different than he has said at grand jury" (McDermott:15). The grand jury testimony was given in secret, without the intimidating presence of Jon Burge. McDermott was now face-to-face with Burge in a courtroom that likely included other concerned police officers as well as reporters.

McDermott's testimony followed from his responses to earlier subpoenas. The unusual circumstances led defense lawyer, Richard Beuke, to request a surprising sidebar to explain why McDermott needed immunity from prosecution.

> Mr. Beuke: Judge, it is our theory here that I don't know when this guy is telling the truth, when he's telling a lie. He's acknowledged that he had lied under oath on several different occasions. What I think it is crucial for this jury to understand is that when he made certain decisions to testify in front of the grand jury in 2008, that there were certain things in his own mind. One of the things . . . was the fact that [an earlier lawyer] . . . told him if you go in there and say you don't remember anything, you're going to get indicted.

The judge ended the sidebar by allowing this line of questioning—a line of questioning that also involved McDermott's professed fear that, unless he was a cooperative witness, he would not only be indicted but also lose his job, health insurance, pension, and other benefits of his employment with the state's attorney's office.

McDermott's lawyer noted that his client had been granted immunity for his testimony, although McDermott insisted that he actually did not want immunity, because he understood this as requiring him to "talk" or go to jail.

> I wished to remain silent. I was ordered by the Chief Judge to talk. And if I didn't, I would have to go to jail. And the only way they could make me talk is to give me immunity. Nobody has ever told me what I need immunity for (McDermott:85).

Yet, it was McDermott who ultimately entered a request for immunity.

Additional drama, and McDermott would say coercion, was added when McDermott described an interaction he had with U.S. Attorney Patrick Fitzgerald before his grand jury appearance. McDermott explained:

> A: I was seated outside, and one of the U.S. attorney approached me and introduced himself.
>
> Q: ... And did he introduce himself to you?
>
> A: To me, my lawyer. And then he walked away and stood by the door of the grand jury.
>
> Q: What happened after he stood by the door of the grand jury?
>
> A: Oh, there were other U.S. Attorneys there. I think an FBI agent. There is like four or five people.
>
> Q: What happened then?
>
> A: Well, I walked away from my attorney. And as I was walking in the door of the grand jury, they kind of stood around me, and the U.S. Attorney kind of made a comment ...
>
> Q: What did he say to you?
>
> A: He said, oh, by the way, it is not just perjury. If I think you're holding back on anything, it is obstruction (McDermott:87–88).

Fitzgerald then entered the grand jury with McDermott, accompanied by the assistant U.S. attorneys and the FBI agent.

The prosecution brought McDermott into the case to corroborate the torture of Shadeed Mu'min. Burge interrogated Mu'min in his office about a robbery. Mu'min testified that Burge pulled a .44 Magnum gun from his desk, told him that he had removed all the bullets except one, pointed the weapon at Mu'min's forehead, and then pulled the trigger three times.

At least some of this occurred when McDermott was standing in the doorway of Burge's office. When Mu'min refused to talk, Burge allegedly yanked a vinyl cover from a typewriter and pressed it against Mu-min's nose and mouth. This was allegedly done three times, with Burge having to revive Mu'min twice by blowing air into his mouth. Only then did Mu'min agree to talk about the robbery (Walecka:22–23).

McDermott was a promising witness for the prosecution, and his testimony could break the code of silence. However, between McDermott's grand jury appearance and the Burge trial, he decided that he had been pressured to testify in ways that threatened his job security and family. McDermott now claimed that he had doubts about whether Burge had the requisite criminal intent to torture Mu'min.

As McDermott's testimony moved toward its conclusion, prosecutor April Perry sought to clarify contradictions between his trial and grand jury testimony about the criminal intent necessary to establish Burge's perjury. With Burge and others looking on, and with the judge answering objections, the prosecution asked:

> Q. Sir, you know that Lieutenant Burge's goal was to coerce a confession, isn't that right?
>
> A. ... I don't know what his intentions were ... it might have been something else ... a three minute interview with a suspect is not my idea of a confession ... I don't know what his intentions were.

Q: Sir, when you were before the grand jury, were you asked these questions, and did you give these answers?

"Question: When you say you were surprised, you don't know why he was doing this in front of you.

Answer: Right.

Question: Would you have expected him to do it in his office if you weren't there?

Answer: I don't think I knew him that well to do something basically incriminating in front of me.

Question: And when you say incriminating, incriminating in what sense from your perspective?

Answer:" — [silence] (McDermott:134–135).

The prosecutor broke the silence by inferring "coercing a confession" and McDermott answered, "Yes."

Ms. Perry, for the prosecution, further addressed McDermott's revised characterization of Burge's criminal intent with regard to Burge holding something over Mu'min's face and whether the interaction was a one-sided confrontation or a two-sided "scuffle."

Q: Sir, isn't it true that there was no struggling or physical fight put up by Mr. Mu'min until he had something placed over his head?

A: There was nothing placed over his head. It was a scuffle, and it was like 20 seconds long, and it was 25 years ago.

Q: Sir, in the grand jury were you asked these questions, and did you give these answers?

"Question: As far as it being a confrontational situation, this was a one-sided confrontation, correct? This was Burge confronting Mu'min. Mu'min not resisting or confronting Burge in any way, correct?

Answer: He could have been, I don't know. I'm sure he wasn't cooperating fully with the interrogation if that's what you want to say is a confrontation.

Question: Well, would it be fair to say at most—

Answer: I would say it was one-sided.

Question: And would it be fair to say at most, maybe perhaps after this bag placed over his head, he might have struggled a little bit?

Answer: Yes.

Question: But not prior to that point?

Answer: That's correct."

Q: Did you give those—were you asked those questions, and did you give those answers?

A: Yes (McDermott:135–137).

The prosecution offered McDermott's combined testimony about the coerced confession and the simulated suffocation as corroborating Mu'min's account of the *actus rea* (i.e., criminal act) and *mens rea* (i.e., criminal intent) of his torture by Burge.

As this part of the trial moved toward its conclusion, the prosecution made two further and somewhat theatrically delivered points. The first was a response to McDermott's contention that U.S. Attorney Fitzgerald placed undue pressure on him as he entered the grand jury by warning him that he could be charged with obstruction of justice and perjury if he gave purposefully untruthful testimony. The prosecution asked McDermott whether if, in offering his warning, Fitzgerald had used any inappropriate language, yelled at him, or physically touched him in any way. Then, drawing an obvious reference to actions of Burge, the prosecution asked if Fitzgerald had pointed a gun in his direction or put a bag over his head. McDermott answered "no" to each question (McDermott:134–137).

The final point was even more theatrical and involved the prospect of another sidebar. McDermott repeatedly said he was treated unfairly before the trial. In apparent anger, McDermott mixed a complaint that he was not allowed to properly prepare for his testimony with his indignation that the court let criminal offenders lie without consequences.

> I knew it was—you were going to talk about 30 or 40 years of possible abuse. And I also knew that the vast majority of these offenders lie, and you guys aren't doing nothing about it. So, no, they didn't tell me any specific case that I worked on ahead of time so I could review my reports and so I could answer with some kind of a refreshed memory (McDermott:142).

The prosecution would later remind McDermott that this approach to interviewing police witnesses was essentially the same as that used by police officers in interrogating suspects. First, however, the prosecution framed the issue in terms of Shadeed Mu'min. In doing so, it generated a response about the police code of silence.

> Q: So certainly no one told you that the government was interested in hearing about Shadeed Mu'min, did they?
>
> A: I know it was listed. I know I went down to OPS [Office of Professional Standards]. I know it was brought up at the police board. This was all public record decades ago, and your office did nothing about it. So I knew that you would ask me about Shadeed Mu'min . . .
>
> Q: Are you finished?
>
> A: I'm Answering your question ma'am.
>
> Q: No, sir. My question was: Did anyone tell you the government was going to be asking about Shadeed Mu'min?
>
> A: You didn't tell me what you were going to ask me.
>
> Q: . . . Sir, isn't it true the reason that these cases were not brought earlier is because people like yourself didn't come forward earlier?

> Mr. Beuke: Objection, Judge, can we have a sidebar?
> The Court: I'll sustain (McDermott:142–143).

It seemed obvious that the prosecutor knew her question would provoke an objection and that she had anticipated that she could make her point without receiving an answer from McDermott. The prosecutor's unanswered question summarized a perspective on the trial that the prosecution sought permission to develop in several sidebars. Namely, that the central elements of this case were racially targeted episodes of torture that were covered up by a code of silence. For the prosecution, this was central to the case.

John Burge as the Businessman's Policeman

Chicago Mayor Jane Byrne met Jon Burge on the night of the Fahey and O'Brien shootings. She described Burge as like "a businessman rather than a policeman" (Byrne deposition (see Chapter Six):1). There was a likely explanation: Burge's mother was an advice columnist (Baer 2020:21) and published a book, *This Business of Dressing for Business*. Burge could also be engaging. In the company of outsiders, he was well spoken, usually dressed in a suit, and professional in manner and demeanor. When asked in court about torture, his denials were typically calm and unwavering. It was easy to see why the police department and state's attorney's office valued his work.

Burge (170) steadfastly insisted he had never seen a suspect's rights violated in Area 2. The prosecution therefore asked:

> Q: Sir, can you explain to the ladies and gentlemen of the jury why, after Andrew Wilson was arrested and being taken back to Area 2, you had to tell someone to handle him with kid gloves? Can you tell us why you even had that concern if you had never seen anything of the sort before?
> A: I didn't have to tell anybody that. I said that to preclude any possibility . . . I wanted to make sure that Mr. Wilson was treated in the nicest possible way . . . (Burge:170–171).

For good measure, Burge added, "that was my choice, Counselor."

Yet there were flashes in Burge's testimony that his views about policing were unorthodox. For example, when asked to evaluate injuries of the kind Wilson received, Burge's answers were startling:

> Q: Sir, isn't it true that, when you first became aware that Andrew Wilson had injuries, you laughed at it and made light of it?
> A: Yes.
> Q: You became aware that he had [significant] injuries, isn't that right?

A: You said significant injuries, counselor. He never had significant injuries; they were superficial injuries.

Q: And you don't believe second degree burns are significant injuries?

A: No, sir.

Q: You don't believe burns to the chest are significant injuries?

A: I don't believe he had any burns to the chest. But they would not be significant injuries. No, they are superficial.

Q: You don't believe a laceration to the back of the head that requires stiches is significant?

A: No (Burge:196).

The prosecution also probed Burge about an exchange during Michael McDermott's testimony about the interrogation of Shadeed Mu'min.

Q: Is there anything you did with Shadeed Mu'min that Michael [Mcdermott]—that someone, a reasonable person—could have misconstrued as you putting plastic over his face?

A: I don't believe so. But I did have the ability to observe his testimony, and I have known Mike for a long time, and I have a very high opinion of him, and he appeared, appeared to me, to be terribly distraught and under great pressure at the time he testified.

Q: And that's because there is a big code of silence within the Chicago Police Department, isn't there?

A: Not to my knowledge, sir.

Q: You have heard of that term, correct?

A: ... Yeah, I have heard it from a bottom-feeding lawyer (Burge:246–247).

Burge quickly added, "No inference to you, sir."

Undeterred, the prosecution continued, "Have you ever reported any Chicago police officer for abusing someone's rights?" Burge answered: "I have never had the occasion arise." The prosecution then asked, "Sir, are you familiar with Detective Frank Laverty?" and then asked, "Detective Laverty created a problem at Area 2, isn't that correct?" Defense counsel jumped to his feet: "Your honor, objection. We're going to need a sidebar" (Burge:247–248).

A Sidebar about Street Files and the Code of Silence

The mention of Frank Laverty caused a stir in the courtroom. Judge Lefkow (Burge:248) turned to the courtroom onlookers to say: "Just a Minute . . . Ladies and Gentlemen, there will be no talking in the courtroom." It seems likely from what followed that some in the courtroom recognized the name of Frank Laverty. In 1985, Laverty had received an award from a police watchdog group, Citizens Alert.

Detective Laverty had clashed with Burge in a case that revealed the police kept secret "street files" containing evidence they withheld from defense counsel, a practice that spoke to the charge of obstruction of justice. Realizing the contentiousness of the issue, and that it was late on a Friday afternoon, Judge Lefkow dismissed the jury for the weekend and began the sidebar discussion.

The secret existence of the street files became known through Detective Laverty's investigation of an Area 2 rape case involving an African American police officer's son, George Jones, who was falsely accused and convicted of rape (Meisner 2016). Laverty had uncovered exculpatory evidence in his investigation of the case. Two detectives, James Houtsma and Victor Tosello, had confronted Laverty and accused him of "messing up their case." According to Laverty, Tosello responded by threatening to "blow him away" (Meisner 2016).

Laverty reported his findings to Assistant State's Attorney Lawrence Hyman, among others, and he assumed this would lead to a dismissal of the case. Instead, he discovered in a radio report that the case had resulted in a conviction. Laverty contacted the defense lawyers and presented his exculpatory testimony at what was intended to be a sentencing hearing. The result was not only dismissal of the case, but also the revelation that Laverty's letter and evidence remained in a street file that was never transmitted to the state's attorney's office or defense counsel. George Jones was exonerated and was the plaintiff in a later civil suit resulting in an $800,000 verdict against the city and eleven police officers.

A follow-up investigation revealed that many other street files, beyond those involving George Jones, had been withheld. An appellate court declared this practice unconstitutional. In a sworn deposition, Laverty reported he had told Jon Burge the case was "screwed up" and that he therefore had let Jones' attorneys know this. Burge responded by punishing Laverty: " . . . You're working afternoons and . . . nobody is going to work with you and the state's attorneys aren't going to approve charges on your cases, and you're going to be dumped as a detective." Laverty was then transferred to an administrative section of the department (Meisner 2016). Officer Byrd would also provide a sworn statement, discussed further below, describing how Burge had further humiliated Laverty at Area 2 with the apparent purpose of punishing his violation of the code of silence (Taylor 2019:52–53).

After hearing a brief sidebar synopsis of the Laverty case, the judge was clearly coming to a conclusion. The prosecutors—Betsy Biffl, April Perry, and David Weisman—made their final plea.

> Ms. Biffl: This witness [Burge] has personal information that goes to the atmosphere in Area 2. He [Burge] is the one that volunteered—he wanted to run his mouth about McDermott and feeling the pressure. This is relevant to that comment.
> Ms. Perry: . . . It is a classic opening the door (259).

The defense counsel— Marc Martin and William Gamboney—argued, in response, that it was a door that should not be opened.

> MR. MARTIN: It is opening the door—we objected to the question.
> THE COURT: Is this a door we want to open?
> MR. GAMBONEY: And then we're going to—I suspect Jon Burge is going to deny that he ever did anything like that . . . I mean, *it is just inflaming the issue . . .*
> THE COURT: Well, he's under pressure too.
> MR. WEISMAN: And that is true, your honor . . .
> MR. MARTIN: *And that is impeachment on a collateral matter,* Judge.
> MS. PERRY: *It is not collateral. This guy had a stranglehold over Area 2 and what people were allowed to say and what they weren't and what he was allowed to say and what he felt like he should —*
> MR. MARTIN: What did Laverty have to do with it?
> MS. PERRY: *Which is what this entire trial is all about.*
> THE COURT: . . . I want to step back from this and think it through myself so we'll take a five-minute break (259–260; emphasis added).

When the sidebar reconvened, Judge Lefkow said she had decided this was a "collateral matter" and therefore not directly relevant to the perjury and obstruction charges. She explained her decision this way:

> All right. Well, I think this is a very close question. And as I understand what Mr. Weisman is saying it impeaches the denial about the code of silence, and I would concede that it probably does. But it is, you know, highly prejudicial for the defense, I think, and would open an area of inquiry that could easily open up some collateral issues. So I'm going to sustain the objection to this line of testimony (260–261, emphasis added).

The prosecution quickly regrouped by requesting—since it was Friday afternoon—that it be allowed to prepare a brief over the weekend with short "alternative-type" questions that would "not go down the road" of collateral issues.

The key issue, of course, was the judge's ruling against probing the code of silence and the prosecution's view that this code was not collateral but central to the case of showing how Burge covered up racial torture in Chicago's Area 2. However, deferring to the authority of the judge, the prosecution now proposed to ask instead about a "trait of character," arguing from a well-known rule in the federal statutes. The prosecution argued that character trait was put at issue when Burge testified that he was "a responsible good supervisor as a police officer, that he maintained good gun handling practices with respect of Shadeed Mu'min . . . " (Burge:266). This assertion contradicted a sworn statement from Officer Doris Byrd (see below) that Burge had mocked Laverty in front of other detectives with his drawn weapon.

The result, when court reconvened, was a quick volley of questions from the prosecution.

> Q: At some point during that four or five months [when Laverty worked under Burge], did you un-holster your gun when Frank Laverty was in the room with you?
> A: Not to my knowledge, no, sir.
> Q: Did you point the gun at Frank Laverty?
> A: No, sir.
> Q: Isn't it true that you said "Pow" or "Bang" pointing the gun at the back of Frank Laverty's head?
> A: Said "Pow" or "Bang"?
> Q: Yes, sir.
> A: No, Sir (Burge:276–277).

Sounds of the Sidebar Silencing

What the jurors and the courtroom observers could not know was that Judge Lefkow's sidebar had allowed the preceding questions and Burge's denial while simultaneously disallowing questions about their meaning in terms of the code of silence. Her justification was that questions about the code of silence would have been "collateral" and in this sense "prejudicial" to assessing the charges against Burge.

The jurors and courtroom observers also could not have known that, in the sidebar, Judge Lefkow acknowledged that allowing introduction of evidence about the code of silence was a "very close question." The jurors and observers additionally could not have known that six years earlier, Officer Byrd had given a sworn statement to Flint Taylor about Burge's imposed code of silence in Area 2 (Byrd 2004). This sworn statement supported the prosecution's argument about Frank Laverty and the code of silence.

> Byrd: One day we were in the room and Laverty was in there looking for a file. And when he left out the room, Burge drew his weapon and pointed it at the back of Laverty and said, 'Bang.'
> Taylor: Was that a message? Did you take that as a message about what would happen if police officers came forward and broke the code of silence and exposed police misconduct?
> Byrd: Yes.

Yet the prosecution did not introduce this sworn statement in the Burge perjury trial. To have done so would presumably have been futile and an overt challenge to Judge Lefkow's authority.

It is also important to note the weakness of the defense objections to introducing such evidence in a perjury case. Introducing an excessive number of gruesome crime scenes photos is often regarded as "prejudicial" or "inflammatory" in cases of criminal violence, but this case simply involved Byrd's testimony of Burge's use of a single spoken word. And since the code of silence is widely regarded as central to the problem of obtaining truthful police testimony, it is difficult to regard Byrd's description of the Laverty incident as "collateral" to the question of Burge's truthfulness. As Perry said in the sidebar, it is, "what this entire trial is all about."

Had Perry been allowed, she could have emphasized that the direct relevance of the code of silence was in relation to the role of Andrew Wilson in the Burge case. It was, as Flint Taylor noted, Laverty who had initially taken Wilson into custody.

> By February 12, the investigation had zeroed in on a group of young men who lived close to the murder scene. A contingent of Area 2 detectives, including Frank Laverty . . . went to the men's house and took six of them into custody. Laverty was about to transport them to Area 2 when Burge approached him and directed him to relinquish custody because Burge intended to take them to police headquarters at 11th and State for interrogation . . . Laverty pointedly told his boss that, 'He's cuffed, he ain't hurt, he ain't been touched' . . . Burge scowled at Laverty and went off with a few trusted detectives and the captured suspects to 11th and State . . . (Taylor 2020:36).

Laverty was also important in the consideration of Wilson's tortured confession and its exclusion from his 1982 retrial.

In the retrial, Jon Burge informed the court that all the notes and a memo resulting from the manhunt leading to the arrest of Wilson had been destroyed. The face sheets from twenty-five street files were found, but not their contents. The destruction of this "street file evidence" played a major role in the Illinois Supreme Court's exclusion of Wilson's confession as evidence for his retrial [People v. Wilson 1987)]. Consideration of this evidence built on Laverty's exposure a year earlier of the withheld street file in the George Jones case (Taylor 2019:66, 71). Destruction of files was an *ongoing* practice in Burge's supervision of Area 2, and it was therefore of central importance with regard to the charges of perjury and obstruction against Burge.

Burge's involvement in the George Jones case and the repeated mention of Frank Laverty's name may indirectly have raised questions in the jurors' minds; especially if they were aware of the Jones case and his exoneration, the $800,000 civil case verdict, and the secret street files that were exposed by this case, followed by the appellate court decision disallowing concealment of these files by police. Yet, the prosecution could not *directly state in court* that the code of silence was at the heart of this case. *The code of silence was buried in the sidebar beyond the hearing of the jury and courtroom observers.*

The disturbance in the courtroom in response to the mention of Frank Laverty's name suggested awareness among onlookers of the Jones case. The *Chicago Tribune* had published a series of articles about the debacle of the George Jones mistrial, concluding that the police and prosecution had engaged in "deliberate misconduct" (Conroy 1990b). A juror from the Jones trial was later quoted in the *Chicago Lawyer* as saying, "I was amazed at how lackadaisical the police and the State's attorneys were about everything" (cited in Bogira 2005:166). The awkwardness of the sidebar conducted beyond the jurors' hearing, and the abbreviated questioning about Laverty allowed when court reconvened, in combination with the above memories of the Jones case, likely renewed and perpetuated legal cynicism among the jurors, courtroom onlookers, and others connected directly or indirectly to the Chicago Police torture case.

Lawrence Ralph (2020: Part II) has emphasized the marginality of African American police officers who worked under Burge in Area 2, and their need to navigate around him. Ralph argued, "by paying attention to their marginality, you can better see the entire government structure that allows torture to take place" (59). Ralph highlighted the experience of William Parker, a Black officer, who, in the company of a group of detectives at Area 2, heard the screams of a suspect in an adjoining room. When Parker opened the door to the room, he saw the suspect chained to a red hot radiator, whimpering and pleading to Jon Burge for mercy. Burge ordered Parker to leave, telling him the situation was "none of his business." When Parker returned to the adjoining room, he found the detectives just as he had left them: glued to their typewriters and busily ignoring the situation. Within the year, Parker was transferred to another precinct and demoted. It was a graphic portrayal of how the code of silence operated and was enforced at Area 2 by Jon Burge.

As we noted earlier, Doris Byrd had candidly explained that, like other Black officers in Area 2, she had taken Laverty's treatment as a warning. Ralph went on to explain: "when your minority status marginalizes you and makes you different, the ambitions of others [e.g., Jon Burge] can put you in a horrible bind" (64). This led to a defensive strategy, as described by Ralph:

> Whenever you got wind that the A Team was on the verge of giving a criminal suspect the "Vietnamese treatment," you hit the street to pursue leads, or you took your paperwork home . . . You . . . came up with a name for this willful circumvention: 'the ostrich approach' . . . You . . . became experts in burying your heads in the sand, seeing and not seeing, learning to know what not to know (78–79).

Ralph's analysis suggests that what at first might seem like a "bottom up," heads in the sand, or "ostrich approach," is actually better understood as a "top-down" marginalized minority adaptation to the vagaries of a legal system that did not have the interests of either Black suspects or Black officers at heart. If there is an "ostrich approach" in this story, it is likely the top-down, "close decision" by the judge to exclude testimony about the ongoing code of silence that Burge enforced at Area 2.

The case of William Parker illustrated that openly challenging Burge's code of silence was a losing proposition. What was needed was a system that could protect whistleblowers like Parker and others and allow them to give voice to their complaints. The secrecy of judicial sidebars added another layer that was now hiding the problem from public view. Circumvention by concerned but marginalized officers was a predictable result.

The Court Room Workgroup, Silent Signals, and Missing Questions

As Burge's testimony ended, the prosecution asked if he had noticed anything missing in the court reporter's transcription of Andrew Wilson's confession. Burge said no. The question anticipated testimony from a court reporter, Mike Hartnett. Hartnett worked closely with the felony review unit in the state's attorney's office and he played a key role in transcribing confession statements.

Hartnett received a call from the head of the felony review unit, Larry Hyman, on the day of Andrew Wilson's interrogation. Hartnett arrived at about ten that morning. The timing was significant because Wilson had already been interrogated and had given a preliminary statement. However, as noted earlier, when Hyman entered the picture, Wilson unexpectedly complained that he had been tortured. Hyman immediately had Wilson removed from his presence (Taylor 2019:40).

At about six that evening, after Hartnett had taken statements from two other people, Hyman asked him to assist in taking a confession from Andrew Wilson. Hyman likely knew Wilson had been tortured in between, although Hartnett did not indicate this in his testimony. Neither Hyman nor Hartnett were likely in the habit of asking questions or looking for problems. Hartnett's answers to questions about his work in Area 2 suggested he was a compliant participant in what law enforcement researchers call the "courtroom work group" (Eisenstein and Jacob 1977). For example, Hartnett's answer to prosecution questions about transcribing confessions revealed his understanding that his role as a court reporter was directly connected to the Cook County States Attorney's Office.

> Q: Okay. Would the state's attorney's office have had the ability to let you go if they were unhappy with your performance?
> A: I would assume so, yes.
> Q: Okay. And at the state's attorney's office, you took direction from them, correct? It wasn't some external office that gave you assignments.
> A: Right.
> Q: Okay. So I assume you got to know the assistant state's attorneys fairly well, especially the ones in felony review (Hartnett:31).

This last question obviously included Larry Hyman. But more importantly, it included Area 2's Jon Burge. Hartnett was familiar enough with Burge to refer to him by first name.

> Q: How well would you say that you knew him?
> A: ... Jon was pleasant. Walk in, he'd always say hello, see if you wanted coffee or what not (31).

Thus, Hartnett was a familiar link between Area 2 and the state's attorney's office.

> Q: You were actually assigned specifically to this case, the investigation involving the murder of the two police officers, is that right?
> A: I was.
> Q: ... Was that because they needed somebody to be on call for that case?
> A: I think so, because of the nature of the case, and they said you are assigned to the case.
> Q: All right. And was that indicative of the seriousness with which the investigation was being taken?
> A: I would think so, yes (37–38).

Hartnett seemed to understand how important this case was to the state's attorney's office and the courtroom leadership group of Area 2.

Harnett's testimony focused on the way in which Wilson's confession was taken and how this varied from normal procedure.

> Q: And did every statement [in a standard confession] start with the reading of Miranda rights?
> A: Well, somewhere in the beginning. Usually they set the stage where we were and what not first ....
> Q: And was there a standard ending to all statements as well?
> A: Usually there was, yes.
> Q: Okay. And that was to ask the person if their statement had been taken voluntarily, is that right?
> A: Correct (34).

The prosecution was establishing that voluntariness was a standard closing element of a confession statement. But the Wilson brothers were handled differently. The prosecution asked Hartnett to explain in sequence how voluntariness was and was not addressed in three statements he took that day at Area 2 from Jackie Wilson, Derrick Martin, and Andrew Wilson. Jackie Wilson came first.

> Q: All right. And when you took the statement of Jackie Wilson ... do you recall whether he was asked at the end of his statement whether it had been given voluntarily?
> A: I'd have to look again to see if it is ....
> A: I don't see it on Jackie's. It would usually be near the end.
> Q: Right. And he wasn't asked anything about is this voluntary, was he?

> A: No (54–55).

The prosecution reiterated that the three statements were taken in sequence, on the same day, and all under the direction of Larry Hyman. It then asked about Derrick Martin.

> Q: You took the statement of Derrick Martin between the statements of Jackie Wilson and Andrew Wilson, correct?
> A: Yes.
> Q: Okay. So on—do you see in Derrick Martin's statements whether he was asked if he was giving that statement voluntarily?
> A: Yes. On Page 17.
> Q: Okay. Now you said that you—now, he was just a witness, correct? He wasn't a suspect?
> A: Correct . . .
> Q: But Larry Hyman asked this witness if his statement was given voluntarily, didn't he?
> A: Yes (55–56).

Andrew Wilson's statement was last in the sequence.

> Q: Now, I'm going to show you Andrew Wilson's statement, which I'll mark Government Exhibit 28.
> A: Thank you.
> Q: And I'll ask you to look at that and tell us if he was asked if that statement was given voluntarily.
> A: No (56).

The missing voluntariness question in the confession statements of the Wilson brothers under the direction of Hyman was an important issue throughout the thirty-year cover-up of the torture scandal.

The prosecution reinforced the importance of failing to ask about voluntariness by asking Hartnett about being called in cases seeking to suppress admission of coerced confessions.

> Q: You were sometimes called to testify in motions to suppress, is that right?
> A: Yes . . .
> Q: And you were called to testify about the circumstances of the interview, correct?
> A: That is correct.
> Q: And that the person had been read their rights, correct?
> A: Yes.

> Q: And were you asked about whether they appeared injured or not during the hearings?
> A: Yes.
> Q: And whether they had been asked about the voluntariness of the interview, is that right?
> A: Correct (36–37).

Specifying, "whether they appeared injured," of course, was to connect the issue of voluntariness to concerns about torture and coercion.

It is conceivable that failing to ask about voluntariness could be accidental, rather than intentional, and so the prosecution explicitly asked about "forgetfulness."

> Q: Did you ever point out to an assistant state attorney, hey, you forgot to ask him this or you didn't include the voluntary part? Did you ever do that?
> A: If an attorney forgot one of the rights, I would stop writing on my court reporter machine, and then we'd have to start all over.
> Q: So was that sort of a silent signal to them?
> A: Yes.
> Q: Now, how about at the end when they would go through the questions about the voluntariness? Did you do the same thing that you would stop if they had missed those?
> A: No.
> Q: What was the difference there?
> A: Well, the difference with the rights is if they forgot one of the rights, it was automatic, you were supposed to stop because the alleged defendant was supposed to be given their Miranda rights (35–36).

There were, of course, additional reasons to believe that the failure to ask about voluntariness was a serious problem in the Wilson brothers' cases. Just how problematic was suggested in the lengths Hyman went to avoid testifying about his handling of the Wilson brother cases. Like the detectives in Area 2, Hyman sought refuge in taking the Fifth Amendment.

John Conroy (2006) wrote a scathing article for the *Chicago Reader* about Hyman's role in the Wilson case. It coincided with the 1990 Office of Professional Standards report and the 2006 special prosecutor report that concluded Andrew Wilson had been tortured in Burge's Area 2. Conroy (2003) observed that Hyman would have known what the state's attorney's leadership group, specifically RM Daley and Richard Devine, knew about the mistreatment of Andrew Wilson and the failure to include the voluntariness questions in the statements taken from the Wilson brothers. Hyman left Area 2 in the late afternoon after taking statements from Jackie Wilson and Derrick Martin, and before returning to take the statement from Andrew Wilson. Had he gone to consult with Daley and Devine?

Conroy (2007) reported, in a separate article, that *The Reader* surveyed fourteen defense lawyers who, collectively, had more than 200 years of experience trying over 900 murders. The survey asked the lawyers if they had ever observed a prosecutor similarly fail to ask the voluntariness questions. None reported that they had. The unaddressed question in the 2006 special prosecutor's report was whether Hyman would have decided to omit questions about the voluntariness of Wilson's confession without advice from the top of the chain of command in the state's attorney's office.

The prosecution closed its questioning of Hartnett by asking his attitude about a suspicious injury he had observed on Wilson's face.

> Q: You testified previously, did you not, that he [Andrew] said, that you said it looked like he's been roughed up on that side of his face. Do you remember testifying to that in the grand jury?
> A: Yes, right on the side, correct.
> Q: So given that he looked like he'd been roughed up or popped on the right side, did you take a photograph of the right side of his face? ...
> A: No, I took one straight ahead. ....
> Q: And you weren't particularly concerned with whether Andrew Wilson had been roughed up, were you?
> A: Not after what he told me, no, ma'am.
> Q: And, in fact, you told the grand jury that you didn't give a damn what happened to Andrew Wilson, didn't you?
> A: That's correct (50–51).

The prosecution closed its cross examination of Hartnett with a series of telling questions:

> Q: And you agree that it's unusual that at the end of the statement that Andrew Wilson was not asked if he'd been treated well?
> A: I do.
> Q: You agree it's routine to ask those questions.
> A: Yes.
> Q: And yet did you say anything to Larry, 'Hey, you forgot to ask him if it was voluntary?'
> A: No.
> Q: Did you say, 'Hey, it looks like he's been roughed up? Shouldn't we ask those questions?'
> A: No.
> Q: And you didn't go out and ask Lieutenant Burge, 'Hey, do you know what happened to him because he looks like he's been popped, and I don't want any problems with the statement?'
> A: No.

> Q: You just did your thing and typed it up, right?
> A: I did my job and left, yes (58–59).

The prosecution took one more opportunity to hammer home this point in a brief re-cross examination.

> Q: … you see an injury on him, he doesn't speak up, so you just keep your head down and type, right?
> A: Yes.
> Q: And if you'd given a damn about him, maybe you would have asked something, right?
> A: I've never asked in any case.
> Q: Okay. You just keep you head down, don't you?
> A: I just do my job, yes, ma'am (67).

From the perspective of the courtroom workgroup, doing your job, for many of the people involved in this case, meant observing the code of silence. The question left hanging over this trial was whether the code of silence not only reinforced a regime of racial torture, but furthermore reinforced the influence of RM Daley's law from the top to the very bottom of the justice system.

"What Was This Case About?"

The City of Chicago and the Fraternal Order of Police paid millions of dollars to defend Jon Burge, and the price tag, which also included civil court settlements and defense lawyer fees, just kept growing. When the Chicago business publication *Crain's* (Daniels 2018) calculated these expenses for the period from 2010 to 2016, it came to nearly a half billion dollars. The carrying costs of the resulting debt is a monetary reminder that this history is deep and long-lasting. What led the city to invest so heavily in defending and settling police torture cases? Indeed, in its summation, the prosecution asked, "What was this case about?"

The Burge case was obviously about more than lying in a 2003 civil case. For the prosecution, the point was to convict and punish gruesome acts of racism that, for decades, had been far more apparent to Blacks than to Whites in Chicago. In a discussion of race in America, Eduardo Bonilla-Silva (1997) emphasized that, over time, American racial subordination has become less overtly and directly racist and is now often more covert and indirect; however, the Burge torture regime and the cases described in the following Epilogue are a reminder of the limits to which this is true. As Bonilla-Silva noted: "The unchanging element is that Blacks' life chances are significantly lower than those of Whites, and ultimately a racialized social order is distinguished by this difference in life chances" (470). The Burge torture regime dramatically demonstrated how elements of an American racialized social system continued to damage the lives of Black Americans in Chicago.

Prosecuting Burge for perjury could never have sufficiently addressed the scale of the inter-sectional race and gender specific consequences of Chicago police torture, even if this was the best and maybe the only way to convict Jon Burge of a crime. In 2011, the court sentenced Burge to four and a half years in prison. He was released three years later, even though many of his torture victims were still languishing on death row.

Were the charges of perjury and obstruction of justice really the only possibilities given the five-year state statute of limitations for torture? We have argued that a more useful description of the criminality and its thirty-year cover-up was as a code of silence that enabled racist torture. For the purposes of developing a social scientific understanding of its causes and effects, this description of Burge's crime is far more useful than its legal designation.

Our analysis suggests that the cover-up of the Burge crimes was a top-down result of a code of silence among high-ranking city officials, police department officers, and detectives, and the efforts of courtroom actors to maintain that code and protect its practitioners. This code enabled the Burge regime's use of racist torture as an ongoing part of RM Daley's three decades of law and order politics in Chicago. This code was—and still is—a key instrument in the toolkit that enforced exclusion and containment of Chicago's hyper-segregated South and West Side African American communities (Hagan, McCarthy, and Herda 2018). And it is a quintessential illustration of how the legally cynical consequences of iron-fisted repression live on in this American city where, in James Baldwin's words, "history is not the past."

This chapter has demonstrated how the law, as implemented through court structure and practices and judicial rulings, is a powerful instrument in an enforcement arsenal used to reinforce and perpetuate exclusion and containment of African Americans. In cases like these, judges simultaneously reinforce police actions that conceal, permit, and perpetuate practices such as racist torture and brutality. In this case, this was done by the judicial refusal to allow the prosecution to ask crucial witnesses questions that would have shown how Jon Burge divided Area 2 detectives along lines of race and developed a White "A Team" of officers who targeted Black suspects for purposes of extracting confessions. A narrow judicial interpretation of perjury and obstruction of justice left little room for prosecutors to bring forward evidence of how a code of silence enabled a thirty-year cover-up of the torture of more than a hundred African American suspects.

Even Black officers assigned to the Area 2 station house that Jon Burge dominated, such as Doris Byrd, who ultimately provided sworn testimony outside of court about Burge's torture tactics and his imposition of a code of silence, were left without the opportunity to be heard in the Burge trial. The judge who ruled against development of this line of testimony confined the prosecution's arguments about the code of silence imposed by Jon Burge in Area 2 to the secrecy of a courtroom sidebar. This was a top-down judicial imposition of courtroom control—an illustration of how top-down law enforcement stimulates and facilitates policies and practices that breed legal cynicism in affected populations. The central role of sidebar secrecy effectively prevented a lengthy trial, and it allowed the resulting judgment to obscure the essence of the Burge case as a historic illustration of how racial brutality and torture are perpetuated by a systemic code of silence in a quintessentially American law enforcement setting. And it provided little or no encouragement for marginalized minority officers to challenge a racially brutalized code of silence where and when they encountered it.

The final dialogue cited in this chapter, between a persistent prosecutor and an uncaring and cynical court reporter, further illustrates how racism can be mobilized in a tightly coupled criminal justice system. It is a system that, in this instance, included a courtroom workgroup that others have argued stretched all the way from Area 2's Jon Burge to the elected and appointed occupants at the top of the Cook County state's attorney's and Chicago's mayor's offices (Conroy 2006; Taylor 2019).

One of the many consequences of the use of torture by Burge and other police officers, and its cover-up by Chicago officials, was to reinforce legal cynicism in minority neighborhoods. In these settings, legal cynicism reflects a collective understanding of a general orientation of the police, and the legal system more broadly, toward Black lives and neighborhoods. This orientation ranges from general disinterest and neglect to hyper-surveillance, intimidation, mistreatment, and, in some cases, fatal violence. This mistreatment has a long history that is inextricably bound to racial segregation, exclusion, and containment. It is a history that persists to this day as a living part of Chicago and its place as a quintessential American city.

The City Settles for Silence

One of the many disappointing aspects of the Jon Burge trial was its failure to address, in legal terms, the connection between Burge and RM Daley. As we noted in Chapter Six, U.S. Attorney Patrick Fitzgerald publicly alluded to the connection between Burge and top officials in Chicago's law enforcement hierarchy. He said that although the 2006 Special Prosecutor's Report had revealed little new information, it could nonetheless "provide the pry bar" leading to new trials, for example, "for civil rights violations, violations of the RICO statute, and possibly perjury." His reference to the RICO statute—with its focus on conspiracy, corruption, and racketeering—implied legal avenues that Fitzgerald, as a Department of Justice U.S. Attorney, could pursue against RM Daley. However, following the Burge trial, Fitzgerald left the U.S. Attorney's office for private practice, and his successor did not pursue these possibilities.

In 2007, two cases increased pressure on Daley, and there was speculation he would not run for a seventh term. In one case, Chicago's city council agreed to a $19.8 million settlement with four Black inmates—Madison Hobley, Stanley Howard, Aaron Patterson, and Leroy Orange—who had been pardoned from death row. The plaintiffs had sought to have Daley deposed as a material witness, but he was able to evade the deposition when city council agreed to the nearly $20 million dollar settlement. In a second case, Flint Taylor and the People's Law Office had joined with Locke Bowman (of the MacArthur Justice Center at Northwestern Law School) in introducing a 73-page civil rights conspiracy motion to include Daley as a defendant in a torture case involving Darrell Cannon as the plaintiff. Cannon had confessed to a crime he did not commit after being tortured. He spent twenty-four years in prison before being exonerated.

Taylor and Bowman represented Cannon in a lawsuit against Burge, his superiors, Richard Devine, and the City of Chicago. They later amended the suit to include Daley and Jane Byrne. Daley was added because of his conduct, both as state's attorney and as mayor, in the conspiracy to cover up torture, while former mayor Jane Byrne was included because of her support for the lawless Wilson manhunt (Taylor 2020:365). The motion was ultimately dismissed, but Taylor and Bowman refused to end their pursuit to bring Daley and others to justice.

Daley was also in trouble on other fronts. The 2008 financial crisis created intense budget pressures, and by 2009 Daley's polling numbers were plummeting. Daley's reputation was badly tarnished by the Hired Truck Scandal discussed in the prologue to this book, and he was now at the center of a follow-up scandal involving a seventy-five-year, $1.157 billion dollar lease to a private company of the city's 36,000 parking meters. The city's inspector general, appointed by Daley, issued a highly critical analysis of the lease, emphasizing the city's failure to carefully analyze its costs as well as its benefits. The lease was an ill-considered scheme to solve the city's short-term budget problems associated with the exploding 2008 financial crisis involving subprime housing loans on Chicago's South Side discussed in Chapter Four. The inspector general's report concluded that the parking meter system was actually worth far more than the lease would pay over its seventy-five-year term. It was a misguided effort to temporarily cover the Daley era's growing budget crisis.

Daley's financial scandals were driving his declining popularity with White Chicago voters. In the fall of 2010, Daley accepted the inevitable and announced he would not seek re-election in 2011. His planned departure from the mayor's office did not, however, deter Taylor and Bowman in their efforts to spotlight his role in the torture scandal. Their next opportunity to do this involved another torture victim case, with Michael Tillman as the plaintiff. Tillman had been exonerated after serving nearly thirty years on death row on the basis of a tortured confession. In 2011, the Tillman case was heard by District Court Judge Rebecca Pallmeyer. In 2011, Pallmeyer dramatically broke new ground by filing a decision that placed Daley at center stage as a defendant. Pallmeyer's decision was particularly threatening because it alleged Daley's central role in the three-decade code of silence that had concealed the racial torture tactics of Jon Burge.

Judge Pallmeyer's decision cogently summarized Tillman's case. She wrote: "[The] plaintiff alleges that, as mayor and state's attorney, Defendant Richard Daley had personal knowledge of the alleged abuses perpetrated by Burge and other Defendants at Area 2. (Taylor 2020:444). She added:

> [the] plaintiff also alleges that Daley, against the advice of his senior advisors, 'personally insisted' throughout his tenure that the City of Chicago continue to finance the defense of Burge . . . and other Area 2 detectives, despite his personal knowledge that Burge committed acts of torture.

Judge Pallmeyer's inclusion of Daley as a defendant was a breakthrough that threatened to overcome previous obstacles to his accountability.

For all apparent intents and purposes, Daley appeared to finally have become a lame duck incumbent of the mayor's office. And, as he likely feared, Judge Pallmeyer's 2011 addition of Daley as a defendant in the Tillman case provided further opportunity to press for another embarrassingly painful deposition, which Judge Pallmeyer now moved to schedule.

In May 2011, Daley attended his last city council meeting. A few weeks later, Rahm Emanuel, his still loyal protégé and now successor, was inaugurated as the new mayor of Chicago. Daley had played a major role in Emanuel's career, and, once in office, Emanuel indicated his openness to settling the Tillman case. Just as Daley had used the city's coffers to pay for the defense of Burge and others, Emanuel was now opening the same dwindling coffers to settle the threat posed to defendant Daley by the Tillman case. The terms of the settlement were substantial, $5.37 million, and Tillman, who had suffered the tortured confession that led to his decades in prison, was anxious to reach an agreement. This agreement included no apology—much less a confession—from the former mayor, and Daley was now also off the hook for a new deposition.

In the American system of justice, lawyers are ethically obliged to honor the wishes of those they represent, and Michael Tillman was in much the same position as many of Taylor's earlier clients who had passed this way before him. He wanted a quick settlement, not a protracted trial. Judge Pallmeyer had rendered the semblance of a judgment by including Daley as a defendant in the Tillman case, and enumerating the abundance of reasons why. So when the city council finally approved Tillman's settlement in July 2012, Taylor made sure to arrange an opportunity for Tillman to address the press and emphasize RM Daley's culpability. In Michael Tillman's (2012) well-chosen words:

> If he had done what he should have, I would not have been tortured, lived with the fear of the death penalty, or sent to prison. To me, this settlement proves that Daley, Jon Burge, and Burge's torture crew did me terribly wrong.

Tillman was clearly morally right, but Daley was left with an opening to still dubiously claim that he had not been legally found "criminally wrong." What does this say about our system of justice?

Daley's evasion of prosecution and punishment for his central role in the Burge torture scandal is consistent with a key hypothesis of this book: the law operates with a light touch for those in the upper reaches of the social hierarchy, characteristically concealing as much or more than it reveals, and leaving legal cynicism abundant room to flourish.

Epilogue: 16 Shots—Front and Back

The Chicago police torture that lies at the heart of this book took place during the 1970s through the 1990s. Many of the people responsible for it are dead or no longer at the center of Chicago politics. In 2010, Richard M. Daley announced he would step down after almost a quarter-century as mayor of Chicago, and in 2018 Jon Burge died. Yet abuse by Chicago police and the role of politicians in obscuring this abuse did not end with these events. Instead, as we show below, it persists, adding to Chicago's historical reputation as a racially treacherous "City on the Make" (Algren 1951). Police abuse, particularly of Blacks and other racial and ethnic minorities, is part of this city's present as well as its past.

The Shooting of Laquan McDonald

In 2012, Rahm Emanuel succeeded Richard M. Daley as mayor of Chicago. Vestiges of the Daley regime were already apparent in Emanuel's first term—most notably in his response to the 2014 shooting of seventeen-year-old Laquan McDonald. The police report described the shooting as justifiable because McDonald refused to drop a knife he was carrying (Mitchell 2014). Press reports based on police-provided information reported an officer shot McDonald in the chest (Futterman and Kalven 2014). Yet the Cook County Medical Examiner found multiple bullet wounds to McDonald's front and back and declared his death a homicide (Mitchell 2014). Emanuel refused to release a police dash-cam video of the shooting, leading to charges of a cover-up and calls for his resignation.

A Police Execution

The killing was a video-recorded police execution. It was one more in a long list of assaults and killings of Black residents by White police officers, a pattern consistent with our exclusion-containment theory and resulting legal cynicism in Chicago's South and West Side neighborhoods. Mayor Emanuel was obviously worried about the explosive political repercussions of a video showing a brazen police killing in the presence of more than a half-dozen onlooking officers. He was nearing a 2015 re-election battle and subsequent runoff against Latinx opponent "Chuy" Garcia.

Emanuel won the runoff. Six months later a Cook County judge ordered the release of the video: Emanuel finally relented, Officer Jason Van Dyke was charged with murder, and three of Van Dyke's fellow officers were charged with covering up the killing with false witness statements (Smith 2019). Emanuel's handling of the killing had markings of the same kind of code of silence and cover-up that characterized RM Daley's law and order regime.

The police initially labeled McDonald's death a legitimate use of force (Macek 2016). A Fraternal Order of Police spokesperson immediately rushed to the murder scene and claimed McDonald, armed with a knife, had lunged at officers and that the offiers were "forced to defend themselves" (Ford 2014). The concealed video would eventually show the opposite: McDonald had veered away from the officers while holding a knife that was only three inches long. Police Superintendent Gary McCarthy nonetheless insisted that the officers faced "a dangerous situation" and could have been killed during the incident (Goodman 2019; Zorn 2018a). Emanuel initially backed Superintendent McCarthy, but when the withheld video went public, it undermined McCarthy's claim and Emanuel fired him.

The first call to release the video came from University of Chicago law school Professor Craig Futterman and *Invisible Institute* journalist Jamie Kalven (2014). They explained that "CPD policy requires officers to activate their in-car cameras when in pursuit" and added that "It's also possible that surveillance cameras at the Burger King on the northwest corner . . . captured relevant footage." Kalven would go on to produce an award-winning documentary about the McDonald case, *16 Shots*, with director Richard Rowley (Goodman 2019; Zorn 2018b).

Mary Mitchell (2014) published an early column in the *Chicago Sun-Times*, building on Futterman and Kalven's piece and drawing attention to the litany of killings by police. She captured the moment saying, "The only thing that separates the 17-year-old [Laquan McDonald] from Staten Island's Eric Garner and Ferguson's Michael Brown is geography." She quoted Futterman's take on the video: "We're being told that there is a video being kept under lock and key of the young man being shot down like a dog in the street." Adam Collins, handling questions from City Hall, reported that the shooting was being investigated by the Independent Police Review Authority [IPRA], which appeared less than independent when it was revealed that it was in regular email communication with City Hall.

Mitchell (2016) recognized the importance of both the murder of McDonald and the refusal to release the police video: "Indeed, it is eerily ironic this case is unfolding in Chicago—the city where Mamie Till Mobley made the ultimate sacrifice by allowing the world to see what hatred did to her son. A young black male unjustifiably killed by police is the Emmett Till of our time." "Allowing the world to see" must have been exactly what Emanuel feared most: a visual record of the gruesome murder of this seventeen-year-old Black youth in a city that was so racially divided.

As in the Daley and Burge case, there was a fundamental question: Would responsibility lead all the way to the top, in this case to Emanuel as mayor, or would it stop at lower levels? Emanuel fired Police Superintendent Gary McCarthy (Zorn 2018a) and did not actively campaign for Cook County State's Attorney Anita Alvarez's re-election. Alvarez was defeated in a primary challenge by Kim Fox—the first African American elected state's attorney in Cook County. Like Daley before him, Emanuel would later use the power of his position to arrange for his own more dignified departure by announcing he would not seek re-election in 2018.

Emanuel Continues to Withhold the Video and Negotiates a Settlement

Following his successful 2015 runoff election, Emanuel continued his refusal to release the video. Instead, like Daley, he used the power of his office to commit city funds, which critics called "hush money," to divert attention from his refusal to release the video. Emanuel offered a combined ten million dollars that included a financial settlement for the McDonald family, to head off a wrongful death suit, and an historic reparations agreement to compensate the victims and family members who had suffered from the Burge torture crimes (Davey 2015).

Emanuel insisted his choices were sound and principled. However, the release of a wave of email communications involving city officials suggested a more complicated story (Chicago City Hall 2016). The non-profit magazine, *In the These Times,* organized the messages into five files and provided an overview summary (Burns 2016) under the title "The Laquan McDonald Email Dump Shows Rahm Emanuel's Administration in Crisis Mode." As noted, Emanuel's announcement looked like political cover for his continued refusal to release the dash-cam video. Among the emails were messages from the *Chicago Sun-Times'* Fran Spielman (Chicago City Hall 2016)., File 1, Page 321) seeking background for a forthcoming column in which she concluded: "The timing may or may not have been coincidental. But it was certainly fortunate politically."

Emails indicated settlement negotiations began with the McDonald family just weeks after Emanuel failed to get a majority vote in the mayoral election, setting up his April runoff with Garcia. Recognizing Emanuel's vulnerability, the McDonald family's lawyer, Jeffrey Neslund (Chicago City Hall 2016, File 1, Page 90–103), contacted Tomas Platt, Deputy Corporation Counsel for the city. He let Platt know they were in possession of the police dash-cam video and that the family wanted a financial settlement to head off the additional trauma of a civil trial.

Neslund laid out a damming case for settlement with a series of assertions:

- The dash-cam established that Laquan was walking at an angle 10–15 feet away from the officers and that Officer Van Dyke continued to fire his weapon for 16 seconds and fired 16 shots at McDonald, who was laying helplessly in the street.
- Officer Van Dyke continued to fire his weapon into Laquan McDonald rather than allow other officers to employ non-lethal force, including a requested Taser.

- The case was new evidence of the city's continuing pattern, practice, and procedures for rubberstamping fatal police shootings of African Americans as 'justified,' while this shooting was both an execution and a hate crime.
- Among the ten officers on the scene, only Officer Van Dyke resorted to deadly force.
- A civilian witness who screamed out at the scene for Officer Van Dyke to stop shooting was taken to a police station against her will and questioned for six hours, as detectives tried to coerce her into changing her statement, claiming it "did not match the video," which they refused to show her.
- This witness was detained until four in the morning, as she consistently reiterated that McDonald had been running *away* from the officers.
- Nearly 90 minutes were missing from 13 surveillance cameras at a nearby Burger King, which the police had accessed and examined for several hours.

Based on the above, and on behalf of the McDonald family, Neslund demanded a $16 million settlement to resolve all claims within seven days.

The $16 million demand obviously was linked to the damning sixteen shots, but the city's lawyers did not rush to an agreement. When the city finally delivered its $5 million counter-offer—the day before city council would vote on it—it included a clause prohibiting the release of the dash-cam video until the case was resolved by the courts (Chicago City Hall 2016, File 1 Page 184). Neslund objected, saying, "We do not agree . . . that the release of the video would have an adverse impact."

Tom Platt (Chicago City Hall 2016, File 1, Page 196) answered for the city with a compromise that conceded little to the McDonalds' objection to the confidentiality provision, insisting: "we cannot limit this bar to specify any time period, but we will agree to modify this sentence to allow release of the probate subpoenaed materials if the materials are . . . disclosed as required by law or court order." The reference to a court order would prove prophetic.

City Council Backs a Settlement and Reparations

A $10 million settlement and reparations agreement, which we discuss further below, was presented and passed by city council in the spring of 2015. The *New York Times* responded in two ways. Monica Davey (2015), the *Times'* Chicago Bureau Chief, provided a summary of the announcement. Later the same week, the *Times* Editorial Board (2015) followed by linking the Emanuel and Daley eras in an op-ed titled, "The Violent Legacy of Chicago's Police." Editorial Board member Brent Staples had been in contact with the city's law department and had introduced himself as a former writer for the *Chicago Reader*. Staples would have known about Emanuel's connection to Richard M. Daley, dating to Emanuel's role as Daley's chief fundraiser in 1988.

The editorial reached back to the era of police torture and linked it to the present shooting:

> The shooting of Mr. McDonald, who was 17, brought back bitter memories of the days when Mayor Richard J. Daley and the Police Department ruled Chicago with an iron hand. Between 1972 and 1991, lawyers say, about 120 mainly African-American men were picked up by Mr. Burge's 'midnight crew,' shocked with cattle prods, beaten with telephone books and suffocated with plastic bags until they confessed to crimes.

Underscoring that the settlement and reparations were necessary and justified, the editorial also pointed out that Chicago was already in deep financial debt and that Emanuel had recently closed fifty schools and mental health clinics in the same neighborhoods where the Burge and Van Dyke cases took place. Activists insisted that reparations, schools, and mental health centers were *not* an either/or proposition; they were all desperately needed. We discuss the historic reparations agreement more extensively below.

Meanwhile, the editorial emphasized Emanuel's continuing refusal to release the dash-cam video of Van Dyke's shooting and to explain the whereabouts of the eighty-six minutes of surveillance video from the nearby Burger King restaurant that had gone missing after police officers had accessed its computers. The editorial called Emanuel's claim, that the dash-cam video could not be released because it was part of the ongoing investigation of McDonald's death, "a flimsy excuse" and concluded "the public deserves to see this evidence." It then returned to the violent legacy of the Daley era, saying that this was "a department that has a history of violating the public's trust."

The day the *Times* editorial appeared, Adam Collins copied it to his colleagues in the city's law department, asking, "Remember when we said it was a mistake not to take the easy opportunity to set the record straight on some basic points being asked by Mary Mitchell?" (Chicago City Hall 2016, File 1). Collins was apparently referring to the Burger King video controversy, about which the *Sun-Times'* Mary Mitchell had continued to inquire. On April 14, 2015, Mitchell had written Collins to ask the following:

> Can you confirm that the only officer being investigated by IPRA and the feds for the Laquan McDonald fatality is the shooter? I'm told CPD detectives removed 86 minutes of videotape from Burger King surveillance cameras (without warrant) designed to cover up the shooting. Are these detectives being investigated? (Chicago City Hall 2016, File 1)

The official response was the same answer given previously to all such questions: the case was under investigation and therefore the city government could not comment. The *Times'* editorial declared this response "flimsy." In a sworn statement about the missing Burger King video, an employee responsible for the Burger King video cameras reported that "I am aware of only two (2) possible explanations: (a) inadvertent moving of the data, rather than copying the data; or (b) intentional deletion" (Chicago City Hall 2016, File 1, page 106).

It later became clear that State's Attorney Alvarez had decided against pursuing the Burger King video. A November 2015 email (Chicago City Hall 2016, File 5, Page 90) explained that, "Earlier, Cook County State's Attorney Anita Alvarez said Burger King's cameras did not capture the shooting," and that "it doesn't appear that [their video had] been tampered with." When asked to elaborate, Alvarez said that forensic testing was done to look for tampering and there was no evidence of this. Apparently, Alvarez did not regard the "gap" in the Burger King video as a promising basis for prosecution.

The law department's singular focus on the Burger King video seemed odd given the other concerns raised in the *New York Times* editorial. Maybe this was the only part of the city's collapsing case that the law department felt it could effectively answer. Police Superintendent McCarthy had blamed the gap on a system "malfunction," and there was no apparent way to disprove this.

A Freelancer Frees the Police Video

In August of 2015, freelance journalist Brandon Smith (2015) filed a little-noticed civil suit against the police department for release of the dash-cam video. Several months passed before the case came to a head. Then, on a Thursday afternoon in November 2015, a Cook County judge, Frank Valderrama, ruled that the video Emanuel had successfully kept under wraps for more than a year must be released within a week (Davey and Smith 2015a). The same afternoon, the city's lawyers introduced a motion to hold the video on appeal, but Judge Valderrama denied the motion, saying the state's Freedom of Information Act provided no grounds for delay.

The next day was Black Friday, the lucrative post-Thanksgiving shopping day. An estimated one thousand demonstrators crowded sidewalks and marched through the middle of Chicago's Magnificent Mile shopping area. All of Chicago's major media outlets covered the demonstration, as did national newspapers, including the *Washington Post* and the *New York Times*. Monica Davey and Mitch Smith (2015) reported that politicians Jessie Jackson, Bobby Rush, and Danny Davis joined with the marchers, shouting, "Sixteen shots! Thirteen months." Sixteen demonstrators lay alongside one another on the pavement blocking the front of Nordstrom's department store, and more carried signs and blocked the entrance to Macy's department store and the Water Tower Mall. It was persuasive.

On Tuesday of the following week, Officer Jason Van Dyke was charged with first-degree murder, and a few hours later the city finally released the long-withheld police video. The following month, a grand jury indicted Van Dyke on six counts of first-degree murder. The video was overwhelming evidence, but Van Dyke pled not guilty.

Chicago Tribune reporters noted that it was the first time in thirty-five years that courts charged a Chicago police officer with first-degree murder (Meisner, Gorner, and Schmadeke 2015). Others speculated it was the first time a Chicago police officer had *ever* been charged with murdering a *Black* person. Van Dyke was ultimately tried for first-degree murder and a count of aggravated battery for each of the sixteen shots identified in the auditor's report.

In a dramatic and ironic move, since he had himself withheld the police dash-cam video for more than a year, Emanuel gave a December 2015 speech at City Hall saying Chicago's police department was in the grip of a "code of silence" (Davey and Smith 2015b). Emanuel spoke passionately about the continuing power of the code "to cover up the bad actions of . . . colleagues." He said the Chicago Police Department needed "complete and total reform" (Smith 2018). But, in the minds of many, Mayor Emanuel's call for reform was "blame shifting" and it ignored the long legacy of the Mayor's office complicity in maintaining the code. *It was, after all, the same code that had helped Mayor Daley protect Commander Jon Burge and his officers from prosecution for torturing more than a hundred Black men.*

The Van Dyke Trial and its Fallout

The trial of Jason Van Dyke began in March 2017. The most dramatic moment involved the testimony of a fellow police officer, Joseph McElliott, captured in the documentary *16 Shots*. When McElliott was called to the witness stand, two rows of police officers stood up and walked out of the courtroom. It was a dramatic protest against a fellow officer breaking the code of silence. The prosecutor introduced McElliott and asked, "On October 20th did you respond to a dispatch call?" He said he had, and the prosecutor followed by asking, "Why didn't you fire your weapon?" McElliott paused before answering in halting but measured tones: "He [Laquan McDonald] didn't make any direct movements at me and I felt my partner was protected for the most part inside the vehicle." This testimony matched the video and reiterated that Van Dyke was the only officer who had discharged his revolver.

Jason Van Dyke took the stand and offered his own account. He wiped away a tear as he acknowledged, "I shot him." His testimony is also recorded in the documentary *16 Shots*. He insisted that McDonald had not put down the knife he was holding, and that he was trying to push himself up from the ground where he had fallen after sustaining the sixteen shots. Van Dyke was confused in describing his own movements toward McDonald, and he had difficulty controlling his emotions. Jamie Kalven, sitting in one of the front rows of the courtroom, would later recall that Van Dyke's testimony suggested that he may have been terrified when he shot McDonald. Yet similar fear had not provoked shots from the drawn weapons of any of the other officers.

In October 2018, Van Dyke was found guilty of second-degree murder and sixteen counts of aggravated battery. The following January he was given a prison sentence of 6.75 years (Smith and Bosman 2019). Yet this was not the end of the story.

The continuing problem that the Laquan McDonald case presented was the persistent influence of the code of silence in Chicago's police department. In the midst of the McDonald case, Attorney General of Illinois, Lisa Madigan, concluded that the code was so problematic that she wrote the U.S. Department of Justice [DOJ] requesting an investigation. The resulting report was extraordinary in its scope and detail (U.S. 2017). The section of the report dealing directly with the code of silence began with a dramatic account of the nature of this problem in Chicago and elsewhere.

> The Mayor [Emanuel] has acknowledged that a 'code of silence' exists within CPD, and his opinion is shared by current officers and former high-level CPD officials interviewed during our investigation. Indeed, in an interview . . . the President of the police officer's union admitted to such a code of silence within CPD, saying 'there's a code of silence everywhere, everybody has it . . . so why would the [Chicago police] be any different.' One CPD sergeant told us that, 'if someone comes forward as a whistleblower in the Department, they are dead on the street' (75).

The report underscored the extent to which police embraced the code of silence: "even more telling are the many examples where officers who simply witness misconduct and face no discipline by telling the truth choose instead to risk their careers to lie for another officer" (75).

The report linked the more general problem of the police code of silence to specific aspects of the Laquan McDonald case that were still unfolding. It demonstrated how the department's Rule 14, which prohibits making false statements, was not enforced and was largely ignored. Referring specifically to the McDonald case as an example, the report found that Rule 14 charges were not initially pursued "against any of the officers who witnessed the shooting and completed reports that seem inconsistent with the video footage, nor against the supervisors who approved such reports" (77).

With this lapse in enforcement made so apparent, the state's attorney's office had little choice but to bring a follow-up case. This second case addressed apparent departmental collusion in the construction of false police witness statements about the McDonald killing. This was in some ways a substitute for addressing other problems associated with the wider range of video and audio materials that had gone missing or proved inaccessible during the McDonald case.

The DOJ report emphasized that the department had done very little in previous years to secure the recording of police conduct on audio and video. The video of the McDonald shooting was recorded on only two of the five car cameras on the scene, and none recorded usable audio. The department was not effectively monitoring the use of this equipment. An unanswered question was whether the dash cameras were simply not working or whether someone had purposefully tampered with them. The report noted officers appeared to have frequently removed batteries and disassembled microphones. Officers also appeared to have sabotaged the monitoring system by neglecting to check that their dash-cam mics were synchronized with the video recorders.

In 2018, charges were eventually brought against three officers. Writing for the *New York Times*, Monica Davey (2018) asked why only three officers were charged, given that nine officers witnessed the killing of Laquan McDonald. Indeed, the Chicago Police Department had eventually requested firing five of the nine officers because of their dubious reports about the killing. Davey noted that witness testimonies were suspiciously similar to one another, yet at variance with the dash-cam video that was now in the public domain. Davey (2018) highlighted the prosecution's skepticism about the witnesses' statements: "As prosecutors tell it, Chicago police officers shooed away eyewitnesses after the shooting on Oct. 20, 2014, and then made up a narrative to justify the shooting."

In an earlier piece, Davey (2015) had pointed to a common thread in the officers' accounts: that McDonald had held on to his knife and continued to make threatening movements, notwithstanding his fatal injuries. The three defendants' official reports all made this claim, asserting that McDonald had tried to stab officers as he rose up off the ground—with sixteen shots piercing his body. As Davey (2018) noted: "The problem was that the dash-cam video presented as evidence in the trial of Jason Van Dyke trial did not match the narratives the officers provided."

All three officers charged denied they were part of a code of silence that was intended to justify the shooting of Laquan McDonald. David March was the officer assigned to record the statements, and he insisted that he had just written down what the other officers had told him. David Walsh, who was among the three, was Van Dyke's partner on the night of the shooting.

A defense lawyer insisted that differences between the accounts provided by the officers and the video were simply a matter of the different angles from which the shooting was observed, perceived, and recorded. In January 2019, Judge Domenica Stephenson acquitted all three defendants, essentially adopting the defense argument that, "Two people with two different vantage points can witness the same event" (Bosman and Davey 2019).

The judge's decision left unexplained how all three officers had come to report that McDonald rose up off the ground and tried to stab three officers after being shot sixteen times, while the dash-cam video showed him lying motionless on his side in the street. Judge Stephenson's decision contrasted with both the findings of the DOJ report and the Van Dyke verdict. Activist William Calloway, who played a major role in organizing demonstrations and demanding the follow-up trial, summarized the disappointment in the verdict: "We're devastated. I mean, we've been fighting for justice for Laquan for four years" (NBC Chicago 2019).

The need to continue the fight against the injustices perpetrated by the Chicago police became clear in the aftermath of the Laquan McDonald case. Two very different Chicago mayors—Rahm Emanuel and Lori Lightfoot—agreed that the Chicago Police Department was seriously compromised by a code of silence that often protected its officers more than the citizens they were sworn to protect. Just over a year into her new job as Chicago's mayor, Lori Lightfoot told the *New York Times Magazine,*

"What I have learned is that the cultural dysfunction in the Police Department is so deep that it's going to take enormous effort to disrupt it" (Marchese 2020: 12).

For Mayor Lightfoot, this "enormous effort" took on full meaning when in December 2020, Chicago newspapers reported that, in February 2019, near the end of Mayor Emanuel's second term, ten police officers had broken down the apartment door of a South Side social worker, Anjanette Young (Savini 2020). Young was preparing to go to bed when the police burst in, pointed a rifle at her, placed her in handcuffs, and made her stand naked for forty minutes with officers looking on in her living room. *It was the kind of raid we have associated with exclusion-containment policing.* The invading officers were looking for weapons based on an "unconfirmed lead" from an "unidentified source" and had not thoroughly checked their information before breaking into the wrong apartment.

It took a Chicago CBS2 television investigation—which had uncovered many similar kinds of Chicago raids—more than a year to break the story by convincing a judge to release the police-cam video (Savini, Assad, Youngerman, and McCann 2020). Anjanette Young also had trouble accessing and showing the video for a civil case. During her tenure as chair of the Chicago Police Accountability Task Force, Mayor Lori Lightfoot had worked on a policy that requires the city to release police videos within sixty days, but the Chicago police had refused Young's request (Spielman 2020). Young eventually secured the video through a Freedom of Information Act request in conjunction with her filing a federal civil suit, but then a lawyer for the city delayed airing the footage in court. Mayor Lightfoot later fired the lawyer. The trauma of the mistaken warrant, followed by the break-in, and the indignity of the resulting handcuffing left Young understandably bitter. "They didn't serve me," she said. "They didn't protect me. They didn't care about me" (Cramer 2020). *It was the kind of encounter that undermined belief in the police promise "to serve and protect" and was a predictable source of legal cynicism.*

Mayor Lightfoot had been informed about the incident a year earlier when she asked to see case files from problematic warrant searches (Charles and Spielman 2020). However, when this case broke, her office said she did not recall it. It was a reminder of how the code of silence endures. However, once reminded, Lightfoot did not deny it: she acknowledged the oversight, called the incident a "colossal mess," condemned and then fired the lawyer whose motion had kept the video from public view, and promised: "we will do better, and will win back the trust that we have lost this week" (Charles and Spielman 2020).

Remembrance and Reparations

Rahm Emanuel and Lori Lightfoot's agreement that the Chicago Police Department's code of silence posed a problem that was not easy to resolve coincided with their agreement about a second problem: the growing stream of civil cases and million-dollar settlements stemming from Jon Burge and his "midnight torture crew." Chicago

City Council's passage of the 2015 $5 million reparations program represented a step forward in addressing some of the wrongs of Chicago's long-lasting racial torture scandal. However, as we suggest below, the specific form of the reparations sidestepped bigger questions of whether Chicago's decision had broader implications for other important policy proposals such as those at the heart of Ta-Nehisi Coates' 2014 *Atlantic Magazine* essay, "The Case for Reparations." .

Chicago's African American activist lawyer Standish Willis was an early advocate for reparations (Taylor 2015). Willis had grown up on the West Side of the city and was a gang leader during his youth. However, his life took a positive turn when he joined the Air Force and went on to earn a law degree. During this period, Willis also organized the African American Defense Committee against Police Violence.

In 2005, while at home with the flu, Willis heard a news report about a *Committee Against Torture* [CAT] hearing being held at the United Nations headquarters in Geneva. The hearing focused on U.S. soldiers who had tortured detainees at Iraq's Abu Ghraib prison, and Willis immediately saw the potential relevance of this international forum for his work on police violence in Chicago.

Willis had already been working for compensation of victims of Chicago police torture, as well as pushing for the long-promised special prosecutor's report on the Jon Burge torture case. He was able to enlist support in these efforts from Illinois Congressman Danny Davis and the National Conference of Black Lawyers. However, his most dramatic coup was getting a hearing about the Chicago case scheduled with the CAT at the U.N. High Commission on Human Rights in Geneva. Although he was unable to travel to Geneva for the 2006 hearing, two other Chicago legal activists—Joey Mogul and Susan Gzessch—attended in his place. Their appearance, and a resulting inquiry by the CAT, refocused Chicago media attention on the Burge case and increased pressure for the federal perjury case we analyzed in Chapter Seven.

Meanwhile, local activists were calling for an Illinois Reparations for Police Torture Victims Act and the establishment of a Chicago-based Center for Torture Victims and Families, as well as the appointment of an Illinois Innocence Inquiry Commission to hear the cases of torture victims. These proposals were taken to a hearing held in Chicago by the U.N. Committee on the Elimination of Racial Discrimination. This hearing was followed by passage of the Illinois Torture Inquiry and Relief Commission Act to review torture claims linked to Jon Burge.

Following Burge's 2010 criminal conviction for perjury and obstruction, the lawyer activist Joey Mogul went on to establish an organization, the Chicago Torture Justice Memorials [CTJM], whose goal was to assure that the racist torture led by Jon Burge would not be forgotten. Mogul drafted a city ordinance modeled in name and substance after the proposals of Stan Willis for victim and family torture reparations.

Flint Taylor (2013) added his unique advocacy skills to the growing Chicago reparations movement with an article in the *Huffington Post*. Taylor posed this question:

> What if Mayor Emanuel, on behalf of the city and its police department . . . stood in front of the old Area 2 "House of Screams" at 91st and Cottage Grove and issued a

joint apology to all of Chicago's citizens, together with a pledge to create a reparations fund to compensate those still-suffering survivors of Chicago police torture
who were cheated out of lawsuits by the cover-up of the scandal?

Attorney Mogul followed up by revising the proposed reparations ordinance to include an official apology, compensation to the survivors, tuition-free education for
them at Chicago City Colleges, and the establishment of a community center to
provide psychological counseling, health care services, and vocational training to
those affected. The draft repeated calls for a reparations fund, for the Chicago Public
Schools to incorporate torture cases into its educational curriculum, as well as for the
creation of public torture memorials.

In 2014, advocacy organizations and activist lawyers submitted a new brief to the
CAT in Geneva, asking it to call on the U.S. government to support the reparations
ordinance. Attorney Shubra Ohri traveled to Geneva with a growing group called We
Charge Genocide, to present the case to the CAT. Their presentation built on Article
14 of the U.N. CAT that mandated reparations for victims of police torture.

The CAT now played a key role, recommending that the "State party" [i.e., Illinois]
should "provide redress to torture survivors by supporting the passage [of the]
Ordinance entitled Reparations for the Chicago Police Torture Survivors" (Taylor
2016:346). Attorney Mogul's Chicago Torture Justice Memorials (CTJM) organization leveraged resulting Chicago media attention to get more council members
to sign on to the ordinance. Mayor Emanuel lent his full support to the ordinance,
announcing before Council: "This is another . . . essential step in righting a wrong,
removing a stain on the reputation of this great city" (Smith and Davey 2015). The following year, Chicago City Council approved the ordinance, including $5.5 million in
financial compensation. In spring, 2021, a design was selected for a 1600-square-foot
memorial that would reflect the CTJM movement's success in assisting survivors of
police violence to begin to live their lives again.

Truth, Lies, and Reparations

The plea for a visible public remembrance through the creation of a justice memorial was at the core of the movement's argument that the public must understand and
"never forget" what the thirty-year torture scandal represented: the deeply embedded
nature of racism in this quintessential American city. Reparations without remembrance would encourage empty promises, perpetuating the kind of lies about racism
and American law enforcement that we emphasized in the prologue to this book.

In the prologue and following chapters, we presented our exclusion-containment
theory of legal cynicism to explain how RM Daley's tightly coupled system of law
and order operated. According to our theory, Daley's machine-like system benefited
and protected White residential neighborhoods and the central business districts of
Chicago, while simultaneously excluding Black and Brown Chicagoans from these

areas and containing them in highly segregated and tightly controlled neighborhoods. Burge's torture team was a vicious part of this exclusion-containment machinery, and it created a residue of repressive neighborhood surveillance and cynical legal memories that persist to this day. In short, the torture and brutality associated with Burge and his memory disseminated the highly contradictory message which, in the prologue, we noted was increasingly seen as a lie.

While Chicago's police department proudly promises to serve and protect all of the city's residents, its day-to-day policing activities have historically more narrowly involved monitoring the exclusion and containment of disadvantaged minority youth and adults in the city's most highly segregated neighborhoods—separating them from the cultural and economic resources available to the city's advantaged White citizens. In today's Chicago, as in other similar American cities, the pressing question is how the historical exclusion-containment legacy of this form of policing can be fully changed.

The chapters of this book have analyzed the top-down, racialized, and exclusionary policies and practices that have ingrained legal cynicism in Chicago's South and West Side minority communities. This cynicism has grown out of the exclusionary creation of community boundaries, targeted torture tactics, broad patterns of police misconduct, and official protective cover-ups that are reinforced by tightly coordinated and nontransparent police and courtroom practices. We have presented evidence that a pervasive code of silence was created and imposed by these means as a protective umbrella that successfully stigmatized and subordinated disadvantaged minorities through the exclusion and containment of their segregated neighborhoods.

The result is a multi-layered, interwoven, and tightly coupled system of exclusion and containment which, to be overcome, requires its exposure and elimination. This will require complete transparency in law enforcement policies and practices, as well as an openness to change which American cities have only sporadically and haltingly allowed. The challenging implication is that relatively little progress is going to be possible without a confrontation and acknowledgment of the deeply embedded repressive histories of Chicago and other U.S. cities. This will require confronting the history that has brought us to this point.

Our earlier chapters show that the roots of this system lie in its hyper-segregation of minority—and especially Black—neighborhoods. Although Chicago's reparations ordinance is an important first step, this situation is unlikely to change further unless there is an acknowledgment of the history from which this hyper-segregation emerged. This city's unique ordinance was made possible by carefully enumerating Chicago's African American torture victims and through the support of Mayor Rahm Emanuel, who was eager to overcome the damage to his political career that had resulted from his withholding of the video evidence of the police killing of Laquan McDonald.

The Chicago reparations can ideally serve as a starting point for a nationwide reparations program for victims of police violence. The Chicago reparations' restorative potential is limited by its restriction to police torture victims and their families. As a result, it represents only a partial contribution to solving Chicago's—and this nation's—larger problems of police violence, race relations, and resulting feelings of legal cynicism about policing emphasized in this book. Much more is needed. New York University law professor Bryan Stevenson, the creator of the Legacy Museum and the National Memorial for Peace and Justice in Birmingham explains why this is the case. He has underscored the, "smog in the air that's created by the history of slavery and lynching and segregation," and has insisted that to break through this smog "we're going to have to be willing to tell the truth" (Brown 2018).

The History of "The Lie" and the Need to "Begin Again"

Eddie Glaude Jr.'s (2020) writing about James Baldwin has grounded our book's focus on problems related to and about policing in Chicago and other American cities. We would be remiss if we did not acknowledge the broader politics of policing that is increasingly being brought into the consciousness of White Americans through a growing body of scholarship about our nation's history and its relationship to our present circumstances. This scholarship includes, for example, Ta-Nehisi Coates' (2014) influential essay on "The Case for Reparations" and Nikole Hannah-Jones' (2019) provocative introduction to the New York Times's 1619 Project. This and a growing body of related work exposes White ignorance about our nation's past and exemplifies why we must reach more deeply into our nation's beginnings to fully understand Glaude's insistence that we must Begin Again.

Coates' work uniquely deepens our awareness of the roots of the exclusion-containment policies that contributed to the patterns we have documented in this book. His essay presents an overview of our nation's dysfunctional housing policies, which are historical sources of policing practices in today's hyper-segregated neighborhoods. Coates (2018:178) emphasized that, during the Great Migration, African Americans encountered living conditions in the north that were only marginally better than those in the south: ". . . mayors, civic associations, banks, and citizens all colluded to pin black people into ghettos, where they were overcrowded, overcharged, and undereducated . . . Police brutalized them in the streets. And the notion that [B]lack lives, [B]lack bodies, and [B]lack wealth were rightful targets remained deeply rooted in the broader society." In this important passage, Coates presaged how Black Americans are today still subjected to exclusion-containment policing, including the sixteen shots that killed Laquan McDonald.

Coates (2014: 54) linked his analysis of American housing policy to a chronology of debts that this nation owes its African American descendants:

Two hundred fifty years of slavery. Ninety years of Jim Crow. Sixty years of separate but equal. Thirty-five years of racist housing policy. Until we reckon with our compounding moral debts, American will never be whole.

This is Coates' backgrounding of what Glaude (2020) calls America's need to *Begin Again*. And this chronology is similarly the source of Hannah-Jones' (2019) insistence that we must relearn American history and its lessons, for example, through the *1619 Project*. Coates and Hannah-Jones have demonstrated that the American moral debt is so deep and misunderstood that White Americans must reeducate themselves about the many untruths still taken for granted in justifying our history.

Hannah-Jones' ambitious project insisted that we retrace American history, not just to 1776 and the drafting of our nation's founding documents, or to Plymouth Rock, but to the arrival of the ships that brought the first slaves to Jamestown in 1619: "They were among the 12.5 million Africans who would be kidnapped from their homes and brought in chains across the Atlantic Ocean in the largest forced migration in human history until the Second World War" (2019:16). Called the Middle Passage, almost two million perished in the crossing, and those who survived are described as "born on the water"—ruthlessly stripped of their native cultures and languages through their uprooting and enslavement.

These first arriving Africans and their descendants joined in the process of growing and picking the cotton that by the late nineteenth century would produce two-thirds of the world's cotton crop—and fully half of America's rapidly growing exports—which would have been impossible without slave labor. Hannah-Jones (see also Wilkerson 2020) noted that this labor was the beginning of an American caste system in which "enslaved people were not recognized as human beings but as property that could be mortgaged, traded, bought, sold, used as collateral, given as a gift and disposed of violently" (2019:17). Our nation's founding documents did not recognize these new arrivals as American citizens, but instead as members of a slave race—thus creating a separate caste unprotected from abusive treatment by our constitution. Hannah-Jones counted ten of our first twelve presidents as having been enslavers, presiding over a nation where slaves were brutally tortured and killed. One wonders, did Jon Burge also self-servingly trace his own supervision of torture to a similar sense of White entitlement?

The reminder that America's slaves were treated as property helps us understand how today's hyper-segregated housing policies have endured as such prominent features of urban American life, and why legal cynicism in these neighborhoods about resulting methods of law enforcement is so intense. These are all important reasons why Ta-Nehisi Coates likely chose housing policy—using examples drawn from Chicago—to make his "Case for Reparations."

Coates' focus on housing policy underscores the outsized role it has played in initiating the "wealth gap" that still describes America's racialized stratification hierarchy. Coates told this story through the life experience of Clyde Ross, who, in his nineties, was still living in the West Side Chicago neighborhood of North Lawndale in the house he purchased with his wife in 1961. Ross was a World War II veteran and second-wave member of the Great Migration who traveled in 1947 from Mississippi to Chicago.

The Rosses bought their house "on contract" at double its market value. They had no choice but to enter into an exploitative housing contract because African Americans had little or no access to legitimate home mortgages or the popular G.I. postwar loans until the 1970s. Neighborhoods where they could purchase homes were "redlined" by banks and legitimate lenders, while other neighborhoods were "preserved" by "restrictive covenants." Coates (2018:168) described the contract: "the seller kept the deed until the contract was paid in full—and unlike a normal mortgage, Ross would acquire no equity in the meantime. If he missed a single payment, he would immediately forfeit his $1,000 down payment, all his monthly payments, and the property itself."

The profits were as disproportionate for the contractors as they were extortionate for the purchasers. The neighborhoods available to Blacks under these punitive terms were either fast becoming or were already highly segregated, offering little benefit from the nation's increasing home prices. Through sheer tenacity, Clyde Ross and his wife were able to hold on to their home, but they would never be in a position to accumulate much wealth from the rapid rise in home prices that Whites experienced after World War II. Today, White Americans have an enduring and still growing net worth on the order of twenty times that of Black Americans (Sharkey 2013).

The cumulative debt owed to African Americans is undeniable, yet the sheer scale of this debt, and therefore the difficulties of how reparations might be paid, also compound the problem. As Coates (2018:178) noted, "broach the topic of reparations today and a barrage of questions inevitably follows: Who will be paid? How much will they be paid? Who will pay?" These are questions about implementation that skip over—and thereby implicitly concede—the justice of the reparation claims.

At this point in his argument, Coates' "Case for Reparations" takes an important turn, based on a House of Representatives Bill known as HR 40. This bill was annually introduced in the House by the now deceased Congressman John Conyers Jr. It called for a "Commission to Study Reparation Proposals for African Americans." Coates (2018:179) maintained that, if we actually cared about the justness of this cause and its possible solutions, "we would support this bill, submit the question to study, and then assess the possible solutions."

What scholars like Bryan Stevenson, Nikole Hannah-Jones, Ta-Nahishi Coates, and Eddie Glaude have demanded is a national engagement with the kinds of issues we have discussed, accepting, as Coates does, the uncertainty of this conversation:

No one can know what would come out of such a debate. Perhaps no number can fully capture the multi-century plunder of black people in America. Perhaps the number is so large that it can't be imagined, let alone calculated and dispensed. But I believe that wrestling publicly with these questions matters as much as—if not more than—the specific answers that might be produced. An America that asks what it owes its most vulnerable citizens is improved and humane. An America that looks away is ignoring not just the sins of the past but the sins of the present and the certain sins of the future. More important than any single check cut to any

African Americans, the payment of reparations would represent America's maturation out of the childhood myth of its innocence into a wisdom worthy of its founders (2018: 206–207).

Glaude has insisted that this kind of maturation is required for Americans to *Begin Again*.

As Clyde Ross saw it, "the reason [B]lack people are so far behind now is not because of now, it's because of then" (Coates 2018:206). These are not, of course, just problems of law and crime, yet they are vastly disproportionate in their association with law and crime, and the costs continue to mount. Consider today's African American death toll from the ravages of Covid-19 that reflect the continuing cumulative damage from "then" in yet another new form. Black Americans living in hyper-segregated neighborhoods and packed together in our nation's overcrowded prisons have suffered and died at orders of magnitude higher than White Americans (Figueroa et al. 2021), due to their disproportionate exclusion and containment within the cumulative disadvantage of their imposed historical circumstances (Jackman and Shauman 2019).

Quoting from an unfinished essay by James Baldwin, Glaude (2020:150) concluded: "the horror is that America . . . changes all the time, without ever changing at all." Real change requires confronting our past and understanding how it shapes the present as well as our future.

Data Sources and Measures

1990 Census data (Chapters Two, Four, Five)
2000 Census data (Chapter Four)
2010–2014 American Community Surveys (Chapter Five)
Census tract measures

1) Quartile measures of African American segregation; derived from number of African Americans/population
2) Quartile measures of Hispanic segregation; derived from number of Hispanics/population
3) Concentrated disadvantage: (1) the number of children under 18; (2) the percent of residents below the poverty line; (3) the percent receiving public assistance; (4) the percent living in a female-headed household; and the (5) percent unemployed
4) Immigrant concentration: percent foreign born
5) Residential stability: percent of residents with housing tenure for five years or more
6) Population density: number of residents

1994–1995 Project on Human Development in Chicago Neighborhoods (Chapters Two, Four, Five)

1) Legal cynicism: Extent of agreement with the following statements: (1) laws are made to be broken; (2) the police are not doing a good job in preventing crime in this neighborhood; and (3) the police are not able to maintain order on the streets and sidewalks in the neighborhood. 1 = strongly disagree 2 = disagree 3 = neither agree nor disagree 4 = agree 5 = strongly agree

2001–2003 Chicago Community Adult Health Study (Chapters Two, Four, Five).

1) Collective efficacy: Could neighbors be counted on to intervene if (1) a fight broke out in front of your house; (2) children were skipping school and hanging out on a street corner; (3) children were spray painting graffiti on a local building; (4) children were showing disrespect to an adult; and (5) a local fire station was threatened with budget cuts. 1 = very unlikely 2 = unlikely 3 = neither unlikely or likely 4 = likely 5 = very likely.
Extent of agreement with the following statements: (6) people around here are willing to help their neighbors; (7) people in this neighborhood can be trusted; (8) people in this neighborhood generally get along with each other; (9) this is a close-knit neighborhood; and (10) people in this neighborhood share the same values. 1 = strongly disagree 2 = disagree 3 = neither disagree or agree 4 = agree 5 = strongly agree.
2) Tolerance of deviance: How wrong is it for teenagers around thirteen years of age to: (1) smoke cigarettes; (2) use marijuana; (3) drink alcohol; (4) get into fistfights. 1 = not wrong at all 2 = a little wrong 3 = wrong 4 = very wrong 5 = extremely wrong.
3) Procedural justice: Extent of agreement with the following statements: (1) the police are fair to all people regardless of their background; and (2) police in your local community can be trusted. 1 = strongly disagree 2 = disagree 3 = agree 4 = strongly agree.
4) Police mistreatment: "Have you ever been unfairly stopped, searched, questioned, physically threatened or abused by the police?" 0 = no 1 = yes

1980–1994 Homicides in Chicago, 1965–1995 (Chapter Two)

1) Yearly count of homicides 1980–1993

2003 Chicago Board of Election Commissioner (Chapter Two)

 Percentage of votes cast for each candidate in Chicago wards, 2003 mayoral election

2003 Missouri Census Data Center (Chapter Two)

1) Crosswalk to link ward election results to census tracts

2006–2008 "Million Dollar Blocks," Chicago Justice Project (Chapters Four, Five)

1) Incarceration: Count of people who received a custodial sentence (i.e., jail, boot camp, or prison). Based on SAS obtained zip codes and geo-coordinates and ArcGIS and 2000 Census tract shapefiles to match records to a census-tract number.

2006–2008 Record Information Service (Chapters Four, Five)

1) Residential foreclosures: Count of all single-family foreclosure repossessions. Based on SAS obtained zip codes and geo-coordinates and ArcGIS and 2000 Census tract shapefiles to match records to a census-tract number.

Tables

Chapter 2 Table 1 Descriptive Statistics by 1990 Tract Level Percent African American Quartiles (N=621 tracts)

Variables	First quartile		Second quartile		Third quartile		Fourth quartile		Min.	Max.
	Mean	SD	Mean	SD	Mean	SD	Mean	SD		
Legal cynicism (PHDCN)	-0.338	0.493	-0.187	0.459	0.155	0.418	0.286	0.311	-1.261	1.398
Percent vote for Mayor Daley 2003	86.853	4.517	80.672	7.257	62.868	11.461	53.601	7.459	41.430	96.430
Concentrated disadvantage 1990	-0.715	0.408	-0.569	0.538	0.179	0.726	0.811	0.948	-1.454	3.473
Percent Hispanic 1990	26.685	28.158	32.174	28.391	17.701	22.564	0.280	0.428	0	97.907
Percent foreign-born 1990	24.058	13.206	24.984	14.408	11.182	11.335	0.602	0.851	0	65.271
Residential stability 1990	59.546	20.484	38.386	18.981	35.020	22.270	37.386	26.750	0	97.257
Population size 1990	3973.433	1892.098	4113.276	2591.423	4026.340	2426.167	3554.613	2426.766	209	16279
Homicide 1980–1994	4.427	5.546	7.590	8.286	20.882	16.468	29.426	20.106	0	116
Positive AA quartile change	0.267	0.444	0.102	0.304	0.431	0.497	0	0	0	1
Negative AA quartile change	0.000	0.000	0.263	0.442	0.124	0.331	0.439	0.498	0	1
Positive Hispanic quartile change	0.363	0.482	0.128	0.335	0.137	0.345	0.194	0.396	0	1
Negative Hispanic quartile change	0.000	0.000	0.160	0.368	0.085	0.280	0.045	0.208	0	1
Concentrated disadvantage change	0.210	0.268	-0.120	0.357	-0.043	0.445	0.031	0.464	-2.481	1.539
Percent foreign-born change	8.336	9.091	1.812	7.576	1.217	6.295	0.635	1.549	-19.711	30.462
Residential stability change	-0.517	3.924	2.487	5.343	3.377	10.298	0.653	5502.000	-14.439	62.541
Population size change	560.472	678.777	327.038	634.524	58.850	590.158	-317.794	487.204	-2951	3157.000
Procedural justice (CCAHS)	0.381	0.549	0.212	0.511	-0.209	0.520	-0.386	0.506	-2.477	2.340
Collective efficacy (CCAHS)	0.173	0.351	0.039	0.294	-0.085	0.365	-0.109	0.350	-1.474	1.131
Tolerance for deviance (CCAHS)	-0.053	0.752	0.263	0.962	-0.005	0.879	-0.155	0.826	-1.828	2.735

Abbreviations: SD=standard deviation; Min.=minimum; Max.=maximum; AA=African American; PHDCN= Project on Human Development in Chicago Neighborhoods; CCAHS=Chicago Community Adult Health Study

Chapter 2 Table 2 OLS Regression, Legal Cynicism 1994–1995 (N=621 tracts)

Variable	b	SE
Second quartile African American 1990	0.080	(0.041)
Third quartile African American 1990	0.344***	(0.050)
Fourth quartile African American 1990	0.384***	(0.079)
Second quartile Hispanic 1990	−0.105	(0.059)
Third quartile Hispanic 1990	−0.041	(0.068)
Fourth quartile Hispanic 1990	0.180*	(0.073)
Concentrated disadvantage 1990	0.156***	(0.029)
Percent foreign-born 1990	0.006***	(0.002)
Residential stability 1990	0.000	(0.001)
Population size 1990	−0.000**	(0.000)
Homicide 1980–1994	0.007***	(0.001)
Constant	−0.349***	(0.087)
Adjusted R^2	0.529	
BIC/df	485.83/12	

Abbreviations: b=regression coefficient; SE=robust standard error; BIC=Bayesian Information Criterion; df=degrees of freedom

*** $p<0.001$, ** $p<0.01$, * $p<0.05$ (two-tailed)

Chapter 2 Table 3 OLS Regression, Votes for Mayor Daley, 2003 (N=621 tracts)

Variable	b	SE
Legal cynicism (PHDCN)	−2.917**	(0.896)
Second quartile African American 1990	−6.564***	(0.983)
Third quartile African American 1990	−19.174***	(1.188)
Fourth quartile African American 1990	−25.695***	(2.002)
Second quartile Hispanic 1990	3.568**	(1.324)
Third quartile Hispanic 1990	6.166***	(1.556)
Fourth quartile Hispanic 1990	8.648***	(1.797)
Concentrated disadvantage 1990	−0.596	(0.666)
Percent foreign-born 1990	0.027	(0.037)
Residential stability 1990	−0.003	(0.020)
Population size 1990	0.000	(0.000)
Positive African American quartile change	−4.703***	(0.945)
Negative African American quartile change	4.139***	(1.088)
Positive Hispanic quartile change	1.768	(0.952)
Negative Hispanic quartile change	−1.570	(1.551)
Concentrated disadvantage change	−0.249	(1.012)
Percent foreign-born change	0.178***	(0.052)
Residential stability change	0.086	(0.056)
Population size change	0.001*	(0.001)
Homicide 1980–1994	0.041	(0.033)
Procedural justice (CCAHS)	0.138	(0.634)
Collective efficacy (CCAHS)	−1.333	(1.056)
Tolerance for deviance (CCAHS)	0.265	(0.355)
Constant	76.022***	(2.069)
Adjusted R²	0.788	
BIC/df	4340.22/24	

Abbreviations: b=regression coefficient; SE=robust standard error; PHDCN=Project on Human Development in Chicago Neighborhoods; CCAHS=Chicago Community Adult Health Study; BIC=Bayesian Information Criterion; df=degrees of freedom

*** p<0.001, ** p<0.01, * p<0.05 (two-tailed)

Chapter 4 Table 1 Negative Binomial Regression, 911 Calls 2006–2008 (N=673 tracts); Equation 1

Variables	Theft		Drugs		Violence	
	b	SE	b	SE	b	SE
Second quartile African American 1990	0.146**	(0.054)	0.109	(0.113)	-0.012	(0.062)
Third quartile African American 1990	0.664***	(0.072)	1.866***	(0.168)	0.760***	(0.080)
Fourth quartile African American 1990	0.781***	(0.110)	1.757***	(0.237)	0.880***	(0.121)
Second quartile Hispanic 1990	-0.105	(0.086)	-0.471*	(0.219)	-0.122	(0.089)
Third quartile Hispanic 1990	0.066	(0.104)	-0.138	(0.271)	0.098	(0.107)
Fourth quartile Hispanic 1990	0.204	(0.106)	0.244	(0.250)	0.200	(0.112)
Concentrated disadvantage 1990	-0.157***	(0.046)	0.687***	(0.139)	0.141**	(0.050)
Percent foreign-born 1990	-0.009***	(0.002)	-0.012**	(0.004)	-0.004	(0.002)
Residential stability 1990	-0.002	(0.001)	0.001	(0.004)	0.000	(0.001)
Population size 1990	0.000***	(0.000)	0.000***	(0.000)	0.000***	(0.000)
Log normal alpha	-1.434***	(0.089)	-0.022	(0.059)	-1.134***	(0.076)
Constant	4.428***	(0.129)	2.544***	(0.383)	4.904***	(0.132)
BIC/df	8143.80/12		7203.11/12		9365.35/12	

Abbreviations: b=regression coefficient; SE=robust standard error; BIC=Bayesian Information Criterion; df=degrees of freedom

*p>.05; **p>.01; ***p>.01 (two-tailed)

Chapter 4 Table 2 Negative Binomial Regression, 911 Calls 2006–2008 (N=673 tracts); Equation 2

Variables	Theft		Drugs		Violence	
	b	SE	b	SE	b	SE
Second quartile African American 1990	0.136*	(0.055)	0.084	(0.116)	-0.036	(0.063)
Third quartile African American 1990	0.618***	(0.077)	1.632***	(0.161)	0.658***	(0.083)
Fourth quartile African American 1990	0.726***	(0.111)	1.507***	(0.240)	0.763***	(0.117)
Second quartile Hispanic 1990	-0.088	(0.083)	-0.387	(0.214)	-0.090	(0.086)
Third quartile Hispanic 1990	0.070	(0.103)	-0.104	(0.267)	0.111	(0.105)
Fourth quartile Hispanic 1990	0.177	(0.106)	0.056	(0.250)	0.149	(0.109)
Concentrated disadvantage 1990	-0.188***	(0.047)	0.520***	(0.139)	0.074	(0.051)
Percent foreign–born 1990	-0.010***	(0.002)	-0.013**	(0.005)	-0.006*	(0.002)
Residential stability 1990	-0.002	(0.001)	0.002	(0.003)	0.000	(0.001)
Population size 1990	0.000***	(0.000)	0.000***	(0.000)	0.000***	(0.000)
Legal cynicism (PHDCN)	0.131*	(0.057)	0.691***	(0.114)	0.278***	(0.064)
Log normal alpha	-1.449***	(0.092)	-0.071	(0.059)	-1.169***	(0.079)
Constant	4.469***	(0.129)	2.683***	(0.383)	4.990***	(0.130)
BIC/df	8131.09/13		7168.71/13		9337.32/13	

Abbreviations: b=regression coefficient; SE=robust standard error; PHDCN=Project on Human Development in Chicago Neighborhoods; BIC=Bayesian Information Criterion; df=degrees of freedom

*** $p<0.001$, ** $p<0.01$, * $p<0.05$ (two–tailed)

Chapter 4 Table 3 Mediation, 3rd and 4th Quartiles African American, Legal Cynicism, and 911 Calls 2006–2008

Variables	Direct effect		Indirect effect		Total effect	
	b	SE	b	SE	b	SE
Theft						
Third quartile African American 1990	1.854***	(0.153)	1.046*	(0.021)	1.940***	(0.150)
Fourth quartile African American 1990	2.082***	(0.257)	1.056*	(0.028)	2.200***	(0.266)
Drugs						
Third quartile African American 1990	5.103***	(0.883)	1.271***	(0.065)	6.482***	(1.136)
Fourth quartile African American 1990	4.435***	(1.280)	1.337***	(0.093)	5.932***	(1.714)
Violence						
Third quartile African American 1990	1.930***	(0.172)	1.100***	(0.028)	2.125***	(0.186)
Fourth quartile African American 1990	2.145***	(0.279)	1.124***	(0.038)	2.411***	(0.320)

Abbreviations: b=regression coefficient; SE=Bootstrap standard errors

*** p<0.001, ** p<0.01, * p<0.05 (two-tailed)

Chapter 4 Table 4 Negative Binomial Regression, 911 Calls 2006–2008 (N=673 tracts); Equation 3

Variables	Theft		Drugs		Violence	
	b	SE	b	SE	b	SE
Second quartile African American 1990	0.243***	(0.058)	0.459***	(0.102)	0.161**	(0.059)
Third quartile African American 1990	0.626***	(0.078)	1.591***	(0.156)	0.685***	(0.085)
Fourth quartile African American 1990	0.897***	(0.120)	1.642***	(0.242)	0.894***	(0.126)
Second quartile Hispanic 1990	-0.020	(0.075)	-0.292	(0.156)	-0.048	(0.077)
Third quartile Hispanic 1990	0.160	(0.095)	0.091	(0.197)	0.176	(0.098)
Fourth quartile Hispanic 1990	0.262*	(0.104)	0.179	(0.208)	0.190	(0.104)
Concentrated disadvantage 1990	-0.126**	(0.044)	0.716***	(0.113)	0.167***	(0.050)
Percent foreign-born 1990	-0.012***	(0.002)	-0.019***	(0.005)	-0.011***	(0.002)
Residential stability 1990	-0.001	(0.001)	-0.002	(0.003)	-0.002	(0.001)
Population size 1990	0.000***	(0.000)	0.000***	(0.000)	0.000***	(0.000)
Legal cynicism (PHDCN)	0.146**	(0.049)	0.619***	(0.110)	0.262***	(0.055)
Positive AA quartile change	0.182**	(0.058)	0.292*	(0.118)	0.163**	(0.061)
Negative AA quartile change	-0.205**	(0.070)	-0.753***	(0.141)	-0.270***	(0.073)
Positive Hispanic quartile change	0.057	(0.055)	0.213	(0.121)	0.045	(0.055)
Negative Hispanic quartile change	0.057	(0.144)	0.336	(0.409)	0.111	(0.188)
Concentrated disadvantage change	0.065	(0.069)	1.037***	(0.146)	0.397***	(0.074)
Percent foreign-born change	-0.009**	(0.003)	-0.008	(0.006)	-0.005	(0.003)
Residential stability change	0.005	(0.004)	0.020	(0.010)	0.003	(0.005)
Population size change	0.000***	(0.000)	0.000*	(0.000)	0.000***	(0.000)
Log normal alpha	-1.567***	(0.098)	-0.265***	(0.066)	-1.369***	(0.093)
Constant	4.325***	(0.127)	2.631***	(0.306)	5.032***	(0.141)
BIC/df	8104.42/21		7074.42/21		9249.45/21	

Abbreviations: b=regression coefficient; SE=robust standard error; AA=African American; PHDCN=Project on Human Development in Chicago Neighborhoods; BIC=Bayesian Information Criterion; df=degrees of freedom

*** p<0.001, ** p<0.01, * p<0.05 (two-tailed)

Chapter 4 Table 5 Negative Binomial Regression, 911 Calls 2006–2008 (N=673 tracts); Equation 4

Variables	Theft		Drugs		Violence	
	b	SE	b	SE	b	SE
Second quartile African American 1990	0.217***	(0.053)	0.487***	(0.102)	0.142*	(0.056)
Third quartile African American 1990	0.572***	(0.077)	1.531***	(0.152)	0.633***	(0.084)
Fourth quartile African American 1990	0.828***	(0.116)	1.610***	(0.237)	0.832***	(0.123)
Second quartile Hispanic 1990	-0.030	(0.074)	-0.242	(0.154)	-0.046	(0.076)
Third quartile Hispanic 1990	0.130	(0.094)	0.122	(0.190)	0.162	(0.097)
Fourth quartile Hispanic 1990	0.230*	(0.102)	0.183	(0.203)	0.174	(0.102)
Concentrated disadvantage 1990	-0.149***	(0.044)	0.681***	(0.112)	0.146**	(0.050)
Percent foreign-born 1990	-0.011***	(0.002)	-0.017***	(0.005)	-0.010***	(0.002)
Residential stability 1990	0.000	(0.001)	-0.002	(0.003)	-0.001	(0.001)
Population size 1990	0.000***	(0.000)	0.000***	(0.000)	0.000***	(0.000)
Legal cynicism (PHDCN)	0.119*	(0.048)	0.598***	(0.109)	0.237***	(0.054)
Positive AA quartile change	0.185**	(0.057)	0.322**	(0.116)	0.165**	(0.060)
Negative AA quartile change	-0.206**	(0.068)	-0.770***	(0.133)	-0.269***	(0.073)
Positive Hispanic quartile change	0.051	(0.053)	0.223	(0.115)	0.041	(0.053)
Negative Hispanic quartile change	0.048	(0.142)	0.344	(0.398)	0.097	(0.183)
Concentrated disadvantage change	0.022	(0.066)	0.962***	(0.143)	0.357***	(0.073)
Percent foreign-born change	-0.009**	(0.003)	-0.006	(0.006)	-0.005	(0.003)

Continued

Chapter 4 Table 5 *Continued*

Variables	Theft		Drugs		Violence	
	b	SE	b	SE	b	SE
Residential stability change	0.005	(0.004)	0.018	(0.010)	0.003	(0.005)
Population size change	0.000***	(0.000)	0.000*	(0.000)	0.000***	(0.000)
Procedural justice (CCAHS)	-0.075*	(0.033)	-0.174*	(0.073)	-0.076*	(0.033)
Collective efficacy (CCAHS)	-0.240***	(0.062)	-0.033	(0.123)	-0.179**	(0.065)
Tolerance for deviance (CCAHS)	-0.026	(0.022)	-0.121**	(0.040)	-0.027	(0.022)
Police mistreatment (CCAHS)	0.028	(0.037)	0.022	(0.082)	0.045	(0.043)
Log normal alpha	-1.613***	(0.099)	-0.286***	(0.066)	-1.397***	(0.094)
Constant	4.304***	(0.123)	2.607***	(0.312)	5.006***	(0.138)
BIC/df	8099.91/25		7084.90/23		9256.54/25	

Abbreviations: b=regression coefficient; SE=robust standard error; AA=African American; PHDCN=Project on Human Development in Chicago Neighborhoods; CCAHS= Chicago Community Adult Health Study; BIC= Bayesian Information Criterion; df=degrees of freedom

*** p<0.001, ** p<0.01, * p<0.05 (two-tailed)

Chapter 4 Table 6 Negative Binomial Regression, 911 Calls 2006–2008 (N=673 tracts); Equation 5

Variables	Theft		Drugs		Violence	
	b	SE	b	SE	b	SE
Second quartile African American 1990	0.150**	(0.052)	0.325***	(0.094)	0.053	(0.054)
Third quartile African American 1990	0.337***	(0.068)	1.075***	(0.148)	0.346***	(0.074)
Fourth quartile African American 1990	0.495***	(0.104)	1.210***	(0.235)	0.436***	(0.106)
Second quartile Hispanic 1990	-0.045	(0.067)	-0.330*	(0.146)	-0.090	(0.069)
Third quartile Hispanic 1990	-0.001	(0.090)	-0.108	(0.183)	-0.014	(0.091)
Fourth quartile Hispanic 1990	0.115	(0.097)	0.098	(0.194)	0.040	(0.098)
Concentrated disadvantage 1990	-0.260***	(0.041)	0.216	(0.118)	-0.031	(0.047)
Percent foreign-born 1990	-0.006**	(0.002)	-0.005	(0.005)	-0.004	(0.002)
Residential stability 1990	-0.006***	(0.001)	-0.007*	(0.004)	-0.007***	(0.002)
Population size 1990	0.000***	(0.000)	0.000	(0.000)	0.000***	(0.000)
Legal cynicism (PHDCN)	0.008	(0.045)	0.224*	(0.100)	0.069	(0.048)
Positive AA quartile change	0.090	(0.054)	0.232*	(0.093)	0.063	(0.054)
Negative AA quartile change	-0.105	(0.063)	-0.392**	(0.134)	-0.113	(0.067)
Positive Hispanic quartile change	0.022	(0.051)	0.134	(0.105)	0.011	(0.050)
Negative Hispanic quartile change	-0.022	(0.136)	0.055	(0.395)	-0.024	(0.169)
Concentrated disadvantage change	-0.099	(0.063)	0.544***	(0.147)	0.178*	(0.069)
Percent foreign-born change	-0.005	(0.003)	0.006	(0.006)	0.000	(0.003)
Residential stability change	0.004	(0.004)	0.013	(0.009)	0.002	(0.004)

Continued

Chapter 4 Table 6 *Continued*

Variables	Theft		Drugs		Violence	
	b	SE	b	SE	b	SE
Population size change	0.000***	(0.000)	−0.000	(0.000)	0.000***	(0.000)
Procedural justice (CCAHS)	−0.024	(0.032)	−0.034	(0.065)	−0.010	(0.030)
Collective efficacy (CCAHS)	−0.206**	(0.064)	−0.048	(0.100)	−0.148*	(0.065)
Tolerance for deviance (CCAHS)	−0.007	(0.021)	−0.005	(0.035)	0.001	(0.021)
Police mistreatment (CCAHS)	−0.000	(0.036)	−0.003	(0.076)	0.009	(0.039)
Incarceration 2006–2008	0.009***	(0.001)	0.034***	(0.003)	0.014***	(0.002)
Incarceration 2006–2008 squared	−0.000***	(0.000)	−0.000***	(0.000)	−0.000***	(0.000)
Foreclosures 2006–2008	0.016***	(0.002)	0.010*	(0.005)	0.016***	(0.002)
Foreclosures 2006–2008 squared	−0.000***	(0.000)	−0.000***	(0.000)	−0.000***	(0.000)
Log normal alpha	−1.772***	(0.107)	−0.557***	(0.074)	−1.618***	(0.103)
Constant	4.626***	(0.121)	2.732***	(0.328)	5.327***	(0.133)
BIC/df	8022.16/29		6927.11/29		9132.95/29	

Abbreviations: b=regression coefficient; SE=robust standard error; AA=African American; PHDCN=Project on Human Development in Chicago Neighborhoods; CCAHS=Chicago Community Adult Health Study; BIC=Bayesian Information Criterion; df=degrees of freedom

*** p<0.001, ** p<0.01, * p<0.05 (two-tailed)

Chapter 4 Table 7 Mediation, 3rd and 4th Quartiles African American, Legal Cynicism, Incarceration, Foreclosures, and 911 Calls 2006–2008

Variables	Direct effect		Indirect effect		Total effect	
	b	SE	b	SE	b	SE
Incarceration						
3rd quartile AA 1990 =>911 theft	1.402***	(0.097)	1.059**	(0.023)	1.485***	(0.109)
4th quartile AA 1990 =>911 theft	1.661***	(0.179)	1.067*	(0.039)	1.772***	(0.204)
3rd quartile AA 1990 =>911 drug	2.919***	(0.487)	1.246**	(0.089)	3.638***	(0.672)
4th quartile AA1990=>911 drug	3.272**	(0.976)	1.281*	(0.160)	4.191***	(1.436)
3rd quartile AA 1990=>911 violence	1.414***	(0.108)	1.097**	(0.035)	1.555***	(0.131)
4th quartile AA 1990=>911 violence	1.554***	(0.176)	1.110*	(0.061)	1.725***	(0.225)
Legal cynicism=>911 theft	1.001	(0.047)	1.061***	(0.016)	1.071	(0.049)
Legal cynicism=>911 drug	1.257*	(0.129)	1.255***	(0.065)	1.577***	(0.173)
Legal cynicism=> violence	1.073	(0.052)	1.100***	(0.024)	1.180**	(0.060)
Foreclosures						
3rd quartile AA 1990 =>911 theft	1.402***	(0.097)	1.111***	(0.025)	1.567***	(0.114)
4th quartile AA 1990 =>911 theft	1.661***	(0.179)	1.167***	(0.041)	1.939***	(0.218)
3rd quartile AA 1990 =>911 drug	2.919***	(0.487)	1.065+	(0.038)	3.110**	(0.513)
4th quartile AA1990=>911 drug	3.272**	(0.976)	1.098+	(0.057)	3.592***	(1.049)
3rd quartile AA 1990=>911 violence	1.414***	(0.109)	1.111***	(0.028)	1.571***	(0.125)
4th quartile AA 1990=>911 violence	1.555***	(0.121)	1.168***	(0.038)	1.815***	(0.121)
Legal cynicism=>911 theft	1.009	(0.047)	1.021	(0.013)	1.030	(0.049)
Legal cynicism=>911 drug	1.257*	(0.129)	1.013	(0.012)	1.273*	(0.132)
Legal cynicism=> violence	1.073	(0.052)	1.021	(0.013)	1.096	(54.000)

Abbreviations: b=regression coefficient; SE=Bootstrap standard errors

*** $p<0.001$, ** $p<0.01$, * $p<0.05$ (two-tailed)

+ $p<.10$ (two-tailed)

Chapter 4 Table 8 Negative Binomial Regression, 911 Calls 2006–2008 (N=673 tracts); Equation 6

Variables	Theft		Drugs		Violence	
	b	SE	b	SE	b	SE
Second quartile African American 1990	0.071	(0.037)	0.344***	(0.092)	0.100*	(0.048)
Third quartile African American 1990	0.240***	(0.049)	1.087***	(0.140)	0.351***	(0.063)
Fourth quartile African American 1990	0.346***	(0.075)	1.290***	(0.220)	0.347***	(0.095)
Second quartile Hispanic 1990	-0.019	(0.046)	-0.268	(0.145)	-0.082	(0.064)
Third quartile Hispanic 1990	0.041	(0.062)	-0.021	(0.181)	0.005	(0.081)
Fourth quartile Hispanic 1990	0.108	(0.070)	0.230	(0.189)	0.045	(0.090)
Concentrated disadvantage 1990	-0.103**	(0.038)	0.161	(0.109)	0.013	(0.043)
Percent foreign-born 1990	-0.002	(0.002)	-0.004	(0.004)	-0.001	(0.002)
Residential stability 1990	-0.003**	(0.001)	-0.006	(0.003)	-0.003	(0.002)
Population size 1990	0.000**	(0.000)	0.000	(0.000)	0.000***	(0.000)
Legal cynicism (PHDCN)	0.011	(0.033)	0.229*	(0.095)	0.050	(0.042)
Positive AA quartile change	0.038	(0.043)	0.217*	(0.089)	0.034	(0.049)
Negative AA quartile change	-0.073	(0.044)	-0.392***	(0.119)	-0.063	(0.063)
Positive Hispanic quartile change	0.050	(0.035)	0.178	(0.096)	0.049	(0.042)
Negative Hispanic quartile change	0.024	(0.085)	0.040	(0.372)	-0.046	(0.152)
Concentrated disadvantage change	-0.032	(0.050)	0.405**	(0.139)	0.088	(0.062)
Percent foreign-born change	-0.001	(0.002)	0.006	(0.006)	0.003	(0.003)
Residential stability change	-0.005	(0.003)	0.009	(0.009)	0.001	(0.003)
Population size change	0.000	(0.000)	-0.000	(0.000)	0.000***	(0.000)
Procedural justice (CCAHS)	0.004	(0.024)	-0.023	(0.060)	0.008	(0.027)

	b (SE)	b (SE)	b (SE)
Collective efficacy (CCAHS)	-0.040 (0.043)	0.016 (0.096)	-0.063 (0.053)
Tolerance for deviance (CCAHS)	0.012 (0.013)	-0.002 (0.034)	0.016 (0.017)
Police mistreatment (CCAHS)	0.011 (0.024)	0.023 (0.070)	-0.011 (0.032)
Incarceration 2006–2008	0.006*** (0.001)	0.024*** (0.003)	0.007*** (0.001)
Incarceration 2006–2008 squared	-0.000*** (0.000)	-0.000*** (0.000)	-0.000*** (0.000)
Foreclosures 2006–2008	0.011*** (0.002)	0.010* (0.005)	0.005 (0.003)
Foreclosures 2006–2008 squared	-0.000*** (0.000)	-0.000*** (0.000)	-0.000*** (0.000)
Police reported crime 2006–2008	0.003*** (0.000)	0.006*** (0.001)	0.002*** (0.000)
Log normal alpha	-2.258*** (0.140)	-0.628*** (0.072)	-1.813*** (0.113)
Constant	4.375*** (0.097)	2.512*** (0.296)	5.032*** (0.129)
BIC/df	7725.52/30	6887.21/30	9009.86/30

Abbreviations: b=regression coefficient; SE=robust standard error; AA=African American; PHDCN=Project on Human Development in Chicago Neighborhoods; CCAHS= Chicago Community Adult Health Study; BIC=Bayesian Information Criterion; df=degrees of freedom

*** p<0.001, ** p<0.01, * p<0.05 (two-tailed)

Chapter 5 Table 1 Bivariate Negative Binomial Regression, Police Complaints 2012–2014 (N=673 tracts)

Variables	b	SE
Police complaints 1980–1994	0.322***	(0.040)
Legal cynicism (PHDCN)	0.831***	(0.096)
Second quartile African American 1990	−0.147	(0.148)
Third quartile African American 1990	0.959***	(0.134)
Fourth quartile African American 1990	1.145***	(0.126)
Second quartile Hispanic 1990	−0.362**	(0.129)
Third quartile Hispanic 1990	−0.905***	(0.114)
Fourth quartile Hispanic 1990	−0.931***	(0.128)
Police reports of crime 2012–2014	1.066***	(0.049)
Police mistreatment (CCAHS)	0.266***	(0.033)
Concentrated disadvantage 1990	0.422***	(0.057)
Percent foreign-born 1990	−0.025***	(0.003)
Residential stability 1990	−0.003	(0.002)
Population size 1990	0.000***	(0.000)
Positive African American quartile change	0.364**	(0.118)
Negative African American quartile change	−0.594***	(0.142)
Positive Hispanic quartile change	−0.084	(0.121)
Negative Hispanic quartile change	0.078	(0.129)
Concentrated disadvantage change	0.303**	(0.110)
Percent foreign born change	−0.008	(0.006)
Residential stability change	−0.022***	(0.006)
Population size change	−0.000***	(0.000)
Incarceration 2006–2008	0.017***	(0.002)
Incarceration 2006–2008 squared	0.000***	(0.000)
Foreclosures 2006–2008	0.029***	(0.004)
Foreclosures 2006–2008 squared	0.000	(0.000)
Procedural justice perceptions (CCAHS)	−0.575***	(0.077)
Collective efficacy (CCAHS)	−0.613***	(0.131)
Tolerance for deviance (CCAHS)	−0.134*	(0.060)

Abbreviations: squared b=regression coefficient; SE=robust standard error; AA=African American; PHDCN=Project on Human Development in Chicago Neighborhoods; CCAHS= Chicago Community Adult Health Study

*** p<0.001, ** p<0.01, * p<0.05 (two-tailed)

Chapter 5 Table 2 Negative Binomial Regression, Police Complaints 2012–2014 (N=673 tracts)

Variables	Equation 1 b	SE	Equation 2 b	SE	Equation 3 b	SE
Police complaints 1980–1994	0.178***	(0.026)	0.179***	(0.026)	0.131***	(0.022)
Second quartile African American 1990	-0.257*	(0.114)	-0.301**	(0.114)	-0.226*	(0.115)
Third quartile African American 1990	0.521***	(0.133)	0.345*	(0.143)	0.072	(0.179)
Fourth quartile African American 1990	0.652***	(0.169)	0.461**	(0.174)	0.050	(0.272)
Second quartile Hispanic 1990	-0.076	(0.106)	-0.031	(0.107)	-0.020	(0.130)
Third quartile Hispanic 1990	-0.089	(0.132)	-0.066	(0.134)	-0.062	(0.142)
Fourth quartile Hispanic 1990	0.039	(0.165)	-0.052	(0.169)	0.024	(0.182)
Concentrated disadvantage 1990	0.175**	(0.063)	0.072	(0.067)	0.103	(0.078)
Percent foreign-born 1990	-0.007	(0.004)	-0.009*	(0.004)	-0.009	(0.005)
Residential stability 1990	0.004*	(0.002)	0.004*	(0.002)	-0.002	(0.003)
Population size 1990	0.000***	(0.000)	0.000***	(0.000)	0.000	(0.000)
Legal cynicism (PHDCN)			0.460***	(0.111)	0.257*	(0.114)
Police reports of crime 2012–2014					0.709***	(0.132)
Police mistreatment (CCAHS)					0.019	(0.026)
Positive African American quartile change					0.047	(0.091)
Negative African American quartile change					-0.103	(0.124)
Positive Hispanic quartile change					0.227	(0.125)
Negative Hispanic quartile change					0.008	(0.110)
Concentrated disadvantage change					0.121	(0.077)

Continued

Chapter 5 Table 2 *Continued*

Variables	Equation 1		Equation 2		Equation 3	
	b	SE	b	SE	b	SE
Percent foreign born change					-0.004	(0.005)
Residential stability change					-0.006	(0.005)
Population size change					-0.000	(0.000)
Incarceration 2006–2008					-0.002	(0.003)
Incarceration 2006–2008 squared					-0.000	(0.000)
Foreclosures 2006–2008					0.000	(0.004)
Foreclosures 2006–2008 squared					-0.000	(0.000)
Procedural justice perceptions (CCAHS)					0.048	(0.066)
Collective efficacy (CCAHS)					0.026	(0.111)
Tolerance for deviance (CCAHS)					0.008	(0.038)
Alpha	-0.982***	(0.135)	-1.042***	(0.134)	-1.520***	(0.209)
Constant	-0.038	(0.201)	0.108	(0.208)	-3.132***	(0.663)
BIC/df	2868.39/13		2853.65/14		2812.55/31	

Abbreviations: b=regression coefficient; SE=robust standard error; PHDCN=Project on Human Development in Chicago Neighborhoods; CCAHS=Chicago Community Adult Health Study; BIC=Bayesian Information Criterion; df=degrees of freedom

*** p<0.001, ** p<0.01, * p<0.05 (two-tailed)

Chapter 5 Table 3 Mediation, 1990 3rd and 4th Quartiles African American, Concentrated Disadvantage, and Police Complaints 2012–2014

Variables	Direct effect		Indirect effect		Total effect	
	b	SE	b	SE	b	SE
Legal cynicism						
3rd quartile AA 1990 =>complaints	1.328*	(0.190)	1.172***	(0.051)	1.557***	(0.214)
4th quartile AA 1990 =>complaints	1.469*	(0.179)	1.213***	(0.039)	1.782***	(0.341)
Concentrated disadvantage 1990 =>complaints	1.089	(0.072)	1.107***	(0.030)	1.206**	(0.077)

Abbreviations: b=regression coefficient; SE=Bootstrap standard errors; AA=African American
*** p<0.001, ** p<0.01, * p<0.05 (two-tailed)

References

Ackerman, Spencer. 2016. "'I Was Struck with Multiple Blows': Inside the Secret Violence of Homan Square." *The Guardian*. April 11. (https://www.theguardian.com/us-news/2016/apr/11/homan-square-chicago-police-internal-documents-physical-force-prisoner-abuse).

Adler, Jeffrey S. 2007. "Shoot to Kill: The Use of Deadly Force by the Chicago Police, 1875-1920." *Journal of Interdisciplinary History* 38(2): 233–254.

Alexander, Michelle. 2010. *The New Jim Crow: Mass Incarceration in the Age of Colorblindness*. New York: New Press.

Algren, Nelson. 1949. *The Man with the Golden Arm*. New York: Doubelday.

Algren, Nelson. 1951. *Chicago: City on the Make*. New York: Doubleday.

Algren, Nelson. 1956. *A Walk on the Wild Side*. New York: Farrar, Straus, & Cudahy.

American Civil Liberties Union. 2015. "Stop and Frisk in Chicago." (https://www.aclu-il.org/en/campaigns/stop-and-frisk).

Amnesty International. 2005. *The Rest of Their Lives: Life without Parole for Child Offenders in the United States*. (https://www.hrw.org/reports/2005/us1005/TheRestofTheirLives.pdf).

Andonova, Elizabeth J. 2017. "Cycle of Misconduct: How Chicago Has Repeatedly Failed to Police its Police." *National Lawyers Guild* 73(2):65–102.

Austen, Ben. 2018. *High-Risers: Cabrini-Green and the Fate of American Public Housing*. New York: Harper.

Baer, Andrew S. 2020. *Beyond the Usual Beating: The Jon Burge Police Torture Scandal and Social Movements for Police Accountability in Chicago*. Chicago: University of Chicago Press.

Baldwin, James. 2010. *The Cross of Redemption: Uncollected Writings*. Edited and introduced by Randall Kenan. New York: Pantheon.

Balto, Simon. 2019. *Occupied Territory: Policing Black Chicago from Red Summer to Black Power*. Chapel Hill: University of Carolina Press.

Beckett, Katherine, and Bruce Western. 2001. "Governing Social Marginality Welfare, Incarceration, and the Transformation of State Policy." *Punishment & Society* 3(1):43–59.

Bell, Monica. 2016. "Situational Trust: How Disadvantaged Mothers Reconceive Legal Cynicism." *Law & Society Review* 50(2):314–347.

Bell, Monica C. 2017. "Police Reform and the Dismantling of Legal Estrangement." *Yale Law Journal* 126:2054–2150.

Bell, Monica C. 2019. "The Community in Criminal Justice: Subordination, Consumption, Resistance, and Transformation." *Du Bois Review* 16(1):197–220.

Belluck, Pam. 1998. "End of a Ghetto; Special Report; Razing the Slums to Rescue the Residents." *New York Times*, September 6. (https://www.nytimes.com/1998/09/06/us/end-of-a-ghetto-a-special-report-razing-the-slums-to-rescue-the-residents.html).

Black, Donald. 1983. "Crime as Social Control." *American Sociological Review* 48(1):34–45.

BlackLivesMatter. 2018a. "Her Story." (https://blacklivesmatter.com/about/herstory/).

BlackLivesMatter. 2018b. "Chapters." (https://blacklivesmatter.com/chapter/blm-chicago/).

Block, Carol R., and Richard L. Block. 2005. *Homicides in Chicago, 1965–1995*. Ann Arbor, MI: Inter-University Consortium of Political and Social Research (https://doi.org/10.3886/ICPSR06399.v5).

Blumstein, Alfred, and Richard Rosenfeld. 1998. "Explaining Recent Trends in U.S. Homicide Rates." *Journal of Criminal Law & Criminology* 88(4):1175–1216.

Bobo, Lawrence D., and Victor Thompson. 2006. "Unfair by Design: The War on Drugs, Race, and the Legitimacy of the Criminal Justice System." *Social Research* 73(2): 445–472.

Bocian, Deborah, Wei Li, and Keith S. Ernst. 2008. "Foreclosures by Race and Ethnicity: The Demographics of a Crisis." *Centre for Responsible Lending Report,* June 18. (http://www.responsiblelending.org/mortgage-lending/research-analysis/foreclosures-by-race-and-ethnicity.pdf).

Bogira, Steve. 2005. *Courtroom 302: A Year Behind the Scenes in an American Criminal Courthouse.* New York: Vintage Books.

Bogira, Steve. 2015. "In Freedom of Information Triumph, Chicago Police Misconduct Complaint Records Now Online." *Chicago Reader,* November 10. (https://www.chicagoreader.com/Bleader/archives/2015/11/10/in-freedom-of-information-triumph-chicago-police-misconduct-complaint-records-now-online).

Bonilla-Silva, Eduardo. 1997. "Rethinking Racism: Toward a Structural Interpretation." *American Sociological Review* 62(3):465–480.

Bosman, Julie, and Monica Davey. 2019. "3 Officers Acquitted of Covering Up for Colleague in Laquan McDonald Killing." *The New York Times,* January 17. (https://www.nytimes.com/2019/01/17/us/laquan-mcdonald-officers-acquitted.html).

Braga, Anthony A., Brandon C. Welsh, and Cory Schnell. 2015. "Can Policing Disorder Reduce Crime? A Systematic Review and Meta-analysis." *Journal of Research in Crime and Delinquency* 52(4):567–588.

Brayne, Sarah. 2020. *Predict and Surveil: Data, Discretion, and the Future of Policing.* New York: Oxford University Press.

Brown, Jeffrey. 2018. "A National Memorial Confronts the Terror of Lynching." *PBS News Hour.* April 27. (https://www.pbs.org/newshour/show/a-national-memorial-confronts-the-terror-of-lynching).

Brzeczek, Richard, Elizabeth Brzeczek, and Sharon DeVita. 1989. *Addicted to Adultery: How We Saved Our Marriage/How You Can Save Yours.* New York: Bantam.

Burge, Jon. 2010. "Police Torture Archive, Jon Burge, Chicago." U.S. V Burge. *Invisible Institute.* (https://www.dropbox.com/sh/ch5e6i674shwpr8/AADlPsCmSASfpbWERyCQYVdya?dl=0).

Burns, Rebecca. 2016 "The Laquan McDonald Email Dump Shows Rahm Emanuel's Administration in Crisis Mode." *In These Times,* January 5. (http://inthesetimes.com/article/18729/laquan-mcdonald-rahm-emanuel-emails-foia).

Byrd, Doris. 2004. Sworn Statement of Doris Byrd. Patterson v. Burge, No. 3 4433, November 9, 2004, 6–7, PLOTE.

Byrd, Doris. 2010. "Police Torture Archive, Jon Burge, Chicago." U.S. V Burge. *Invisible Institute.* (https://www.dropbox.com/sh/ch5e6i674shwpr8/AADlPsCmSASfpbWERyCQYVdya?dl=0).

Cameron, A. Colin, and Pravin K. Trivedi. 2013. *Regression Analysis of Count Data,* 2nd edition. New York: Cambridge University Press.

Capehart, Jonathan. 2017. "Opinion: How the Terror of Lynchings in the Past Haunts Us Today and Our Future." *The Washington Post,* June 27. (https://www.washingtonpost.com/blogs/post-partisan/wp/2017/06/27/how-the-terror-of-lynchings-in-the-past-haunt-us-today-and-our-future/).

Carmichael, Jason T., and Stephanie L. Kent. 2014. "The Persistent Significance of Racial and Economic Inequality on the Size of Municipal Police Forces in the United States, 1980-2010." *Social Problems* 61(2):259–282.

Carr, Patrick J., Laura Napolitano, and Jessica Keating. 2007. "We Never Call the Cops and Here Is Why: A Qualitative Examination of Legal Cynicism in Three Philadelphia Neighborhoods." *Criminology* 45(2):445–480.

Charles, Sam, and Fran Spielman. 2020. "After Anjanette Young Raid Snafu, Lightfoot Pledges, 'We Will Do Better.'" *Chicago Sun Times*. (https://chicago.suntimes.com/city-hall/2020/12/17/22187318/chicago-police-raid-anjanette-young-mayor-lightfoot-pledges-do-better).

Chetty, Raj, Nathaniel Hendren, and Lawrence F. Katz. 2015. "The Effects of Exposure to Better Neighborhoods on Children: New Evidence from the Moving to Opportunity Experiment." *Harvard University and NBER.* (http://www.equality-of-opportunity.org/images/mto_paper.pdf).

Chicago 21. 1973. A Plan for Central Area Communities. (https://www.govinfo.gov/content/pkg/CZIC-ht168-c5-c54-1973b/pdf/CZIC-ht168-c5-c54-1973b.pdf).

Chicago City Hall. 2016. Mayor Rahm Emanuel Email Release. (https://docs.google.com/spreadsheets/d/1aWuLqPmzoupsed1P97JBnxBwLgQx-YijsJOg7IhbBXQ/edit#gid=1899370579).

Clarke, Elizabeth. 1996. "A Case for Reinventing Juvenile Transfer: The Record of Transfer of Juvenile Offenders to Criminal Court in Cook County, Illinois." *Juvenile & Family Court Journal* 47(4):3–22.

Clear, Todd R. 2007. *Imprisoning Communities: How Mass Incarceration Makes Disadvantaged Neighborhoods Worse*. New York: Oxford University Press.

Coates, Ta-Nehisi. 2014. "The Case for Reparations." *The Atlantic* 313(5) June 1. (https://www.theatlantic.com/magazine/archive/2014/06/the-case-for-reparations/361631/).

Coates, Ta-Nehisi. 2018. *We Were Eight Years in Power: An American Tragedy*. New York: One World.

Cohen, Adam, and Elizabeth Taylor. 2000. *American Pharaoh: Mayor Richard J. Daley – His Battle for Chicago and the Nation*. Little Brown and Company.

Conroy, John. 1990a. "House of Screams." *Chicago Reader*, January 25. (https://www.chicagoreader.com/chicago/house-of-screams/Content?oid=875107).

Conroy, John. 1990b. "Capital Crimes." *Chicago Reader*, November 29. (https://www.chicagoreader.com/chicago/capital-crimes/Content?oid=876701).

Conroy, John. 1997. "The Shocking Truth." *Chicago Reader*, January 10. (https://www.chicagoreader.com/chicago/the-shocking-truth/Content?oid=892462).

Conroy, John. 2000. *Unspeakable Acts, Ordinary People: The Dynamics of Torture*. Oakland: University of California Press.

Conroy, John. 2001. "A Hell of a Deal." *Chicago Reader*, October 11. (https://www.chicagoreader.com/chicago/a-hell-of-a-deal/Content?oid=906674).

Conroy, John. 2003. "Deaf to the Screams." *Chicago Reader*, July 31. (https://www.chicagoreader.com/chicago/deaf-to-the-screams/Content?oid=912813).

Conroy, John. 2005. "Tools of Torture." *Chicago Reporter* February 4. (https://www.chicagoreader.com/chicago/tools-of-torture/Content?oid=917876).

Conroy, John. 2006. "Doe in the Headlights." *Chicago Reader*, July 19. (https://www.chicagoreader.com/chicago/doe-in-the-headlights/Content?oid=922666).

Conroy, John. 2007. "Police Torture: Is This a Gag?" *Chicago Reader*, September 27. (https://www.chicagoreader.com/chicago/police-torture-is-this-a-gag/Content?oid=926030).

Cooper, Daniel, and Ryan Lugalia-Hollon. n.d. Chicago Justice Project of Chicago's Million Dollar Blocks. (http://chicagosmilliondollarblocks.com/).

Corsaro, Nicholas, James Frank, and Murat Ozer. 2015. "Perceptions of Police Practice, Cynicism of Police Performance, and Persistent Neighborhood Violence: An Intersecting Relationship." *Journal of Criminal Justice* 43(1):1–11.

Cramer, Maria. 2020. "Chicago Mayor Apologizes to Social Worker Who Was Handcuffed Naked." *New York Times*. December 17. (https://www.nytimes.com/2020/12/17/us/chicago-police-raid-anjanette-young.html).

Cruz, Wilfredo. 1982. "Minority Leaders Charge Police with 'Disorderly Conduct.'" *The Chicago Reporter*, October 1. (https://www.chicagoreporter.com/arrests-jump-sharply-minority-leaders-charge-police-with-disorderly-conduct/).

Cui, Lin, and Randall Walsh. 2015. "Foreclosure, Vacancy and Crime." *Journal of Urban Economics* 87:72–84.

Daley, Richard M. 1994a. Crime Bill Press Conference. August 12. Richard J. Daley Library, University of Illinois at Chicago. (https://researchguides.uic.edu/DaleyFamily/RMDfindingaid).

Daley, Richard M. 1994b. Crime Bill Press Conference. August 17. Richard J. Daley Library, University of Illinois at Chicago. (https://researchguides.uic.edu/DaleyFamily/RMDfindingaid).

Daniels, Steve. 2018. "Tallying the Cost of Bad Cops." *Crain's Chicago Business*, July 9, pp. 1, 22.

Davey, Monica. 2015. "Chicago Pays $5 Million to Family of Black Teenager Killed by Officer." *New York Times Magazine*, April 15. (https://www.nytimes.com/2015/04/16/us/chicago-pays-5-million-to-family-of-black-teenager-killed-by-officer.html).

Davey, Monica. 2018. "Police 'Code of Silence' Is on Trial After Murder by Chicago Officer." *New York Times*, December 3. (https://www.nytimes.com/2018/12/03/us/chicago-police-code-of-silence.html).

Davey, Monica, and Mitch Smith. 2015a. "Video of Chicago Police Shooting a Teenager Is Ordered Released." *New York Times*. November 19. (https://www.nytimes.com/2015/11/20/us/laquan-mcdonald-chicago-police-shooting.html).

Davey, Monica, and Mitch Smith. 2015b. "Chicago Protests Mostly Peaceful After Video of Police Shooting Is Released." *New York Times*. November 24. (https://www.nytimes.com/2015/11/25/us/chicago-officer-charged-in-death-of-black-teenager-official-says.html).

Desmond, Matthew. 2016. *Evicted: Poverty and Profit in the American City*. Crown Books: New York.

Desmond, Matthew, Andrew V. Papachristos, and David S. Kirk. 2016. "Police Violence and Citizen Crime Reporting in the Black Community." *American Sociological Review* 81(5):857–876.

Desmond, Matthew, Andrew V. Papachristos, and David S. Kirk. 2020. "Evidence of the Effect of Police Violence on Citizen Crime Reporting." *American Sociological Review* 85(1):184–190.

Desmond, Matthew, and Nicol Valdez. 2013. "Unpolicing the Urban Poor: Consequences of Third-Party Policing for Inner-City Women." *American Sociological Review* 78(1):117–141.

Diamond, Andrew. 2017. *Chicago on the Make: Power and Inequality in a Modern City*. Oakland: University of California Press.

Dodge, L. Mara. 2000. "'Our Juvenile Court Has Become More Like a Criminal Court': A Century of Reform at the Cook County (Chicago) Juvenile Court." *Michigan Historical Review* 26(2):51–89.

Editor. 1969. "No Quarter for Wild Beasts." *Chicago Tribune* November 15, 10. ProQuest Historical Newspapers. University of California Davis.

Editorial Board. 2015. "The Violent Legacy of Chicago's Police." *New York Times*, April 21. (https://www.nytimes.com/2015/04/21/opinion/the-violent-legacy-of-chicagos-police.html?_r=0).

Eisenstein, James, and Herbert Jacob. 1977. *Felony Justice: An Organizational Analysis of Criminal Courts*. Boston: Little & Brown.

Eisner, Manuel, and Amy Nivette. 2013. "Does Low Legitimacy Cause Crime? A Review of the Evidence." In Justice Tankebe and Alison Liebling (Eds.), *Legitimacy and Criminal Justice: An International Exploration*, pp. 308-325. Oxford, England: Oxford University Press.

Ekins, Emily. 2016. "Policing in America: Understanding Public Attitudes toward the Police. Results from a National Survey." Results from the Cato Institute 2016 Criminal Justice Survey. (https://www.cato.org/survey-reports/policing-america).

Emery, Clifton R., Jennifer M. Jolley, and Shali Wu. 2011. "Desistance from Intimate Partner Violence: The Role of Legal Cynicism, Collective Efficacy, and Social Disorganization in Chicago Neighborhoods." *American Journal of Community Psychology* 48(3–4):373–383.

Erie, Steven P. 1988. *Rainbows' End: Irish Americans and the Dilemmas of Urban Machine Politics, 1840-1985.* Berkeley: University of California.

Faber, Jacob William, and Jessica Rose Kalbfeld. 2019. "Complaining While Black: Racial Disparities in the Adjudication of Complaints Against the Police." *City & Community* 18(3):1028–1067.

Fagan, Jeffrey, and Elizabeth Piper Deschenes. 1990. "Determinants of Juvenile Waiver Decisions for Violent Juvenile Offenders." *Journal of Criminal Law & Criminology* 81(2):314–347.

Fan, Andrew. 2016. "The Most Dangerous Neighborhood, the Most Inexperienced Cops." *The Marshall Project,* September 20. (https://www.themarshallproject.org/2016/09/20/the-most-dangerous-neighborhood-the-most-inexperienced-cops).

Felstiner, William L.F., Richard L. Abel, and Austin Sarat. 1980/1. "The Emergence and Transformation of Disputes: Naming, Blaming, Claiming . . ." *Law & Society Review* 15(3–4):631–654.

Figueroa, Jose F., Rishi K.Wadhera,Winta T.Mehtsun, Kristen Riley, Jessica Phelan, and Ashish K.Jha. 2021. "Association of Race, Ethnicity, and Community-level Factors with COVID-19 Cases and Deaths across U.S. Counties." *Healthcare* 9(1):338.

Ford, Quinn. 2014. "Cops: Boy, 17, Fatally Shot by Officer after Refusing to Drop Knife. " *Chicago Tribune,* October 21. (https://www.chicagotribune.com/news/breaking/chi-chicago-shootings-violence-20141021-story.html).

Forman, James Jr. 2017. *Locking Up Our Own: Crime and Punishment in Black America.* New York: Farrar, Straus, and Giroux.

Fortner, Michael. 2015. *Black Silent Majority: The Rockefeller Drug Laws and the Politics of Punishment.* Cambridge, MA: Harvard University Press.

Fountain, John W. 1992. "As Violence Rises, So Do Trials of Teens as Adults." *Chicago Tribune,* February 19. (https://www.chicagotribune.com/news/ct-xpm-1992-02-19-9201160277-story.html).

Fox, Sanford J. 1970. "Juvenile Justice Reform: An Historical Perspective." *Stanford Law Review* 22(6):1187–1239.

Fremon, David K. 1988. *Chicago Politics Ward by Ward.* Bloomington: Indiana University Press.

Futterman, Craig, and Jamie Kalven. 2014. "Laquan McDonald." *Invisible Institute,* December 8. (https://invisible.institute/news/2014/laquan-mcdonald).

Garfinkel, Harold. 1956. "Conditions of Successful Degradation Ceremonies." *American Journal of Sociology* 61(5): 420–424.

Garland, David. 2001. *The Culture of Control: Crime and Social Order in Contemporary Society.* Chicago: University of Chicago Press.

Glaser, Jack. 2014. *Suspect Race: Causes and Consequences of Racial Profiling.* New York: Oxford University Press.

Glaude, Eddie Jr. 2020. *Begin Again: James Baldwin's America and its Urgent Lessons for Our Own.* New York: Penguin/Random House.

Goffman, Alice. 2014. *On the Run: Fugitive Life in an American City.* Chicago: University of Chicago Press.

Gonnerman, Jennifer. 2018. "Framed: How One Woman's Fight to Save Her Family Helped Lead to a Mass Exoneration." *The New Yorker,* May 28. (https://www.newyorker.com/magazine/2018/05/28/how-one-womans-fight-to-save-her-family-helped-lead-to-a-mass-exoneration).

Goodman, Amy. 2006 "Chicago's Abu Ghraib: UN Committee Against Torture Hears Report on How Police Tortured Over 135 African American Men Inside Chicago Jails." *Democracy Now!*

May 9. (https://www.democracynow.org/2006/5/9/chicagos_abu_ghraib_un_committee_against).

Goodman, Amy. 2019. "'16 Shots': Chicago Police Killing of Laquan McDonald Exposed a System Built on Lies." *Democracy Now!* June 17. (https://www.democracynow.org/2019/6/17/16_shots_rick_rowley_showtime_documentary).

Gorner, Jeremy, and Geoffrey Hing. 2015. "Tribune Analysis: Cops Who Pile Up Complaints Routinely Escape Discipline." *Chicago Tribune*, June 13. (https://www.chicagotribune.com/news/ct-chicago-police-citizen-complaints-met-20150613-story.html

Graif, Corina. 2015. "Delinquency and Gender Moderation in the Moving to Opportunity Intervention: The Role of Extended Neighborhoods." *Criminology* 53(3):366–398.

Granovetter, Mark S. 1973. "The Strength of Weak Ties." *American Journal of Sociology* 78(6):1360–1380.

Green, Bob. 1992. "It May be Too Late to Sound an Alarm." *Chicago Tribune*, December 1, C1. ProQuest Historical Newspapers. University of California Davis.

Hagan, John. 1989. "Why Is There So Little Criminal Justice Theory? Neglected Macro- and Micro-Level Links Between Organization and Power." *Journal of Research on Crime and Delinquency* 26(2):116–135.

Hagan, John. 2010. *Who Are the Criminals? The Politics of Crime Policy in the Age of Roosevelt to the Age of Reagan.* Princeton: Princeton University Press.

Hagan, John, and Celesta Albonetti. 1982. "Race, Class, and the Perception of Criminal Injustice in America." *American Journal of Sociology* 88(2):329–355.

Hagan, John, Paul Hirschfield, and Carla Shedd. 2002. "First and Last Words: Apprehending the Social and Legal Facts of an Urban High School Shooting." *Sociological Methods & Research* 31(2): 218–254.

Hagan, John, Joshua Kaiser, and Anna Hanson. 2015. *Iraq and the Crimes of Aggressive War: The Legal Cynicism of Criminal Militarism.* New York: Cambridge University Press.

Hagan, John, Bill McCarthy, and Daniel Herda. 2018. "Race, Legal Cynicism, and the Machine Politics of Drug Law Enforcement in Chicago." *Du Bois Review* 15(1):129–151.

Hagan, John, Bill McCarthy, and Daniel Herda. 2020 "What the Study of Legal Cynicism and Crime Can Tell Us about Reliability, Validity, and Versatility in Law and Social Science Research." *Annual Review of Law and Social Science* 16:1–20.

Hagan, John, Bill McCarthy, Daniel Herda, and Andrea Cann Chandrasekher. 2018. "Dual Process Theory of Racial Isolation, Legal Cynicism, and Reported Crime." *Proceedings of the National Academy of Sciences* 115(28):7190–7199.

Hagan, John, Gabriele Plickert, Alberto Palloni, and Spencer Headworth. 2015. "Making Punishment Pay: The Political Economy of Revenue, Race and Regime in the California Prison." *DuBois Review* 12(1):95–118.

Hagan, John, Carla Shedd, and Monique Payne. 2005. "Race, Ethnicity, and Youth Perceptions of Criminal Injustice." *American Sociological Review* 70(3):381–407.

Hagedorn, John. 2006. "Race Not Space: A Revisionist History of Gangs in Chicago." *Journal of African American History* 91(2):194–208.

Hall, Matthew, Keith Crowder, and Amy Spring. 2015. "Neighborhood Foreclosures, Racial/Ethnic Transitions, and Residential Segregation." *American Sociological Review* 80(3):526–549.

Hamilton, Aretina R., and Kenneth Foote. 2018. "Police Torture in Chicago: Theorizing Violence and Social Justice in a Racialized City." *Annals of the American Association of Geographers* 108(2):399–410.

Hannah-Jones, Nikole. 2019. "Our Democracy's Founding Ideals Were False When They Were Written. Black Americans Have Fought to Make Them True." *New York Times Magazine* August 14. (https://www.nytimes.com/interactive/2019/08/14/magazine/black-history-american-democracy.html).

Harcourt, Bernard E. 1998. "Reflecting on the Subject: A Critique of the Social Influence Conception of Deterrence, the Broken Windows Theory, and Order-Maintenance Policing New York Style." *Michigan Law Review* 97(2):291–389.

Harcourt, Bernard E. 2001. *Illusion of Order: The False Promise of Broken Windows Policing.* Cambridge, MA: Harvard University Press.

Harcourt, Bernard E., and Jens Ludwig. 2006. "Broken Windows: New Evidence from New York City and a Five-City Social Experiment." *University of Chicago Law Review* 73(1): 271–320.

Hartnett, Michael. 2010. U.S. v. Burge. 6.21 and 6.22.10.pdf. Police Torture Archive, Jon Burge, Chicago, 13. U.S. v Burge. *Invisible Institute.* (https://www.dropbox.com/sh/ch5e6i674shwpr8/AADlPsCmSASfpbWERyCQYVdya?dl=0).

Harding, David J., and Peter Hepburn. 2014. "Cultural Mechanisms in Neighborhood Effects Research in the United States." *Sociologia Urbana e Rurale* 103:37–73.

Hawes, Christine, and Terry Wilson. 1992. "Tilden Tries to Heal Wounds: Counselors Help Students Cope with Fatal Shooting." *Chicago Tribune*, November 24, S7. ProQuest Historical Newspapers. University of California Davis.

Hickey, Megan. 2020. "Protesters Demand Closure of CPD Homan Square Facility." CBS. July 24, 2020. (https://chicago.cbslocal.com/2020/07/24/protesters-demand-closure-of-cpd-homan-square-facility/).

Hinton, Elizabeth. 2016. *From the War on Poverty to the War on Crime: The Making of Mass Incarceration in America.* Cambridge, MA: Harvard University.

Hinton, Elizabeth, Julilly Kohler-Hausmann, and Vesla M. Weaver. 2016. "Did Blacks Really Endorse the 1994 Crime Bill?" *New York Times*, April 13. (http://www.nytimes.com/2016/04/13/opinion/did-blacks-really-endorse-the-1994-crime-bill.html?mtrref=undefined&assetType=opinion&_r=0).

Hipp, John R. 2007. "Block, Tract, and Levels of Aggregation: Neighborhood Structure and Crime and Disorder as a Case in Point." *American Sociological Review* 72(5):659–680.

Hirsch, Arnold R. 1983. *Making the Second Ghetto: Race and Housing in Chicago, 1940-1960.* Chicago: University of Chicago Press.

Hoerner, Emily. 2019. "Illinois High Court Hears Defense Prosecutor Debate 50-Year Sentence for Youth." *InjusticeWatch*, January 15. (https://www.injusticewatch.org/news/2019/Illinois-high-court-hears-defense-prosecutor-debate-50-year-sentence-for-youth./).

Holmes, Malcolm D. 2000. "Minority Threat and Police Brutality: Determinants of Civil Rights Criminal Complaints in U.S. Municipalities." *Criminology* 38(2):343–368.

House, James S., George A. Kaplan, Jeffrey Morenoff, Stephen W. Raudenbush, David R. Williams, and Elizabeth A. Young. 2012. *Chicago Community Adult Health Study, 2001-2003 (ICPSR31142-v1).* Ann Arbor, MI: Inter-university Consortium for Political and Social Research [distributor]. (http://doi.org/10.3886/ICPSR31142.v1).

Hunt, Chacyln (n.d.) "Police Torture Archive, Jon Burge, Chicago." OPS.Goldston.Sanders. Police Foundation Reports. *Invisible Institute.* (https://www.dropbox.com/sh/ch5e6i674sh-wpr8/AADlPsCmSASfpbWERyCQYVdya?dl=0)

Hunt, Chacyln (n.d.) "Police Torture Archive, Jon Burge, Chicago." Special Prosecutor. Reports and Evidence. *Invisible Institute.* (https://www.dropbox.com/sh/ch5e6i674shwpr8/AADlPsCmSASfpbWERyCQYVdya?dl=0)

Hunt, Chacyln (n.d.) "Police Torture Archive, Jon Burge, Chicago." U.S. V Burge. *Invisible Institute.* (https://www.dropbox.com/sh/ch5e6i674shwpr8/AADlPsCmSASfpbWERyCQYVdya?dl=0)

Hunter, Marcus Anthony, and Zandria F. Robinson. 2016. "The Sociology of Urban Black America." *Annual Review of Sociology* 42:385–405.

Ignatiev, Noel. 1995. *How the Irish Became White.* New York: Routledge.

Invisible Institute. 2017. "Citizens Police Data Project." (https://beta.cpdp.co/).

Jackman, Mary R., and Kimberlee A. Shauman. 2019 "The Toll of Inequality: Excess African American Deaths in the United States over the Twentieth Century." *Du Bois Review* 16(2): 291–340.

Jackson, David. 2011. "The Law and Richard M. Daley." *Chicago Magazine*, May 13. (https://www.chicagomag.com/Chicago-Magazine/September-1988/The-Law-and-Richard-M-Daley/).

Kahneman, Daniel. 2011. *Thinking, Fast and Slow*. New York: Farrar, Straus and Giroux.

Kane, Robert J. 2002. "The Social Ecology of Police Misconduct. *Criminology* 40(4): 867–896.

Kane, Robert J. 2005. "Compromised Police Legitimacy as a Predictor of Violent Crime in Structurally Disadvantaged Communities." *Criminology* 48(2):469–498.

Kennedy, Randall. 1997. *Race, Crime, and the Law*. New York: Pantheon Books.

Kerstetter, Wayne A., Kenneth A. Rasinski, and Cami L. Heiert. 1996. "The Impact of Race on the Investigation of Excessive Force Allegations against Police." *Journal of Criminal Justice* 24(1):1–15.

Khan-Cullors, Patrisse, and asha bandele. 2017. *When They Call You a Terrorist: A Black Lives Matter Memoir*. New York: St. Martin's Press.

King, Martin Luther, Jr. 2020. Chicago Campaign. *Martin Luther King, Jr. Encyclopedia*. (https://kinginstitute.stanford.edu/encyclopedia/chicago-campaign).

Kirk, David S. 2016. "Prisoner Reentry and the Reproduction of Legal Cynicism." *Social Problems* 63(2):222–243.

Kirk, David S., and Derek S. Hyra. 2012. "Home Foreclosures and Community Crime: Causal or Spurious Association?" *Social Science Quarterly* 93(3): 648–670.

Kirk, David S., and Mauri Matsuda. 2011. "Legal Cynicism, Collective Efficacy, and the Ecology of Arrest." *Criminology* 49(2):443–472.

Kirk, David S., and Andrew V. Papachristos. 2011. "Cultural Mechanisms and the Persistence of Neighborhood Violence." *American Journal of Sociology* 116(4):1190–1233.

Kirk, David S., Andrew V. Papachristos, Jeffrey Fagan, and Tom Tyler. 2012. "The Paradox of Law Enforcement in Immigrant Communities: Does Immigration Enforcement Undermine Public Safety?" *The ANNALS of the American Academy of Political and Social Science* 641(1): 79–98.

Kling, Jeffrey R., Jens Ludwig, and Lawrence F. Katz. 2005. "Neighborhood Effects on Crime for Female and Male: Evidence from a Randomized Housing Voucher Experiment." *Quarterly Journal of Economics* 120(1):87–130.

Koeneman, Keith. 2013. *First Son: The Biography of Richard M. Daley*. Chicago: University of Chicago Press.

Lacey, Samuel. 2010. "Police Torture Archive, Jon Burge, Chicago." *U.S. V Burge. Invisible Institute*. (https://www.dropbox.com/sh/ch5e6i674shwpr8/AADlPsCmSASfpbWERyCQYVdya?dl=0).

Lavin, Cheryl. 1989. "Guilty of Adultery." *Chicago Tribune*, September 13. (https://www.chicagotribune.com/news/ct-xpm-1989-09-13-8901120490-story.html).

Lemann, Nicholas. 1995. *The Promised Land: The Great Migration and How It Changed America*. New York: Vintage Books.

Lenhart, Jennifer, and Louise Kiernan. 1992. "Even Safety of Schools Shattered, Student Slain, 2 Others Wounded in Hallway at Tilden." *Chicago Tribune*, November 21, D1. ProQuest Historical Newspapers. University of California Davis.

Lepore, Jill. 2020a. "The Riot Report: What Government Commissions Say about Protests for Racial Justice." *The New Yorker*, June 22. (https://scholar.harvard.edu/jlepore/publications/riot-report-what-government-commissions-say-about-protests-racial-justice).

Lepore, Jill. 2020b. "The Long Blue Line: Inventing the Police." *The New Yorker*, July 13. (https://www.newyorker.com/magazine/2020/07/20/the-invention-of-the-police)

Lerman, Amy E., and Vesla M. Weaver. 2014. *Arresting Citizenship: The Democratic Consequences of American Crime Control*. Chicago: University of Chicago Press.

Levine, Sam. 2015. "Here's How the Laquan McDonald Shooting Differs from What Police Said Happened." *HuffPost*, November 25. (https://www.huffpost.com/entry/laquan-mcdonald-shooting-video_n_5655ca26e4b08e945fea9488).

Leovy, Jill. 2015. *Ghettoside: A True Story of Murder in America*. New York: Random House.

Liu, Hanhua, Richard Emsley, Graham Dunn, Tyler VanderWeele, and Linda Valeri. 2014. "Paramed: A Command to Perform Causal Mediation Analysis Using Parametric Models." (http://www.haghish.com/statistics/stata-blog/stata-programming/download/paramed.html).

Logan, John R., Zengwang Xu, and Brian J. Stults. 2014. "Interpolating U.S. Decennial Census Tract Data from as Early as 1970 to 2010: A Longitudinal Tract Database." *The Professional Geographer* 66(3):412–420.

Macek, Steve. 2016. "Framing a Shooting (and a Movement)." *Mediapolis: A Journal of Cities and Culture*. (https://www.mediapolisjournal.com/2016/03/framing-shooting-movement/).

Marable, Manning. 1986. "Harold Washington and the Politics of Race in Chicago." *The Black Scholar* 17(6):14–23.

Marchese, David. 2020. "Lori Ligthfoot, Mayor of Chicago, on Who's Hurt by Defunding Police. *New York Times*, June 22. (https://www.nytimes.com/interactive/2020/06/22/magazine/lori-lightfoot-chicago-police.html).

Massey, Douglas S., and Nancy A. Denton. 1993. *American Apartheid: Segregation and the Making of the Underclass*. Cambridge, MA: Harvard University Press.

Massey, Douglas S., and Jonathan Tannen. 2015. "A Research Note on Trends in Black Hypersegregation." *Demography* 52(3):1025–1034.

Matza, David. 1964. *Delinquency and Drift*. New York: John Wiley & Sons.

Mazerolle, Lorraine, Sarah Bennett, Jacqueline Davis, Elise Sargeant, and Matthew Manning. 2013. "Procedural Justice and Police Legitimacy: A Systematic Review of the Research Evidence." *Journal of Experimental Criminology* 9(3):245–274.

McCluskey, John D., and William Terrill. 2005. "Departmental and Citizen Complaints as Predictors of Police Coercion." *Policing: An International Journal of Police Strategies & Management* 28(3):513–529.

McDermott, Michael. 2010. "Police Torture Archive, Jon Burge, Chicago." U.S. V Burge. *Invisible Institute*. (https://www.dropbox.com/sh/ch5e6i674shwpr8/AADlPs CmSASfpbWERyCQYVdya?dl=0).

Meares, Tracey L. 2014. "The Law and Social Science of Stop and Frisk." *Annual Review of Law and Social Science* 10:335–352.

Meisner, Jason. 2016. "Trial to Expose 'Street Files' Used by Police to Hide Evidence Years Ago." *Chicago Tribune*, November 20. (https://www.chicagotribune.com/news/breaking/ct-chicago-police-street-files-trial-met-20161121-story.html).

Meisner, Jason, Jeremy Gorner, and Steve Schmadeke. 2015. "Chicago Releases Dash-cam Vido of Fatal Shooting after Cop Charged with Murder." *Chicago Tribune*, November 24. (https://www.chicagotribune.com/news/breaking/ct-chicago-cop-shooting-video-laquan-mcdonald-charges-20151124-story.html).

Metcalfe, Ralph H. 1972. "The Misuse of Police Authority in Chicago. A Report and Recommendations before the Blue Ribbon Panel." (https://chicagopatf.org/wp-content/uploads/2016/01/metcalfe-report-1972.pdf).

Misra, Tanvi. 2016. "Housing Vouchers, Economic Mobility, and Chicago's Infamous 'Projects'." *Citylab*, March 31. (https://www.citylab.com/equity/2016/03/what-demolitions-of-chicagos-projects-in-1990-reveal-about-housing-vouchers/475809/).

Mitchell, Mary. 2014. "Questions Surround a Chicago Police Fatal Shooting of a Teen." *Chicago Sun Times*, December 16. (https://chicago.suntimes.com/2014/12/16/18598665/questions-surround-a-chicago-police-fatal-shooting-of-a-teen).

Mitchell, Mary. 2016. "Why the City Doesn't Want Video of Laquan McDonald's Shooting Released." *Chicago Sun Times*, June 24. (https://chicago.suntimes.com/2016/6/24/18479492/why-the-city-doesn-t-want-video-of-laquan-mcdonald-s-shooting-released).

Moskos, Peter. 2008. *Cop in the Hood: My Year Policing Baltimore's Eastern District*. Princeton, NJ: Princeton University Press.

Muhammad, Khalil Gibran. 2010. *The Condemnation of Blackness: Race, Crime, and the Making of Modern Urban America*. Cambridge, MA: Harvard University Press.

Muller, Christopher. 2012. "Northward Migration and the Rise of Racial Disparity in American Incarceration, 1880-1950." American Journal of Sociology 118(2):281–326.

Myers, Linnet. 1987. "Brzeczek Acquitted of Theft, Lashes Daley." *Chicago Tribune*, May 15. (https://www.chicagotribune.com/news/ct-xpm-1987-05-15-8702060227-story.html).

Muwakkil, Salim. 2006. "Police Torture and the Need for Repair." *In These Times*, August 3. (https://inthesetimes.com/article/police-torture-and-the-need-for-repair).

Nagin, Daniel S., and Cody W. Telep. 2017. "Procedural Justice and Legal Compliance." *Annual Review of Law and Social Science* 13:5–28.

National Center for Educational Statistics. 2019. *Indicators of School Crime and Safety*. (https://nces.ed.gov/programs/crimeindicators/ind_02.asp).

National Research Council Committee on Proactive Policing. 2017. (https://www8.nationalacademies.org/cp/CommitteeView.aspx?key=49739).

NBC Chicago. 2019. "3 Chicago Cops Not Guilty in Alleged Cover-up of Laquan McDonald Shooting." January 17. (https://www.nbc15.com/content/news/3-Chicago-cops-not-guilty-in-alleged-cover-up-of-Laquan-McDonald-shooting-504513751.html).

New York Times. 1987. The Reagan White House; Transcript of Reagan's Speech: I Take full Responsibility for My Actions. March 5 p. A1, 18. https://www.nytimes.com/1987/03/05/us/reagan-white-house-transcript-reagan-s-speech-take-full-responsibilty-for-my.html

Novak, Tim, and Steve Warmbir. 2004a. "'You Put in Your Eight Hours a Day, but You Just Sit on the Job'." *Chicago Sun Times*, January 23, p. 1. Access World News, Rutgers University Newark.

Novak, Tim, and Steve Warmbir. 2004b. "Hired Trucks Thrive in Daley's Ward." *Chicago Sun Times*, January 26, p.1. Access World News, Rutgers University Newark.

Ouellet, Marie, Sadaf Hashimi, Jason Gravel, and Andrew V. Papachristos. 2019. "Network Exposure and Excessive Use of Force: Investigating the Social Transmission of Police Misconduct." *Crime & Public Policy* 18:675–704.

Papajohn, George. 1992. "Student was in the Wrong Place at Wrong Time." *Chicago Tribune*, November 23, NW A1. (https://www.chicagotribune.com/news/ct-xpm-1992-11-22-9204160765-story.html).

Peck, Jennifer H. 2015. "Minority Perceptions of the Police: A State-of-the-Art Review." *Policing: An International Journal of Police Strategies & Management* 38(1):173–203.

People. 1993. "Death of an Innocent Bystander: The Peacekeeper in his Family, Delondyn Lawson is Cut Down at Random by a Classmate Firing Wildly." *People*, June 14, pp. 48–49.

Platt, Anthony M. 1969. *The Child Savers: The Invention of Delinquency*. Chicago: University of Chicago Press.

Police Accountability Task Force. 2016. *Recommendations for Reform: Restoring Trust between the Chicago Police and the Communities They Serve*. (https://chicagopatf.org/wp-content/uploads/2016/04/PATF_Final_Report_Executive_Summary_4_13_16-1.pdf).

Possley, Maurice. 2020. "Jackie Wilson, Other Cook County, Illinois Exonerations with False Confession." October 16. (https://www.law.umich.edu/special/exoneration/Pages/casedetail.aspx?caseid=5818).

President's Task Force on 21st Century Policing. 2015. Final Report. (https://cops.usdoj.gov/pdf/taskforce/taskforce_finalreport.pdf).

Raba, John. 2010. "Police Torture Archive, Jon Burge, Chicago." U.S. V Burge. *Invisible Institute*. (https://www.dropbox.com/sh/ch5e6i674shwpr8/AADlPsCmSASfpbWERyCQYVdya?dl=0.)

Rachlinski, Jeffrey J., Chris Guthrie, and Andrew J. Wistrich. 2013. "Contrition in the Courtroom: Do Apologies Affect Adjudication?" *Cornell Law Review* 98(5): 1189–1123.

Ralph, James. 1993. *Northern Protest: Martin Luther King, Jr., Chicago, and the Civil Rights Movement*. Cambridge, MA: Harvard University Press.

Ralph, Laurence. 2013. "The Quality of Pain: How Police Torture Shapes Historical Consciousness." *Anthropological Theory* 13(1-2):104–118.

Ralph, Laurence. 2017. "Alibi: The Extralegal Force Embedded in the Law." In Didier Fassin (Ed.), *Writing the World of Policing: The Difference Ethnography Makes*, pp. 248–268. Stanford, CA: Stanford University Press.

Ralph, Laurence. 2020. *The Torture Letters: Reckoning with Police Violence*. Chicago: University of Chicago Press.

Ranney, David. 2003. *Global Decisions, Local Collisions: Urban Life in the New World Order*. Philadelphia: Temple University Press.

Raphael, Steven, and Michael A. Stoll. 2013. *Why Are So Many Americans in Prison?* New York: Russell Sage Foundation.

Rast, Joel. 2002. *Remaking Chicago: The Political Origins of Urban Industrial Change*. DeKalb, IL: Northern Illinois University Press.

Raymond, Adam K. 2017. "Trump Lauds Cops, Rips Immigrants and Media in Speech to FBI." *New York Intelligencer*. December 15. (https://nymag.com/intelligencer/2017/12/trump-lauds-cops-rips-immigrants-and-media-in-speech-to-fbi.html).

Redding, Richard E. 2010. *Juvenile Transfer Laws: An Effective Deterrent to Delinquency?* U.S. Department of Justice, Office of Justice Programs, Office of Juvenile Justice and Delinquency Prevention. (https://www.ncjrs.gov/pdffiles1/ojjdp/220595.pdf).

Regulus, Thomas A., Ann O'Brien Stevens, and Donald Faggiani. 1988. *State School to Stateville: A Report on Mandatory Transfer and Criminal Prosecution of Juveniles in Cook County, IL, January 1980 to June 1988*. Chicago: The Chicago Law Enforcement Study Group.

Reisig, Michael D., Scott E. Wolfe, and Kristy Holtfreter. 2011. "Legal Cynicism, Legitimacy, and Criminal Offending: The Nonconfounding Effect of Low Self-Control." *Criminal Justice and Behavior* 38(12):1265–1279.

Rios, Victor. 2011. *Punished: Policing the Lives of Black and Latino Boys*. New York: New York University Press.

Roberts, Dorothy. 1999. "Foreword: Race, Vagueness, and the Social Meaning of Order Maintenance Policing." *Journal of Criminal Law & Criminology*, 89(3):775–836.

Rogers, Phil. 2018. "18 Convictions Overturned in Cases Tied to Disgraced Police Sergeant." *NBC Broadcasting*, September 25. (https://www.nbcchicago.com/investigations/ronald-watts-new-exonerations-494136631.html).

Rotella, Carlo. 2019. *The World is Always Coming to an End*. Chicago: University of Chicago Press.

Rothstein, Richard. 2017. *The Color of Law: A Forgotten History of How Our Government Segregated America*. New York: W. W. Norton.

Royko, Mike. 1971. *Boss: Richard J. Daley of Chicago*. New York: Plume.

Royko, Mike. 1992. "Facts Don't Add Up to Police Brutality." *Chicago Tribune*, February 27, N3. (https://www.chicagotribune.com/news/ct-xpm-1992-02-27-9201180750-story.html).

Rugh, Jacob S., Len Albright, and Douglas S. Massey. 2015. "Race, Space, and Cumulative Disadvantage: A Case Study of the Subprime Lending Collapse." *Social Problems* 62(2):186–218.

Sampson, Robert J. 2008. "Moving to Inequality: Neighborhood Effects and Experiments Meet Social Structure. *American Journal of Sociology* 114(1):189–231.

Sampson, Robert J. 2012. *Great American City: Chicago and the Enduring Neighborhood Effect.* Chicago: University of Chicago Press.

Sampson, Robert J., and Dawn Jeglum Bartusch. 1998. "Legal Cynicism and (Subcultural?) Tolerance of Deviance: The Neighborhood Context of Racial Differences." *Law and Society Review* 32(4):777–804.

Sampson, Robert J., and Janet L. Lauritsen. 1997. "Racial and Ethnic Disparities in Crime and Criminal Justice in the United States." *Crime and Justice* 21:311–374.

Sampson Robert J., and Charles Loeffler. 2010. "Punishment's Place: The Local Concentration of Mass Incarceration." *Daedalus* 139(3):20–31.

Sampson, Robert J., Steven W. Raudenbush, and Felton Earls. 1997. "Neighborhoods and Violent Crime: A Multilevel Study of Collective Efficacy." *Science* 277(5328):918–924.

Sampson, Robert J., and William Julius Wilson. 1995. "Toward a Theory of Race, Crime, and Urban Inequality." In John Hagan and Ruth Peterson (Eds.), *Crime and Inequality*, pp. 37–56. Stanford, CA: Stanford University Press.

Sampson, Robert J., William Julius Wilson, and Hanna Katz. 2018. "Reassessing "Toward a Theory of Race, Crime, and Urban Inequality": Enduring and New Challenges in 21st Century America." *Du Bois Review: Social Science Research on Race* 15(1):13–34.

Savini, Dave. 2020. "'You Have the Wrong Place:' Body Camera Video Shows Moments Police Handcuff Innocent, Naked Woman During Wrong Raid." *CBS 2 News.* December 17. (https://chicago.cbslocal.com/2020/12/17/you-have-the-wrong-place-body-camera-video-shows-moments-police-handcuff-innocent-naked-woman-during-wrong-raid/).

Savini, Dave, Samah Assad, Michele Youngerman, and Rebecca McCann. 2020. "[un]warranted." *CBS 2 News.* July 29. (https://storymaps.arcgis.com/stories/63ce5770e1ed43bea99d1d8274b94f91).

Schaible, Lonnie M., and Lorine A. Hughes. 2012. "Neighborhood Disadvantage and Reliance on the Police." *Crime & Delinquency* 58(2):245–274.

Schlabach, Betsy. 2018. "Our Emancipation Day": Martin Luther King Jr. in Chicago. Public Books. April 20. (https://www.publicbooks.org/our-emancipation-day-martin-luther-king-jr-in-chicago/).

Schoenfeld, Heather. 2018. *Building the Prison State: Race and the Politics of Mass Incarceration.* Chicago: University of Chicago Press.

Sciandra, Mathew, Lisa Sanbonmatsu, Greg J. Duncan, Lisa A. Gennetian, Lawrence F. Katz, Ronald C. Kessler, Jeffrey R. Kling, and Jens Ludwig. 2013. "Long-term Effects of the Moving to Opportunity Residential Mobility Experiment on Crime and Delinquency." *Journal of Experimental Criminology* 9(4):451–489.

Seron, Carroll, Joseph Pereira, and Jean Kovath. 2006. "How Citizens Assess Just Punishment for Police Misconduct." *Criminology* 44(4):925–960.

Sharkey, Patrick. 2013. *Stuck in Place: Urban Neighborhoods and the End of Progress toward Racial Equality.* Chicago: University of Chicago Press.

Shaw, Clifford R., and Henry D. McKay. 1942(1972). *Juvenile Delinquency and Urban Areas: A Study of Rates of Delinquency in Relation to Differential Characteristics of Local Communities in American Cities.* Chicago: University of Chicago Press.

Shedd, Carla. 2015. *Unequal City: Race, Schools, and Perceptions of Injustice.* New York: Russell Sage Foundation.

Simon, Jonathan. 2007. *Governing Through Crime: How the War on Crime Transformed American Democracy and Created a Culture of Fear.* New York: Oxford University Press.

Simon, Jonathan. 2014. *Mass Incarceration on Trial: A Remarkable Court Decision and the Future of Prisons in America.* New York: New Press.

Simpson, Richard, Ola Adeoye, Daniel Bliss, Kevin Navratil, and Rebecca Raines. 2004. "The NewDaleyMachine,1989-2004."PresentedattheCity'sFutureConference,July2004.(http://citeseerx.ist.psu.edu/viewdoc/download?doi=10.1.1.202.5133&rep=rep1&type=pdf).

Skogan, Wesley G. 1990. *Disorder and Decline: Crime and the Spiral of Decay in American Cities.* New York: The Free Press

Skogan, Wesley G. 2006. *Police and Community in Chicago: A Tale of Three Cities.* New York: Oxford University Press.

Skogan, Wesley. 2007. "Reflections on Declining Crime in Chicago." Unpublished Manuscript, Northwestern University. (http://skogan.org/files/Skogan.Crime_Drop_in_Chicago.April_2007.pdf).

Skogan, Wesley G., Maarten Van Craen, and Cari Hennessy. 2015. "Training Police in Procedural Justice." *Journal of Experimental Criminology* 11(3):319–334.

Small, Mario. 2004. *Villa Victoria: The Transformation of Social Capital in a Boston Barrio.* Chicago: University of Chicago Press.

Small, Mario. 2018. "Understanding When People Will Report Crimes to the Police." *Proceedings of the National Academy of Sciences* 115(32):8057–8059.

Smith, Brad W., and Malcolm D. Holmes. 2003. "Community Accountability, Minority Threat, and Police Brutality: An Examination of Civil Rights Criminal Complaints." *Criminology* 41(4):1035–1064.

Smith, Brad W., and Malcolm D. Holmes. 2014. "Police Use of Excessive Force in Minority Communities: A Test of the Minority Threat, Place, and Community Accountability Hypotheses." *Social Problems* 61(1):83–104.

Smith, Brandon. 2015. "I Filed Suit for the Laquan McDonald Police Video. Its Mundanity Shocked Me." *The Guardian*, November 25. (https://www.theguardian.com/commentisfree/2015/nov/25/i-filed-suit-for-the-laquan-mcdonald-police-video-release-its-mundanity-shocked-me).

Smith, Mitch. 2018. "Chicago Prosecutors Paint Officer as Reckless in the Shooting of Laquan McDonald." *New York Times*, September 17. (https://www.nytimes.com/2018/09/17/us/jason-van-dyke-laquan-mcdonald-trial.html).

Smith, Mitch. 2019. "Four Chicago Police Officers Fired for Cover-Up of Laquan McDonald." *New York Times*, July 19. (https://www.nytimes.com/2019/07/19/us/chicago-police-fired-laquan-mcdonald.html).

Smith, Mitch, and Julie Bosman. 2019. "Jason Van Dyke Sentenced to Nearly 7 Years for Murdering Laquan McDonald." *New York Times*, June 18. (https://www.nytimes.com/2019/01/18/us/jason-van-dyke-sentencing.html).

Snyder, Howard N., and Melissa Sickmund. 1995. *Juvenile Offenders and Victims: A Focus on Violence, Statistics Summary.* Reno, NV: National Center for Juvenile Justice. (https://www.ncjrs.gov/pdffiles1/Photocopy/153570NCJRS.pdf).

Spielman, Fran. 2004. "'I'll Take the Blame Myself' - But Mayor Hints Some Top Officials Could Lose Jobs Over Truck Scandal." *Chicago Sun Times*, January 31. Access World News. Rutgers University Newark.

Spielman, Fran. 2005. "Scandal-weary Daley Dumps Hired Truck Program: Mayor Bans Contractor Gifts, Says One Firm Will Run New Program." *Chicago Sun Times*, February 9, Page 9 Access World News. Rutgers University Newark.

Spielman, Fran. 2008. "Mayor Reverses on Who's to Blame." *Chicago Sun Times*, October 22. Access World News. Rutgers University Newark.

Spielman, Fran. 2020. "Lightfoot Apologizes for Botched Police Raid." *Chicago Sun Times*. December 16. (https://chicago.suntimes.com/2020/12/16/22179377/lightfoot-apologizes-botched-police-raid-anjanette-young-video-search-warrant-wrong-address).

Stein, Sharman. 1992. "Canaryville Beatings Prompt 2 Cop Firings: Police Panel Sides with Teen Victims. *Chicago Tribune*, March 21. ProQuest Historical Newspapers. University of California Davis.

Steinberg, Laurence. 2017. "Adolescent Brain Science and Juvenile Justice Policymaking." *Psychology, Public Policy, and Law* 23(4):410–420.

Street, Paul L. 2007. *Racial Oppression in the Global Metropolis: A Living Black Chicago Experience*. Lanham, Maryland: Rowman and Littlefield.

Sunshine, Jason, and Tom Tyler. 2003. "The Role of Procedural Justice and Legitimacy in Shaping Public Support for Policing." *Law & Society Review* 37(3):513–548.

Sutton, John. 1988. *Stubborn Children: Controlling Juvenile Delinquency in the United States, 1640-1981*. Berkeley: University of California Press.

Taylor, G. Flint. 2013. "It's Time to Heal the Wounds from Chicago Police Torture." June 18. *Huffington Post*. (https://www.huffpost.com/entry/its-time-to-heal-the-woun_b_3455452).

Taylor, G. Flint. 2014. "The Chicago Police Torture Scandal: A Legal and Political History." *CUNY Law Review* 17(2):329–381.

Taylor, G. Flint. 2015. "How Activists Won Reparations for the Survivors of Chicago Police Department Torture." *In These Times*. June 26. (https://inthesetimes.com/article/jon-burge-torture-reparations).

Taylor, G. Flint. 2019. *The Torture Machine: Racism and Police Violence in Chicago*. Chicago: Haymarket Books.

Taylor, Keeanga-Yamahtta, 2016. *From #BlackLivesMatter to Black Liberation*. Chicago: Haymarket Books.

Terrill, William, and Jason R. Ingram. 2016. "Citizen Complaints against the Police: An Eight City Investigation." *Police Quarterly* 19(2):150–179.

Thibaut, John, and Laurens Walker. 1975. *Procedural Justice: A Psychological Analysis*. Hillsdale, NJ: Erlbaum.

Thompson, Cheryl W. 1992. "Teen Slain at Tilden is Mourned." *Chicago Tribune*, November 29, L A7. ProQuest Historical Newspapers. University of California Davis.

Thornton, Jerry. 1992. "Mother of Teen Shot at School Sues Board." *Chicago Tribune*, December 4, S5. ProQuest Historical Newspapers. University of California Davis.

Tillman, Michael. 2012. "Statement." July 23. (https://www.law.northwestern.edu/legalclinic/macarthur/projects/wrongful/documents/TillmanStatement.pdf).

Tuttle, William M. 1970. *Race Riot: Chicago in the Red Summer of 1919*. Champaign, IL: University of Illinois Press.

Tyler, Tom. 2017. "Procedural Justice and Policing: A Rush to Judgment?" *Annual Review of Law & Social Science* 13:29–53.

Tyler, Tom R., and Yuen J. Huo. 2002. *Trust in the Law: Encouraging Public Cooperation with the Police and Courts*. New York: Russell Sage Foundation.

Tyler, Tom, and Jonathan Jackson. 2013. "Popular Legitimacy and the Exercise of Legal Authority: Motivating Compliance, Cooperation, and Engagement." *Psychology, Public Policy and Law* 20(1):78–95.

United Nations. 2006. "Consideration of Reports Submitted by State Parties Under Article 19 of the Convention." Convention against Torture, and Other Cruel, Inhuman or Degrading Treatment or Punishment, Thirty-sixth session, May 1-19. (https://www.refworld.org/docid/453776c60.html).

U.S. Department of Justice, Office of Justice Programs. 2015. Bureau of Justice Statistics. Police-public contact survey, 2015. Inter-university Consortium for Political and Social Research [distributor], 2018-04-11. (https://doi.org/10.3886/ICPSR36653.v1)

U.S. Department of Justice, Civil Rights Division. 2017. *Investigation of the Chicago Police Department*. (https://www.justice.gov/opa/file/925846/download).

Vaisey, Stephen. 2009. "Motivation and Justification: A Dual-Process Model of Culture in Action." *American Journal of Sociology* 114(6):1675–1715.

Van Cleve, Nicole Gonzalez. 2016. *Crook County: Racism and Injustice in America's Largest Criminal Court*. Stanford, CA: Stanford University Press.

Vargas, Robert. 2016. *Wounded City: Violent Turf Wars in a Chicago Barrio*. New York: Oxford University Press.

Venkatesh, Sudhir Alladi. 2000. *American Project: The Rise and Fall of a Modern Ghetto*. Cambridge, MA: Harvard Univeersity Press.

Wacquant, Loïc. 2008. *Urban Outcasts: A Comparative Sociology of Advanced Marginality*. Cambridge: Polity Press.

Wacquant, Loïc. 2009. *Punishing the Poor: The Neoliberal Government of Social Insecurity*. Durham: Duke University Press.

Walecka, K. I. 2010. . "Police Torture Archive, Jon Burge, Chicago." U.S. V Burge. *Invisible Institute*. (https://www.dropbox.com/sh/ch5e6i674shwpr8/AADlPsCmSASfpb WERyCQYVdya?dl=0).

Walker, Alan, and Carol Walker (Eds.). 1997. *Britain Divided: The Growth of Social Exclusion in the 1980s and 1990s*. London: Child Poverty Action Group.

Ward, Geoff. 2016. "Microclimates of Racial Meaning: Historical Racial Violence and Environmental Impacts." *Wisconsin Law Review* 2016(3):575–626.

Waxman, Olivia. 2018. The Surprising Story Behind This Shocking Photo of Martin Luther King Jr. Under Attack. *Time*. January 18. (https://time.com/5096937/martin-luther-king-jr-picture-chicago/).

Weisman, David. 2010. "Police Torture Archive, Jon Burge, Chicago." U.S. V Burge. *Invisible Institute*. (https://www.dropbox.com/sh/ch5e6i674shwpr8/AADlPsCmSASfpb WERyCQYVdya?dl=0.)

Weitzer, Ronald, and Steven Tuch. 2006. *Race and Policing in America: Conflict and Reform*. New York: Cambridge University Press.

Western, Bruce. 2006. *Punishment and Inequality in America*. New York: Russell Sage.

White, Michael D., and Henry F. Fradella. 2016. *Stop and Frisk: The Use and Abuse of a Controversial Policing Tactic*. New York: New York University.

Wilkerson, Isabel. 2010. *The Warmth of Other Suns: The Epic Story of America's Great Migration*. New York: Vintage Books.

Wilkerson, Isabel. 2020. *Caste: The Origins of Our Discontents*. New York: Penguin/ Random House.

Wille, Lois. 1997. *At Home in the Loop: How Clout and Community Built Chicago's Dearborn Park*. Carbondale: Southern Illinois University Press.

Wilson, Terry. 1994a. "Trial Opens in Killing at Tilden." *Chicago Tribune*, January 20, NA 5. ProQuest Historical Newspapers. University of California Davis.

Wilson, Terry. 1994b. "Teen Guilty of Slaying in Tilden High Hallway." *Chicago Tribune*, January 22, N5. ProQuest Historical Newspapers. University of California Davis.

Wilson, William Julius. 1987. *The Truly Disadvantaged: The Inner City, the Underclass, and Public Policy*. Chicago: University of Chicago Press.

Witt, Howard. 1985. "Attack on 2 Blacks Barely Draws Notice." *Chicago Tribune*, July 12, A1. ProQuest Historical Newspapers. University of California Davis.

Zelizer, Julian E. 2016. *The Kerner Report: National Advisory Commission on Civil Disorders*. Introduction by Julian E. Zelizer. Princeton, NJ: Princeton University Press.

Zimring, Franklin. 2017. *When Police Kill*. Cambridge, MA: Harvard University Press.

Zorn, Eric. 2018a. "McCarthy Takes the Fall. Should Alvarez be Next?" *Chicago Tribune*, December 1. (https://www.chicagotribune.com/opinion/editorials/ct-garry-mccarthy-fired-zorn-20151201-story.html).

Zorn, Eric. 2018b. "Coming Soon: A Laquan McDonald Documentary that Makes the Story Even Worse." *Chicago Tribune*, May 4. (https://www.chicagotribune.com/columns/eric-zorn/ct-perspec-zorn-laquan-mcdonald-jason-van-dyke-documentary-0506-20180504-story.html).

Case Citations

People vs. Joseph White. 1994. Cook County Circuit Court, Criminal Division, Illinois.
People v. Wilson. 1987. Supreme Court of Illinois. 116 Illinois. 2d 29. 506N.E. 2d 571.

Index